# The Human Journey

## A Concise Introduction
to World History

### Second Edition

## Volume 1: Prehistory to 1450

### KEVIN REILLY

**Raritan Valley Community College**

ROWMAN & LITTLEFIELD
*Lanham • Boulder • New York • London*

Executive Editor: Susan McEachern
Editorial Assistant: Katelyn Turner
Senior Marketing Manager: Kim Lyons

Credits and acknowledgments for material borrowed from other sources, and reproduced with permission, appear on the appropriate page within the text.

Published by Rowman & Littlefield
An imprint of The Rowman & Littlefield Publishing Group, Inc.
4501 Forbes Boulevard, Suite 200, Lanham, Maryland 20706
www.rowman.com

Unit A, Whitacre Mews, 26-34 Stannary Street, London SE11 4AB, United Kingdom

British Library Cataloguing in Publication Information Available

**Library of Congress Cataloging-in-Publication Data**

Names: Reilly, Kevin, 1941-
Title: The human journey : a concise introduction to world history / Kevin Reilly, Raritan Valley
   Community College.
Description: Second edition. | Lanham, MD : Rowman & Littlefield, [2018] | Includes bibliographical
   references and index.
Identifiers: LCCN 2018004488 (print) | LCCN 2018006430 (ebook) | ISBN 9781538105658 (electronic)
   | ISBN 9781538105634 (cloth : alk. paper) | ISBN 9781538105641 (pbk. : alk. paper) | ISBN
   9781538105597 (electronic v. 1) | ISBN 9781538105573 (cloth v. 1 : alk. paper) | ISBN 9781538105580
   (pbk. v. 1 : alk. paper) | ISBN 9781538105627 (electronic v. 2) | ISBN 9781538105603 (cloth v. 2 : alk.
   paper) | ISBN 9781538105610 (pbk. v. 2 : alk. paper)
Subjects: LCSH: World history—Textbooks.
Classification: LCC D21 (ebook) | LCC D21 .R379 2018 (print) | DDC 909—dc23 LC record available at
   https://lccn.loc.gov/2018004488

♾™ The paper used in this publication meets the minimum requirements of American National
Standard for Information Sciences—Permanence of Paper for Printed Library Materials, ANSI/NISO
Z39.48-1992.

Printed in the United States of America

For Pearl

# Brief Contents

# Contents

# Illustrations

## Figures

## Maps

# Preface

OVER THE years that I have been teaching world history, I have frequently been asked, "How are you able to cover everything?" My answer—after "of course you can't cover *everything*"—is that you have to broaden your focus. Just as a photographer switches to a wide-angle lens to capture a landscape, we must survey larger patterns of change to understand the history of the world. This means rethinking what is important, rather than cutting parts of the old story. When I was a college student and the course was "Western Civilization," instructors solved the problem of coverage, as each passing year made their subject longer and larger, by calving off much of ancient and recent history. Thus, we began with the Roman Empire and barely got to World War II. More recently, those who designed the first Advanced Placement world history course decided to view everything before the year 1000 as prelude. These are arbitrary cuts, not solutions to the problem of understanding the human story. In fact, that problem requires us to dig deeper into the past than we are used to, so that we can understand the formative stage of human development. And it also requires that we try to understand the recent past not only as a chain of important events, but also as the continuation of long-term processes. Thus, while twelve chapters might seem a spare space to describe *The Human Journey*, I have devoted the first chapter to what historians have often dismissed as "prehistory" and used the last two chapters to locate the present—on the surface and in depth. Consequently, the remaining nine chapters—the centerpiece of the story—take on greater meaning: the rise of states and empires as a consequence of the Agricultural Revolution, the classical age that shapes even our own, the development and spread of the universal religions that dominate our world, the stages of globalization from "southernization" to westernization, and the impact of industrialization and democratization.

Too many people to name have made this book possible. In addition to the scholars I have read, only a small fraction of whom are cited here, there were dozens of others who advised me or reviewed parts of this work, many anonymously. I am extraordinarily lucky to count many of them as good friends. It is regrettably impossible to thank the late Jerry Bentley, but Ross Dunn was also an early supporter. Steve Gosch, Sue Gronewold, Marilyn

Hitchens, David Kalivas, Lauren Ristvet, and George Sussman also read all or parts of the manuscript. Discussions with David Christian, Marc Gilbert, Craig Lockard, Heather Streets-Salter, John McNeill, and Adam McKeown helped me as well. Finally, my good friend Bob Strayer played a far greater role than he would allow, from first suggesting the project to contributing at every stage.

At Rowman & Littlefield I am enormously grateful to my editor Susan McEachern. In addition, I'd like to thank Carrie Broadwell-Tkach, Grace Baumgartner, and Karie Simpson in Acquisitions and Alden Perkins in Production.

# 1

# The Long Prologue
## FROM 14 BILLION YEARS AGO

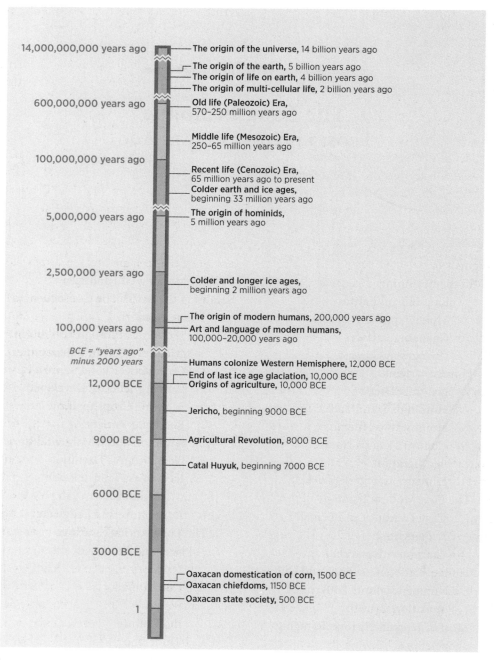

14,000,000,000 years ago — The origin of the universe, 14 billion years ago

The origin of the earth, 5 billion years ago
The origin of life on earth, 4 billion years ago
The origin of multi-cellular life, 2 billion years ago

600,000,000 years ago — Old life (Paleozoic) Era,
570–250 million years ago

Middle life (Mesozoic) Era,
250–65 million years ago

100,000,000 years ago — Recent life (Cenozoic) Era,
65 million years ago to present
Colder earth and ice ages,
beginning 33 million years ago

5,000,000 years ago — The origin of hominids,
5 million years ago

2,500,000 years ago — Colder and longer ice ages,
beginning 2 million years ago

The origin of modern humans, 200,000 years ago
100,000 years ago — Art and language of modern humans,
100,000–20,000 years ago

*BCE = "years ago" minus 2000 years* — Humans colonize Western Hemisphere, 12,000 BCE
End of last ice age glaciation, 10,000 BCE
12,000 BCE — Origins of agriculture, 10,000 BCE

Jericho, beginning 9000 BCE

9000 BCE — Agricultural Revolution, 8000 BCE

Catal Huyuk, beginning 7000 BCE

6000 BCE

3000 BCE

Oaxacan domestication of corn, 1500 BCE
Oaxacan chiefdoms, 1150 BCE
Oaxacan state society, 500 BCE

1

Figure 1.1  Time line of the first 14 billion years.

## Origins

### *In the Beginning*

THE BEGINNING of everything in the universe, everything we know, can know, or even imagine goes back almost 14 billion years ago to an explosion called the Big Bang. Everything our world contains came from that explosion: not only suns and planets but also space and time and even light (though not for another half billion years). Today, that explosion still continues with the expansion of the universe. Astronomers recently trained their telescopes on the edge of that first light, still rocketing out into space, leaving our world in its twilight.

*First Life on Earth.* On the scale of 14 billion years our Earth is breaking news. Along with our sun and solar system, it originated about 5 billion years ago in the debris of some earlier stars. During a cooling process of about a billion years, the bubbling mixture of chemicals on our Earth did something we see as miraculous: it created life about 4 billion years ago. Chemists at the University of Cambridge have recently suggested that the rain of comets that bombarded the young earth could have triggered the activation of life from the necessary ingredients,[1] among them sunlight, water, and carbon. Scientists describe the first life as a kind of pond scum that looked like blue-green foam or algae. By the process of photosynthesis, these cells absorbed sunlight and released oxygen into the atmosphere. Two billion years later, some single cells clustered together to form multicellular organisms. The rest of our story is the tale of life these past billion years.

*Three Explosions of Life.* We tend to think of most long-term historical processes as gradual, or following an even pace, and

perhaps they are. But the growth of life was a series of expansions and extinctions—the multiplication of new life forms followed by five major extinctions and many smaller ones. In broad terms we can distinguish three major explosions of life over the last 550 million years. Scientists call these three stages "Old Life," or "Paleozoic" (550 million to 250 million years ago); "Middle Life," or "Mesozoic" (250 million to 65 million years ago); and "Recent Life," or "Cenozoic" (65 million years ago to the present).

The first stage, the Paleozoic, began with a wild explosion of natural forms, possibly thanks to the oxygen-charged atmosphere. Within 40 million years, nature shot out almost all possible life forms—the basic structures of everything that exists today—but all under the sea. First came worms and other invertebrates, then vertebrates, fish, and vascular plants (with roots, stems, and leaves). Then some dug roots or crawled on to the land. After a brief rest came the conquest of land: first by plants and then insects, trees, and amphibians. By about 300 million years ago, the first winged insects and reptiles appeared.

Two extinctions occurred during the Paleozoic era before the third and largest mass extinction: about 250 million years ago, when something like 90 percent of sea species and 70% of land species suddenly disappeared. Some scientists believe that a meteor may have been the cause;[2] others point to massive volcanic eruptions in Siberia and the release of carbon from the lava burning of Siberian coal fields.[3] The resulting dark global winter lasted millions of years.

The next major era of growth, the Mesozoic, brought the first dinosaurs and mammals. The first birds appeared 200 million years ago and the first flowers 150 million years ago. The Mesozoic profusion of life was interrupted by a fourth extinction event around 200 million years ago, and it ended in a fifth—another mass extinction about 65 million years ago. The cause this time may have been a large asteroid, six miles in diameter, which plowed a huge trench under what is today the Yucatan Peninsula in Mexico.[4] The dust and debris from the explosion may have spread all over the earth. Sixty percent of all the earth's species disappeared, including the dinosaurs. Every animal larger than a cat was wiped out.

After a million years or more of darkness and acid rain came the beginning of the modern or Cenozoic era. North American ferns led the revival of plant life. Eventually, larger plants and trees spread their seeds and took root. With a new forest canopy came the first primates, squirrel-like mammals that took to the trees about 60 million years ago, and the first apes, 57 million years ago. The Cenozoic is sometimes called the "age of mammals" since so many mammals replaced the dinosaurs as the largest creatures on the planet, but it could just as well be called the age of flowers or insects or fish or birds. In fact, we would recognize most of today's animals in early Cenozoic fossils. Some would surprise us, like birds that stood seven feet high and sloths as big as elephants. The Cenozoic is our own era, even if we might not recognize all of its inhabitants.

Some have suggested we are now experiencing a sixth extinction, this one manmade.[5] Instead of the sudden impact of a volcano or asteroid, the earth is being transformed by a single species working with increasing intensity over recent generations: Humans. But it is not gradual. Species

extinction is occurring 1,000 times faster because of humans.[6] We are injecting carbon dioxide into the atmosphere 10 times faster than the worst previous time, 250 million years ago.[7]

*Changing Surfaces.* Anyone who has looked at the shape of Africa and South America on a map has seen how the two continents were once joined. Actually, various landmasses have come together and moved apart continually over the past half billion years. These landmasses have also drifted over the surface of the earth in ways that bear no resemblance to their current configuration.

By the beginning of the Mesozoic era, 250 million years ago, various landmasses around the globe had come together as a single global continent, the bulk of which lay in the Southern Hemisphere. Then it began to split apart. About 200 million years ago, a southern section including what is today Africa, India, Southeast Asia, Australia, and New Zealand broke off and drifted toward the South Pole. Then, around 150 million years ago, the western half split apart and drifted farther west, opening up an area that became the Atlantic Ocean.

Continental landmasses are not the only loose crusts sliding over the surface of the earth. Both lands and oceans sit on large plates that slide around the globe over a more fluid core. These plates sometimes collide, pushing up great mountain ranges, or slide next to each other, causing earthquakes. For example, the collision of India with the rest of Asia raised the Himalayan Mountains. Similarly, the Pacific plate pushed against North and South America, creating the Andes Mountains in South America and triggering earthquakes along the coast from Chile to Alaska.

*Changes in Climate.* Some of these sliding plates also affect climate. In general, the larger a continent, the colder it gets, especially in the interior. This is because large continental landmasses block the moderating warm air and water flows that circulate in the atmosphere and oceans. Near the poles or at high altitudes, such continents build up snow and permanent ice, or glaciers. Large glaciers make the atmosphere even drier and cooler since ice and snow absorb moisture and reflect sunlight away. At the other extreme, islands and small land areas are warmed by circulating air and currents. The many small landmasses of the late Mesozoic and early Cenozoic eras kept global temperatures quite balmy. Fifty million years ago, North Dakota sweltered under tropical forests.

Global temperatures turned colder about 33 million years ago. For most of the past 30 million years, icing and warming periods lasted about the same amount of time. But during the most recent 2.5 million years, ice ages have lasted longer, and warming periods have been much shorter. In the past million years, the warm interglacial periods lasted only about 20,000 years each before the ice returned. Since the last ice age ended about 12,000 years ago, we may be near the end of the current interglacial warming. This time, however, human behavior, especially our burning of fossil fuels—the swamp grasses and giant trees of the Paleozoic era (350 million years ago) turned into coal, gas, and oil—may be slowing or even reversing the natural process. Whether this current "global warming," the first change caused by humans, delays the next ice age or makes the world permanently warmer remains to be seen.

## Human Origins

The similarity of humans and monkeys is evident to anyone who visits a zoo. It is a staple of story and mythology in every society where humans have come into contact with them. The Indian *Ramayana* legend tells of the Princess Sita being carried off by monkeys. The Chinese story *Monkey* imagines a monkey guide for an early Chinese Buddhist missionary. So Charles Darwin was hardly the first person to imagine that humans and monkeys were related.

*Natural Selection.* Darwin added the idea of descent to the recognition of similarity. His argument that humans and monkeys shared ancestors was part of a larger argument that all species changed or evolved. The importance of change was certainly a dominant idea in Darwin's England of the mid-nineteenth century. At the same time that Darwin's contemporaries were discovering fossils of extinct species in English stone, English stone masons were losing work to the new industrial workers. Transplanted farmers forged giant steel beams to carry coal-belching steam locomotives across what had only recently been (according to the poet) a "green and pleasant land." In a world of wrenching mechanical change, Darwin thought that he had found the mechanisms for change in nature. He called them random mutation and natural selection. A species would randomly produce offspring with slight variations. Some of these variants would prove more resilient than others, and a rare one would initiate a new divergence, possibly becoming a new species. In some cases, the old variants would die off, and the new ones would replace them. Nature is a harsh and unpredictable task master; more than 99 percent of the species it produced are now extinct.

In the past 40 years, the new science of molecular biology, the study of the most basic elements—the DNA—of organisms, has given us the tools to go far beyond Darwin's guesswork. For instance, Darwin guessed that humans were closer to African primates, including the African gorilla than they were to Asian monkeys and the orangutan. DNA measurements by molecular biologists now give precise measurement to those differences confirming Darwin's guess.

Molecular biology can measure not only nature's similarities and differences more precisely but also change over time. The principle is that differences in DNA develop at a fixed rate over time so that the greater the differences in DNA between two organisms, the longer the two have grown apart. This has also deepened our understanding of human origins by helping us figure out just when our first human ancestors began their own branch on the family tree of primates. DNA comparisons show that human and African ape branches separated about 25 million years ago and that our last common ancestors with chimpanzees lived about 7 million years ago.

*Hominids Stand Tall.* Our human ancestors are called hominids. While initially not very different from the other tailless chimpanzee-like animals of the time, they gradually developed the physical features we associate with modern humans: less hair, habitual erect posture, bipedalism (walking on two feet), legs longer than arms, flat face, smaller jaw and teeth, larger brains, and longer period of infant growth after birth, among others. Some of these changes had profound consequences for hominid development. Physical changes in the brain, lips, larynx, and tongue enabled the development of a capacity for speech and language. Walking upright led to hands that could carry, manipulate, and use tools. With language and tools came ideas and skills—cultural tricks for survival that meant less dependence on nature and that enabled each generation to give the next a leg up.

*Hominids to Humans.* Combined with DNA analysis, the fossil remains of the past 6 million years allow us to chart the transition of hominids to humans with some degree of accuracy. Finding the particular hominid species that led to the first humans—and to nothing else—is more arbitrary, however. Skeletons of hominids from 4 to 6 million years ago, like the early bipedal *Ardipithecus*, may be our ancestors, but they could also be examples of a hominid that went extinct. These had the stature and brain size of modern chimpanzees. They lived in forests in East Africa, where their hooked big toe allowed them to swing from the trees, crawl on all fours. and possibly walk upright.[8] From a slightly later period, 4 million to 2 million years ago, there are skeletal remains of the hominid *Australopithecus* from East Africa and South Africa. They are upright, three and a half to five feet tall, with a brain capacity of 400 to 500 cubic centimeters and limbs, skull, jaw, and teeth that combine ape and human features. One of these is the 3.2 million-year-old skeleton called Lucy. Recently a possibly related very human-like jawbone from 2.8 million years ago was found in Ethiopia, pushing the claim of first humans to almost 3 million years ago.[9]

Otherwise a more traditional human ancestry story begins with *Homo erectus* (also from East Africa, about 1.9 million years ago) with a brain size of 900 to 1,000 cubic centimeters and a height of five to six feet. *Homo erectus* appears to be the first hominid to travel outside of Africa, as fossil remains have been found in Europe, China, and Java. *Homo erectus* made stone tools, controlled fire, probably used hides for clothing, and may have had spoken language. Most scientists believe that they went extinct without contributing to the genes of modern humans.

*Homo sapiens* appeared in East Africa between 400,000 and 100,000 years ago, with a modern brain size of 1,400 cubic centimeters. They made tools of wood and bone as well as stone. The species was called "*sapiens*" (wise or thoughtful) because its members probably used language symbolically and expressed certain religious and aesthetic ideas. There is evidence, for instance, of burial, body painting, jewelry, carving, and cave painting.

Finally, about 150,000 years ago, humans whose skeletal remains suggest modern human physical features appeared, with brain capacities of 1,400 to 1,600 cubic centimeters. With more than a touch of bravado, scientists named this, our own species, *Homo sapiens sapiens*. (We're so smart we have to say it twice.) For much of the past 100,000 years, these *Homo sapiens sapiens* were not alone. One of our cousins, called the Neanderthal, named after the German town where remains were first discovered, originated about 150,000 years ago and lived in North Africa, Europe, and Southwest Asia. Despite their bad press, Neanderthals had larger heads and brains (1,400 to 1,700 cubic centimeters) than we do and very muscular stout bodies. They buried their dead and survived the cold climate of northern Europe. Before they became extinct 28,000 years ago, recent DNA analysis shows that they contributed to our gene pool.[10] The existence of another cousin, called Denisovan, has recently been discovered in Siberia. A small amount of its DNA can be found in people of New Guinea and the Pacific. In addition, the remains of possibly another human species, called *Homo florensis*, have recently been discovered on the island of Flores in Indonesia, where these people lived until at least 13,000 years ago, possibly much later. Their skeletons show a people who measured only about three feet tall and had heads only a third the size of modern humans. There is no evidence of their interbreeding with our ancestors.

*Culture Trumps Nature.* We have noted the increasing brain size in the history of hominid evolution. Larger brains, supported by thinner frames, allowed humans to advance more by thinking than by the exertion of brute force. But within any species, brain sizes were similar. Modern *Homo sapiens sapiens* did not differ significantly by hat size. And hat sizes had nothing to do with inventiveness. In the world of *Homo sapiens sapiens*, culture (what we learned) was far more important than nature (our biology) in determining what we could do. More than any other creatures of the earth, humans are products of culture; they are also its creators. Rabbits may breed more quickly, but their lives are very similar, generation after generation. Through culture, humans have made—and continue to remake—themselves. And they have been able to do so throughout the world in every environment.

## Global Migration

Humans were not the first of Earth's creatures to spread throughout the world and colonize every continent. They are not even

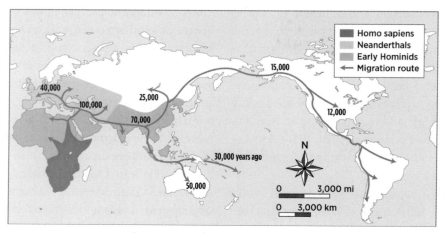

Map 1.1   While hominids began to migrate from Africa to the Middle East and Asia almost 2 million years ago, it is generally believed that modern humans are descended from those who left Africa beginning about 100,000 years ago, arriving finally in the Western Hemisphere 12,000 to 15,000 years ago.

the most numerous of the Earth's approximately 30 million species. It is even possible that other global colonizers will outlast humans—cockroaches, for example. But if that happens, humans will have only themselves to blame because in their brief span on the planet, humans have reshaped it to their every need.

*Humans as Travelers.* So far, we have been imagining a particular branch of hominids as they became human beings—and *then* went out to travel the world. But it might make more sense to see the process of becoming human as part of the process of walking and traveling. Walking meant upright posture, seeing where you are going, better vision and planning, and more things to do with the arms and hands. Traveling meant discovering, confronting, adapting, and inventing.

Most hominid species (probably all) originated in East Africa, but they did not stay there. They traveled throughout Africa and to Australia, to Europe and Asia, and

there is evidence that they did this over and over again, learning new skills and ideas and in the process becoming what we mean by human.

*Homo erectus* was probably the first hominid to travel beyond Africa. A representative of the species left teeth in China almost 2 million years ago.[11] *Erectus* may have traveled to Java by water or an ice-age land bridge as much as 1.8 million years ago. Later generations settled in southern Africa over a million years ago. About 800,000 years ago, new members of *Homo erectus* traveled to Europe, India, and China. *Homo sapiens* migrated out of Africa between 100,000 and 200,000 years ago, followed by our immediate ancestor, *Homo sapiens sapiens*, beginning less than 100,000 years ago.

What knowledge of clothing, sewing, fire, and cooking was prompted by their movement into the forests of northern Asia and Europe? What social skills, language, or communication ability answered the need to make camp in a new area, perhaps colder or wetter, with different animals as potential prey or predator and unrecognizable mushrooms that might cure or kill? What new scraper, spear point, or fishhook was invented to kill the mammoths of the northern Asian grasslands or the seals of the Bering Sea?

We cannot know the specific answers to these questions. We do know that these travelers became remarkably adept at colonizing and conquering new lands. We do not know if *Homo sapiens sapiens* were responsible for the extinction of other human species, like the Neanderthals or *Homo florensis*. Whether or not these or other early humans were annihilated by *Homo sapiens sapiens*, many animal species probably were. Humans were by no means the largest animals, but they used their brains to capture and kill with abandon. So devastating was the human contact with large mammals and birds that we can practically chart the migration of *Homo sapiens sapiens* by looking for the multiple extinctions of these creatures: 50,000 years ago in Australia and 14,400 years ago in northern Eurasia.

Between 18,000 and 15,000 years ago,[12] *Homo sapiens sapiens* crossed the Bering Sea land bridge created by low ice-age ocean levels. They may have followed the path of small groups of earlier humans who settled in the Western Hemisphere much earlier; there is some evidence of human settlements in Chile 30,000 years ago and in South Carolina possibly 50,000 years ago. But the settlement at the end of the ice age, between 18,000 and 15,000 years ago, had a far greater ecological impact. They arrived in a world of huge elephant-like mastodons, woolly mammoths standing over 10 feet to the shoulder and weighing 13 tons, birds with the wing span of a small airplane, bears that weighed

1,500 pounds, giant bison, sloths, horses, camels, and lions. It was a world that makes our own look "zoologically impoverished," the great naturalist Alfred Russell Wallace, Darwin's collaborator, remarked. At some time before 13,000 years ago, these travelers perfected a stone spear point (called Clovis after its discovery in Clovis, New Mexico) that gave the new Americans a deadly advantage over the large mammals.

The resulting impact may have been a "megafaunal overkill,"[13] rivaling the extinction of the dinosaur. Virtually every large animal species on the continent was hunted to extinction before a second human migration came by sea about 8,000 years ago.

## The First Modern Humans

*Homo sapiens sapiens*, the colonizers of every continent but Antarctica over the past 100,000 years, were the first truly modern human beings with regard to the size of their brains, the height of their foreheads, and their general appearance. They were the first of our ancestors who, with the right haircut, diet, and clothes, would fail to surprise us if we saw them on the street or in the shower.

We used to think that the early ancestors of our species were late bloomers, that it took more than 100,000 years before these anatomically moderns became behavioral and thinking moderns. Without much evidence of *Homo sapiens sapiens'* art or invention between the time of their appearance 100,000 to 200,000 years ago and the dramatic cave paintings created 30,000 years ago, archaeologists thought that the first half of our species' existence was fairly uneventful. But no more.

Recent discoveries in sub-Saharan Africa from almost 100,000 years ago reveal an early propensity of our species for artistic expression and abstract thought. We find a wide range of highly specialized tools—scrapers, fishhooks, awls, and needles—for specific functions, and we find them in various shapes, sizes, and media—stone, wood, and bone. These people also carved their tools for aesthetic effect. We also find red ocher pigments often associated with burial, body decoration, and religion.[14] In addition, recent excavations in South Africa uncovered a set of pierced beadlike shells that may have been worn as jewelry 75,000 years ago.[15]

Human clothing may also date from this period. Research on the "molecular clock" of lice[16] indicates that human body lice diverged from human head lice about 75,000 years ago. Since body lice live in clothing and most other mammals support only one kind of lice, the reasoning is that only a widespread human use of clothing would have precipitated such a successful genetic mutation.

As early as 40,000 years ago, people in modern-day Australia engraved thousands of circles on a high sandstone monolith and surrounding boulders. Early human burials date to more than 50,000 years ago; in caves in the Middle East, there are examples of children buried with deer antlers or the skull of a wild boar, indicating some religious or totemic identification of human and animal. All these efforts to beautify, plan, or give meaning suggest if not the origins of art and religion, then at least the beginnings

Figure 1.2 These bison from a cave in the Pyrenees Mountains were painted by hunter-gatherers about 13,000 years ago. The earliest European cave art dates from 32,000 years ago. We can only speculate about their origins, but it is likely that these images of wild animals conveyed a magical or religious aspect of the hunt. *Erich Lessing/Art Resource, NY.*

Figure 1.3 Statues of women, like this from France 25,000 years ago, were also created by Paleolithic artists in Europe and Asia from 30,000 to 12,000 years ago. They are sometimes called "Venus" figurines to suggest a possible religious function related to women's fertility. *Gianni Dagli Orti/The Art Archive at Art Resource, NY. Museo Civico Vicenza.*

*Cave Paintings and Female Figurines.* The full flowering of this human creativity can be seen in the cave paintings and female figurines that date from about 30,000 to 12,000 years ago. These works, discovered in areas of Europe that have undergone extensive excavation, have led many archaeologists to speak of a late or "Upper Paleolithic Cultural Revolution" during this period. Clearly, these Stone Age ancestors had become talented artists, innovative toolmakers, symbolic thinkers, and reflective human beings. All this occurred as they became the effective hunters and voracious meat eaters that swept through the herds of big game that roamed the planet and as they migrated throughout the glacially cold world at the height of the last ice age. Their need to adapt to new environments as they moved and their need to confront conditions of sometimes bitter cold may, in fact, have been challenges that pushed their cultural development. They invented techniques like sewing close-fitting fur garments, weaving fibers and firing pottery, and creating tools like bows and arrows, spear throwers, nets, traps, and multipurpose flint blades.

The best evidence of this "Upper Paleolithic," or late Stone Age, revolution is in the female figurines and animal cave paintings that can be found from Spain to Mongolia, heralding a mature artistic ability, religious rituals, long-range cultural contact and trade, and a considerable increase in population density.

*Cultural Adaptation.* The changes that occurred to our human ancestors between 100,000 and 10,000 years ago were not only the most extensive changes that had ever occurred in such a short time but also changes in the way in which change occurred. These were not physical changes. The human brain

of abstract thought and a fairly developed capacity for expression and communication.

We also see the beginning of cultural differences in this period. Tool kits, the set of tools a group employs, begin to vary from one area to another. They vary not only to serve different purposes—fishing or hunting the big game residing in the forest or grasslands—but also to reflect a local style or tradition. These cultural differences mean that culture was beginning to shape human behavior. Nature had moved to the back seat.

and facial features that typify *Homo sapiens sapiens* reached their current form 100,000 years ago. The changes that occurred after that were cultural: changes in behavior and thought. And they were so critical that they altered the way humans were to change forever after. From then on, cultural changes far outpaced the slow process of physical evolution.

To the extent that the fittest humans survived the past thousands of years, it was because of culture. Warm clothes, better weapons and tools, social support, and the ability to communicate—these cultural attributes of humans provided more leverage in surviving than would any random mutation in genes or physical condition. Even at the height of the last ice age, 18,000 to 20,000 years ago, the human ability to control fire, make warm clothing and housing, and thus stay warm by cultural means far outweighed any potential physical change. It is difficult to imagine a physical change that would have been as effective. The development of a thick coat of fur-like hair would have been a successful adaptation to the ice age but to little else, especially not to the warming that began 12,000 years ago. A far more effective adaptation was the development of the ability to make a fur coat that could be worn or taken off. Physical changes are limiting because they address a single problem. The key adaptation that humans experienced was the ability to think and express themselves with complex language; the special function of culture was the ability to solve new problems as they arose.

## Human Differences: Race and Culture

The overwhelming changes that have occurred to humans over the past few hundred thousand years occurred to them all. The physical changes were species wide and very slow; the cultural changes spread rapidly. But there were some changes, both physical and cultural, that occurred separately or in varying degrees. Oddly, humans have often been more preoccupied by these differences. From the vantage point of a Martian, all humans were changing in the same way, but to human eyes on the ground, it sometimes looked like people were going their separate ways.

The most obvious physical differences among humans are those that are popularly lumped under the heading of race. Skin pigmentation is one of these. Dark pigmentation is obviously an adaptation to bright sun (actually ultraviolet light) in a tropical climate. However, that does not mean that all our African ancestors had dark skin. Today's Africa has an enormous variety of climates and peoples, and all these have changed over the past 100,000 years. But it is likely that one successful adaptation by humans who came from Africa to the cloudy skies of northern Europe was a lightening of skin pigmentation. This is because sunlight supplies necessary vitamin D, and light skin can compensate for limited sunlight. Fish are also a good source of vitamin D, so Inuit (Eskimo) adaptation to Arctic winters over the past 50,000 years has not required white skin. Each natural adaptation may have a single function, but there are numerous possible adaptations to any problem. Recent DNA evidence suggests, for instance, that the light skin of Europeans is a different genetic adaptation than the light skin of Asians.[17]

Human body sizes and shapes also varied as adaptations to climate and environment. In a hot dry climate, like that of North

Africa and the Middle East, a successful adaptation enabling the rapid release of body heat resulted in a small head, long legs with short torso, and a generally tall stature (providing a high ratio of skin surface to body mass). Initial human settlements outside of Africa were limited to the lower, warmer latitudes. But when humans began to move into northern cold and dry climates, the opposite adaptation—large heads, short legs, long torso, and short overall stature—then evolved.

When did these changes occur? Since different species of our human ancestors have traveled out of Africa on numerous occasions over the course of the past 2 million years, there is some debate about when and how modern humans evolved into their current appearances. Some, called "out-of-Africa" theorists, believe that the latest African emigrants, *Homo sapiens sapiens*, who left Africa less than 100,000 years ago, replaced all previous humans in the world without interbreeding with them. According to this theory, all physical differences among human beings would therefore have occurred within the past 100,000 years. Another theory, called "multiregional," associated with Milford Wolpoff,[18] argues that *Homo sapiens sapiens* likely interbred with the descendants of earlier travelers from Africa, possibly including the descendants of *Homo erectus*. According to this view, modern humans evolved differently in different parts of the world even though all mixed with the late-arriving *Homo sapiens sapiens* out of Africa. If Wolpoff is right, human differences evolved over the millions of years of human settlement around the globe. The debate continues: a recent DNA study argues that all modern humans are descended from an Africa migration 65,000 years ago.[19] But

another recent study suggests interbreeding: it reveals that Neanderthal DNA is 99.5 percent similar to the human genome.[20]

What about cultural differences? They are more recent than biological differences. For most of the past 5 million years, cultural changes were monotonously uniform throughout the world. Wherever humans went, they took many of the same tools. *Homo erectus* in East and South Asia used more bamboo and less stone for projectile points than did the stone toolmakers of Africa, Europe, and Central Asia. Stone axes that could be thrown like lethal Frisbees were widely produced west of India, but not, it used to be thought, in East and South Asia.[21] Recently, however, archaeologists have unearthed similar axes made 800,000 years ago in South China, suggesting that the technologies of early humans were quite similar.

Certainly in the past 100,000 years, cultural differences in the world have increased. In this period, the tool kit of central Africa was very different from that of southern Africa. Two areas of France produced different sets of tools. The cave paintings of the Mediterranean were vastly different from those of the Sahara or Australia.

Nevertheless, the emergence of separate cultural zones did not prevent one culture from influencing another. Especially during the Upper Paleolithic era (40,000 to 12,000 years ago), as cultural contacts increased, toolmakers and artists learned to borrow and adapt styles or techniques from others. Thus, the caves of Chauvet, France, were unique in their depiction of rhinos, but that was a minor variation in an animal cave art that spread throughout settled Eurasia. Strikingly similar Venus figurines were carved from 27,000 to 20,000 years ago in

Figure 1.4   Venus of Brassemouy, France 25,000–20,000 BCE. Head of a woman in Paleolithic age. This "Venus" is unusual in its attention to facial detail.  It also reveals the work of Paleolithic women in braiding and textile weaving. *Photo © RMN-Grand Palais (musée d'Archéologie nationale) / Jean-Gilles Berizzi.*

Lespuge, France; Willendorf, Austria; and Kostenski, Russia. They all emphasize the breasts, belly, thighs, and vulva of the female figure, suggesting a common religious attention to fertility.

They are also similar in their depiction of woven string material or textiles, a testament not only to a common style but perhaps also to the common activity of Paleolithic women. Is the similarity of these works a result of imitation or common development? We do not know. Certainly, no one would presume to identify a "French" or "Russian" style in any of these works. The world of national style was still far in the future.

Did all these Upper Paleolithic peoples speak the same language? We do not know that either. Some scientists postulate an original language at the time of leaving Africa, whether by *Homo erectus* 2 million or *Homo sapiens sapiens* 100,000 years ago. But because Africa contains 25 percent of the world's languages, it is likely that there were many languages in Africa before humans left to colonize the world. The current distribution of the world's language groups may only be as old as the spread of agriculture. In any case, languages change much faster than genes. Certainly, the languages we know are very recent, none of them more than a few thousand years old and most of them only a few hundred years old in recognizable form. A shaved Shakespeare in jeans would go unnoticed until he opened his mouth.

## *Do Numbers Count? Patterns of Population Growth*

If you had been viewing Earth from Mars with a good telescope for the past 100,000 years, you would likely be impressed by how humans took over the planet. From a population of about 10,000 at the beginning of the last glacial expansion about 100,000 years ago, humans increased to about 6 million by its end, 10,000 years ago. But you would also be struck by how humans replaced other animals. With the help of a technique of modern archaeology, it would be tempting to conclude that humans multiplied by eating everything in sight. The archaeological technique is the examination of ancient coprolites or fossilized excrement to determine what was eaten.[22] A team of archaeologists studied the coprolites of three long-term human settlements around the Mediterranean Sea in Italy and Israel. All these communities consumed shellfish, tortoises, partridges, hares, and rabbits from almost 200,000 years ago to 10,000 years ago. The archaeologists discovered that the food remains from the early years of settlement showed a diet made up almost entirely of the slow-maturing, slow-moving, and easy-to-catch tortoises and shellfish. By 50,000 years ago, this easy prey had declined to about three-fourths of local meat intake, and about 20,000 years ago, they fell to less than a quarter. Humans increased their numbers at the expense of the abundant, easy-to-capture prey, forcing their descendants to run ever more quickly for the hares and rabbits.

## Most of Human History: Foraging Societies

What were the lives of these first humans like? We call them foragers because that is how they obtained their food. Before the agricultural revolution, 10,000 years ago, all humans foraged for their food: gathering available plants and animals, fishing, and hunting. Some combination of hunting,

fishing, gathering, or foraging for whatever was available in nature has been the primary means of subsistence for most of humanity for most of our history: for all primates up to 10,000 years ago and for many since. Even today, there are isolated pockets of people who engage in little or no agriculture but live on what nature provides. Agriculture has spread so far and wide that today's foragers are relegated to some of the most remote and uninviting environments in the world. We find the Khoisan in the Kalahari Desert of southern Africa, the aboriginal inhabitants of Australia in the arid Outback, the Inuit (Eskimos) in the northern Arctic, the Mbuti Pygmies in the rain forests of central Africa, and many foragers deep in the Amazon rain forest.

*Lifestyles of Foragers.* It is tempting to think that these contemporary hunters and gatherers live as all our ancestors did before the agricultural revolution. No doubt there are some ways in which a foraging lifestyle shapes how people think and behave. But before we try to figure out what these are, we must issue a couple of warnings. First, we must recognize that the lives of today's foragers may be very different from that of their parents, grandparents, or ancestors. Their society has had its own history; it has not been static. Today's hunters and gatherers have not emerged from a pristine pre-agricultural world as if from a time machine. This lesson has been brought home to anthropologists and historians by a series of recent studies of foragers in the world today, beginning with a study of the Khoisan people of the Kalahari Desert.[23] Since the Khoisan are foragers today, it was assumed that their lives were continuations of ancient traditions and that they could consequently be used to speak for all of our past ancestors before the agricultural revolution. On closer inspection, however, it turned out that the Khoisan living today were actually descended from a pastoral people who had known agriculture as well as domesticated animals. Similarly, a recent study of a foraging people in the interior of Borneo revealed that their ancestors had been farmers who became gatherers hundreds of years ago in order to supply forest products to Chinese traders.[24] We can still call these people foragers or hunter-gatherers, but we cannot use them as stand-ins for the human population before agriculture.

Another warning—and one for which this chapter has already prepared the ground—is that the lives of our hunter-gatherer ancestors also changed, sometimes radically, in the tens of thousands, hundreds of thousands, and millions of years before the agricultural revolution. In time and space, the lives of foragers varied too much for us to ask "what was *it* like?" Changes in climate, tool capacity, speech, organizational ability, population density, geographical position, environment, and knowledge changed our ancestors' lives radically.

With those reservations in mind, however, we can use examples from contemporary foragers when they correspond to what we know from archaeological excavations. We have already alluded to their diet, a matter of concern to some modern nutritionists who reason that whatever worked for the first hundreds of thousands of years should be good enough for us today. Vegetarian nutritionists who hoped to find evidence of a meatless Paleolithic diet have continually been disappointed by evidence that the Upper Paleolithic diet always contained meat, but modern critics of animal fat, milk products, and grains have found support for

their contention that the modern diet is a radical departure from that of our ancient ancestors. Food remains of ancient hunter-gatherers show a heavy reliance on lean game animals, fish and crustaceans, nuts, fruits, berries, and leaves. It was a diet high in protein and low in carbohydrates and fats, especially when compared to the dietary changes that came about as a result of the agricultural revolution. It was also a varied diet, consisting of a wider-than-modern variety of plants and animals, many of which no longer exist.

What of their social life? Like modern foragers, our pre-agricultural ancestors probably lived in groups of families or "bands" of a couple dozen to a couple hundred individuals. Bands were further divided into families and groups of relatives. Like modern foragers, many were nomadic, following game seasonally, returning periodically to familiar places, but building homes from available materials (leaves, grasses, mud, or ice) quickly for stays of a few nights to a few months. Not all hunters and gatherers were nomadic, however. Some of our foraging ancestors lived in almost permanent communities, and some Paleolithic sites were inhabited continually. Whether nomadic or settled, they carried few possessions with them, owned little in the way of personal or family property, shared the bounty of a hunt, and made sure that everyone had an adequate and roughly equal supply of food.

*Sexual Division of Labor.* In most cases, men hunted, usually in small groups, while women gathered plants and small animals with the children, closer to home. This sexual division of labor is typical of modern foragers, but few today live in regions of abundance as they once did. Modern hunters sometimes travel for days, even weeks, at a time, bringing back the kill for a special feast. The richer natural environment of the Upper Paleolithic tropical and temperate world might have made meat more frequent, man's work easier, the male presence greater, and men's social role more prominent. In modern foraging societies, especially those in which plant life provides the bulk of the food source, the women's role is correspondingly important. Nevertheless, the Venus figurines of the Upper Paleolithic suggest that the woman's role as provider of life was a matter of considerable concern, perhaps even veneration. Kathleen Gough, an anthropologist who studied foragers in India, wrote that women in hunting societies are "less subordinated in crucial respects" than are women in almost all other societies. "Especially lacking in hunting societies," she writes, "is the kind of male possessiveness and exclusiveness regarding women that leads to such institutions as savage punishment or death for female adultery, the jealous guarding of female chastity and virginity, the denial of divorce to women, or the ban on a woman's remarriage after her husband's death."[25]

Whether or not women were worshipped as life givers, fertility goddesses, or food providers, they played many important roles in Paleolithic society. Besides bearing children and providing what was likely the most reliable source of food by gathering, women were also the ones who cooked the food and distributed it to the family.

Women also probably invented fabric. Paleolithic figurines show that women have learned to make string by twisting fiber and wear garments like skirts from dangling string tied to a band. A recently excavated site in the Czech Republic shows evidence of both weaving and pottery, dating from 28,000 years ago. Both of these activities were traditionally women's work, performed almost exclusively by women in agricultural societies. That these skills developed long before the agricultural revolution 10,000 years ago may be an indication that some Upper Paleolithic societies were much more sophisticated than we have thought.

*Relative Social Equality.* The politics of Paleolithic society probably reflected its relative social equality. Our popular image of one caveman lording it over others is far from the reality. In modern hunter-gatherer bands, decision making is based on consensus. There is often a "headman" or leader, but his position is usually limited and advisory. For instance, the headman in a !Kung Khoisan band depicted in the film *The Hunters* is chosen because his wife is the daughter of a previous headman *and* because he has the confidence of the others in the band. Leadership is neither a full-time activity nor a job that excuses one from other duties. The only other specialty is that of a shaman, healer, or religious intermediary. Among contemporary hunter-gatherers, this individual also emerges through some combination of birth and evidence of special abilities. Among Arctic Eskimos, the role of shaman, which requires a high sensitivity to the spiritual world, typically fell to the individual, male or female, who seemed least adept at hunting and practical skills.

*Leisure Time.* How much time and energy went into providing food? Anthropologists have discovered that most modern foraging bands are able to provide for their basic needs and still have considerable leisure time. In fact, it seems that modern foragers spend less time working and more time at leisure than do people in agricultural or industrial societies. Even in the Kalahari Desert of southern Africa, a desolate and barren landscape to the outsider, the !Kung are able to find enough game, plants, roots, insects, and water to spend most of their time at leisure. Since our Paleolithic ancestors 10,000 to 50,000 years ago were not limited to remote areas or fragile ecosystems and since their world was far richer in flora and fauna, their workweek must have been even shorter. Nevertheless, there is no sign in the archaeological record of individuals of special privilege or distinction. While there are burial sites from this period, it is not until much later (5,000 to 6,000 years ago) that some graves outrank others.

Interpreters of the lives of our foraging ancestors carry heavy burdens. There seems to be much at stake, in part because this "first" stage of human history is seen as the formative beginning and in part because it was such a long period of human history. Inevitably, the sense that our Paleolithic ancestors created "the human condition," shaped "human nature," that they are the "original" or the "real" us, demands more of our ancestors than is possible to accurately determine.

Again, our distinction between biology and culture may be useful. Biologically, we are still like our ancestors tens of thousands of years ago. That may be significant in terms of our diet, our need for exercise, and our vulnerability to the ills of sedentary society. But culturally we are worlds away from our Paleolithic ancestors, and our ideas, feelings, visions, and dreams are shaped by our culture, not our biology.

The difference is manifest if we consider a little hypothetical experiment. Imagine that we were able to exchange two newborn babies: one born 30,000 years ago with one

born yesterday. At the age of 20, the child from the Paleolithic world would be dating, driving, and enjoying college world history courses like everyone else. The child born to modernity but raised in Paleolithic culture would be sniffing the air for the spoor of the wild boar, distinguishing the poisonous mushrooms from the healthy ones, or scanning the backs of beetles for signs of a cold winter. Both would have adapted to their worlds as completely and effortlessly as everyone else because everything they needed—including such physical attributes as muscular strength or the ability to distinguish smells—was taught by their culture. If, on the other hand, we were able to take two 50-year-olds, one from each world, and exchange them, both would be completely lost. Their cultures would have prepared them for skills that were irrelevant and unnecessary. And yet, with time, they too could learn.

*Merging Old and New.* In December 2001, the shamans from a tenth of Brazil's 230 indigenous nations met in the Amazon and drew up a declaration calling on the Brazilian government to "create punishment mechanisms to deter the robbery of our biodiversity."[26] Concerned that they were losing control of their traditional knowledge of Brazilian plants to international pharmaceutical corporations, they called for a "moratorium on the commercial exploitation of traditional knowledge of genetic resources." Their goal was not to deprive foreign scientists and corporations from benefiting from their knowledge but to develop a system that would involve them and pay royalties. "We're not against science, but we don't want to be just suppliers of data," an organizer of the conference, Marcos Terena of the Terena tribe, explained. "We want to be part of the whole process from research to economic results." The modern descendants of forest foragers have learned a lot.

## Subduing the Earth: The Consequences of Domestication

### *The First Breakthrough: Origins of Agricultural/Pastoral Economies*

With her galaxy's most powerful telescope, an astronomer viewing the planet Earth over the past million years would have had no reason to suspect the existence of intelligent life until very recently. Ice covered the poles, periodically pushing toward the equator and then retreating. The last expansion, which began 100,000 years ago, reached its maximum extent, halfway to the equator, about 20,000 years ago. About 10,000 years ago, our astronomer would have seen something new. That is when she could see anything at all, because as the ice retreated, it was replaced by mist and clouds. She would have seen green areas become more uniform in color, shape, and size. It was the stamp of agriculture. First by planting wild roots and seeds about 10,000 years ago and finally by plowing and irrigating fields and hillsides by 5,000 years ago, humans were revealing their presence on the planet.

The intergalactic astronomer could only imagine the scene at ground level. In a couple of temperate, well-watered areas of the planet, women whose mothers had for generations dug the tubers and gathered the grains were putting some of them back into the ground. They were doing it systematically: punching holes in the ground with a digging stick and planting. Soon they were choosing particular plants, putting them in particular places, making sure there was

sufficient sun and water, and clearing the area to improve the yield.

*Control over Food Supply.* At the same time that women began to take control of edible plants, men began to control some of the animals they were in the habit of hunting. The taming or domestication of wild animals, although not visible from distant galaxies, had the same effect as the breeding and growing of favored plants. Men and women were controlling their food supply: increasing it, stabilizing it, and asserting their dominance over nature. From then on, as any sensible astronomer could see, a new planet had produced a species that was about to organize and subdue its small world.

Why then? The retreat of the ice about 12,000 years ago would be part of the

Figure 1.5 Saharan Africa: 6000-4000 BCE, pigment on rock, Tassili n'Ajjer, Algeria. This rock painting from the Sahara Desert shows the relationship between women and agriculture. Notice the grain falling from the stalks that grow like a crown above the woman's head. Consider also how the Sahara was different in the early Neolithic age.

answer. Warmer temperatures (an average of 4 or 5 degrees Fahrenheit) and greater rainfall increased the number of plants that could be turned to human use. Vast fields of wheat and barley sprang up in the Middle East, providing a regular diet of cereals for an expanding population of people. The rising levels of rivers and oceans also increased the varieties and amount of fish available. In China too, rivers and coasts carried more fish and shellfish, and marshlands multiplied the varieties of wild rice.

But that most recent retreat of ice was not a simple cause of the agricultural revolution. People may have learned to consume a wider variety of plants, especially in the Middle East. In northern Syria, there is early evidence of grinding wild grains and the use of a wide array of stone implements for harvesting cereals and other wild food. But there was no agriculture to supplement, much less replace, gathering for another 2,000 years. So agriculture was not just the result of warmer weather.

There is also a problem with the idea that people chose agriculture as an obvious effort to better their lives. The problem is that no one could have foreseen that the long-term effects of agriculture would be beneficial. In fact, the short-term effects were probably not. Archaeologists who have examined skeleton remains of early farmers of about 10,000 years ago have found evidence that the first farmers may not have eaten as well as gatherers had. Their bone fragments show signs that early farmers suffered from inferior nutrition, shorter stature, and earlier deaths than their foraging ancestors. A recent discovery of drilled teeth from a Neolithic site in Pakistan 9,000 years ago might mark our ancestor's first visit to the dentist—a practice made increasingly

necessary by the abrasive minerals produced when grain was ground on stone.[27] In addition, anthropologists have concluded that most farmers worked longer hours than hunters and gatherers.

*Why Agriculture Developed.* So why did they do it? Why did gatherers choose the backbreaking work of planting instead of just plucking fruit from the tree? And why did hunters decide to raise animals instead of just killing the wild ones? Why did they go through the trouble of taming, herding, feeding, and breeding them for meals they might not even live to enjoy?

A clue to the answer may lie in the ice-age confusion. If warmer, wetter weather 12,000 years ago multiplied vegetation and animals, including humans, why did they wait another 2,000 years to become farmers? The agricultural revolution occurred not as the glaciers retreated 12,000 years ago but in the sudden cold snap that followed. So the question is not only why agriculture, but why agriculture then? The answer may be because they had to.

Food production probably replaced hunting and gathering in a two-step process of experiment followed by necessity. First, 12,000 years ago, as the ice melted, increased rains and longer summers added abundant new species of plants and animals. In a world full of choices, gatherers continued weeding, selecting, and harvesting one species over another. But there was no need to plant what nature provided free of charge. Similarly, wild animals could be tamed as a supplement or leisure activity rather than as a necessity: first the wolf that became the dog, then wild sheep and goats were easily herded by people and dogs and provided food and clothing on demand. But in a world full of wild gazelles, shepherding was an unnecessary activity. Populations grew in the warming years; settlements increased, and people gorged on a natural harvest that seemed eternal. Then, in the wake of a dry, cold snap between 11,000 and 10,000 years ago,[28] with more mouths to feed, the party ended. Agriculture and pasture became necessities. We know, for instance, that horses and wild gazelles, an important source of meat and protein, were rapidly disappearing from the Middle East about 10,000 years ago.

*Selecting Crops to Grow.* The astronomer from another planet would have needed a telescope with an extremely sensitive color receptor to notice something else about the spreading green on planet Earth. The shades of green that she saw beginning 10,000 years ago were both different and less varied than the earlier ice-age greens. The farmers were changing the planet's plants and choosing a few to take the place of the many.

Farmers made different choices than nature. Nature selected plants with abundant seeds for survival against birds, pests, and chance. Humans chose to plant fruits, like bananas, with fewer or smaller seeds so that they would not get caught in their teeth. Nature protected some plants—the ancestors of almonds, cabbages, and potatoes, for instance—with a sour taste or poisonous fruit. Humans chose to develop the rare specimen that lacked this protection. Nature took fewer risks, finding safety in the widest variety of species. Humans chose the tastiest or hardiest and replaced the others.

Human choices enabled the human population to grow exponentially. A few choices, like cereal crops bred for maximum number of grains, made all the difference. The grain/seeds of wild grasses were indigestible for humans and eaten only by animals 12,000

years ago. Today, grains like wheat, barley, millet, oats, rice, and corn—processed as cereals, ground as flour, and turned into noodles, breads, and baked goods—feed the world. This is a result of the domestication of these grains, the process of enlarging their size and quantity. The modern ear of corn, for instance, is a product of thousands of years of domestication. Five thousand years ago, it was a grass with small grains on the tip. Mexican Indians enlarged it to a thumbnail size stalk by about 2,000 years ago, and it measured about five inches by the time of the Spanish conquest of Mexico, 500 years ago. Today, the average ear of corn measures eight or nine inches.

In some cases, humans increased the variety of nature. They took the humble ancestor of the cabbage, for instance, and produced a wide variety of descendants. Initially cultivated for the oil of its seeds, some cultivators chose to develop it for its leaves, producing modern cabbage; others chose plants with abundant small buds, leading to Brussels sprouts; and still others cultivated the flower and stems, producing broccoli and cauliflower.

*Reducing Variety.* But the overwhelming impact of the farmer was to reduce nature's riot of species, concentrating on those that humans could eat, especially those that produced the most per planting. Out of 200,000 species of wild plants, humans ate only a few thousand, and of those they domesticated only a few hundred. Today, only 12 of those account for 80 percent of the world's tonnage of crops.[29] These are wheat, corn, rice, barley, sorghum, soybeans, potato, sweet potato, manioc, sugarcane, sugar beet, and banana.

The selection of crops for planting also reduced the genetic variety within a species.

Ninety percent of all the world's apples are descended from only two trees out of the thousands that existed in the forests of Kazakhstan 6,000 years ago.[30] The shallow gene pool that results from ages of interbreeding makes such plants more vulnerable to blights, pests, and diseases. Apple growers, for instance, are returning to the central Asian source to breed hardier apples. Unfortunately, many plants that were discarded have become extinct. Many that have been adapted to human needs can no longer grow without human intervention. Bananas and breadfruit, for instance, can no longer be reproduced from their tiny seeds but require humans to make cuttings from their stalks for reproduction.

In summary, the great revolution of human food production began to transform the world about 10,000 years ago after the end of the last ice age. It was a gradual process that began in discovery and experimentation and culminated in the need of growing populations to confront periodic shortages of wild foods. The result was not only a dramatic increase in human population and a change in human lifestyles but also a reshaping of the natural world.

## *Globalization and Continental Variety*

Food production was the first human step to globalization. First, a planet of hunters and gatherers started to become a planet of farmers and herders. Second, these first farmers and herders in various parts of the world began exchanging recipes, sharing seeds, and using the same or similar animals for food, clothing, and transport.

But some people were left out of this new revolution, in some cases for a long time. Thus, a revolution that eventually created a single world also created the first "haves" and "have-nots." In the beginning, many farmers may not have lived better than foragers. But eventually, farmers formed larger, more complex societies; took the best land; and forced the remaining bands of gatherers to the margins: deserts, barren mountains, dense rain forests, and the Arctic north.

For most of the 10,000 years since the beginning of domestication, the world has belonged to the farmers. Their descendants produced the first cities, states, and empires beginning 5,000 years ago. Their urban revolution of city building, state formation, and the development of complex, literate societies was in one sense a departure from agricultural society and in another sense its fulfillment. The great urban empires of Mesopotamia and Egypt, India, China, and the Americas erected their monuments by taxing and working untold numbers of peasant farmers. They invented writing and trained poets and historians to tell their stories as if they were the only stories to be told. The foragers of the Philippines, Australia, the Amazon, and the African Kalahari and the hunting and fishing peoples of the American Northwest, the Arctic, and the hills of Southeast Asia were relegated to the spectator seats while the great ones strutted their stuff on the world stage.

Nevertheless, not all agricultural societies became urban empires 5,000 years ago, and some of the early empires were not descended from the first farmers. The winners of history are not always the smartest or most talented. It took over 1,000 years for agriculture to spread from its first home in the Middle East to the Mediterranean. Greece and Rome and then Europe were late borrowers who made good use of the invention. And some of the important breakthroughs that enabled agricultural societies to become empires—domesticated horses, wheels, and chariots—first came to light in central Asia, not in the agricultural societies that later turned horse-drawn chariots into engines of empire.

*Geography as Destiny.* Why did some agricultural societies prosper far more than others? Geography partly explains why some agricultural people, borrowers as well as inventors, turned cultivation into high culture. In *Guns, Germs, and Steel*, Jared Diamond argued provocatively that powerful city-based empires grew in Mesopotamia, Egypt, the Mediterranean, Europe, India, and China because these agricultural societies were geographically well placed and close together. They had the good fortune to be where there were many available plants and animals that could be domesticated or to live along the same latitudes as the initial fortunate few who first domesticated them.[31]

The first farmers, those of the Middle East, were blessed with a wide variety of plants and animals, many of which could be domesticated. Wheat and barley were prominent cereal grains of the Fertile Crescent, the area that stretched along the Tigris and Euphrates rivers to the foothills of Turkey and the Mediterranean. The Fertile Crescent also had abundant pulses (edible seeds, like beans, which are rich in protein), specifically peas and lentils.

Perhaps the wild gazelles were hunted almost to extinction because they could not be domesticated. But the people of the Fertile Crescent domesticated sheep, goats, pigs, and cattle. They brought these animals under human control not only for food but also for their wool and hides for clothing and eventually for milk and cheese. They also recognized the utility of certain plants for their fiber content and planted flax for the fiber we know as linen.

China, too, had a rich assortment of wild plants and animals that could be domesticated. The Chinese had access to millet in the northern Yellow River valley and wild rice in the lakes and marshes of the southerly Yangtze River. In addition, soybeans provided protein. For meat, the Chinese domesticated the pig. For fiber, they grew

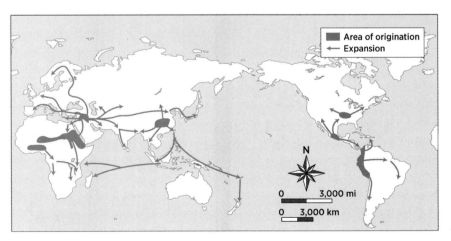

Map 1.2 Agriculture originated independently in nine different regions of the world. What are these, and what plants did they domesticate?

Figure 1.6 The first step of the agricultural revolution was to recognize the nutritive grains that grew in nearby wild plants. These are modern domesticated rice plants. *Photo by Damien Boilley, January 5, 2006.*

hemp for rope and the silkworm for silk cloth.

Other areas of independent domestication offered different combinations of cereals, pulses, animals, and fibers. The African Sahel (the grasslands just south of the Sahara) had the cereal grains sorghum, millet, and African rice and such pulses as cowpeas and African peanuts. In addition, guinea fowls provided meat. Separately, farther south in West Africa, the available domesticates were African yams, oil palms, watermelon, gourds, and cotton. Farther east, in Ethiopia, coffee was first domesticated along with certain local plants.

Native Americans domesticated plants and animals in three areas. The inhabitants of Central America and Mexico domesticated tomatoes, corn, beans, squash, and turkeys. South Americans (in the Andes and Amazon) domesticated potatoes, the grain

quinoa, various beans, and the llama, alpaca, and guinea pig. In addition, the inhabitants of the Eastern Woodlands (today's eastern United States) domesticated a number of local plants that yield starchy or oily seeds, like the sunflower. Independently of all these areas, the farmers in New Guinea domesticated sugarcane, bananas, yams, and taro, but they lacked cereals and animals.

Of these nine separate cases of domestication in the world, only a few produced a wide range of edible plants, a balance of carbohydrates and proteins, and animals for meat, hides, and transportation. The Middle East was the richest area, followed by China and South and Central America. Some areas initiated farming or herding with so few plants and animals that people continued to forage or hunt for much of their food. Ethiopia, West Africa, New Guinea, and North America were such areas. In these cases, domestication was a part-time affair, supplemented by hunting, fishing, and gathering. In addition, Eurasia enjoyed a far greater variety of animals that could be domesticated than did Africa and the Americas.

Thus, the agricultural/pastoral revolution began to create a world in which the accidents of geography enabled some people to benefit from a varied diet and wide range of animals under human control, while others did not. Almost all farming societies grew and prospered at the expense of foragers. But some of the original agricultural societies—again, New Guinea, the West Africans, and the native North Americans—did not develop the complex urban and literate cultures that became the next step for agriculturalists 5,000 years later. The most successful agricultural societies, in addition to the Middle East and China, were probably Egypt, India, and the Mediterranean, all of which piggybacked on the original discoveries in the Middle East or Southwest Asia.

*East–West Transmission Advantages.* What accounts for this difference in fortunes? Again, geography may be the answer. In general, plants, animals, people, and ideas moved more easily along an east–west than a north–south axis. If other climate factors like rainfall and temperature were similar, newly domesticated crops could be easily transplanted on the same latitude because the climate and growing season were similar. The plants and animals that were domesticated in the Fertile Crescent traveled easily from the Tigris and Euphrates westward to Egypt, the Mediterranean and Europe, and eastward to Iran, Afghanistan, and India. In each of those areas, the new farmers and herders added new crops and tamed new animals—Egyptian figs and donkeys; Indian cucumbers, cotton, and humped cattle; and Mediterranean olives and grapes. The result was a remarkably varied basket of cereals, pulses, fruits, and vegetables and numerous animals for food, transport, clothing, and pets, most of which could travel back and forth between Europe and India.

Conversely, plants and animals resisted north–south movement. Horses would not breed easily close to the equator because the even hours of night and day hampered ovulation. Mexican corn took 1,000 years to reach what is today the United States.

Chinese domesticated crops and animals also moved more quickly along the eastbound paths of the great river valleys: millet along the Yellow River and rice along the Yangtze. But north–south movement was slow. Northern domesticated pigs, dogs, and mulberry trees did not transfer easily to the more tropical zones of southern China. Southern Chinese wet rice and tropical fruits did not easily move north, but along with pigs and chickens, they traveled in two directions: south into Southeast Asia and east to the island of Taiwan about 6,000 years ago. There, the southern Chinese cultural complex joined the maritime and fishing traditions of the island, forming a new complex called Austronesian and a culture of maritime expansion. In the Philippines about 5,000 years ago, this culture added such tropical products as bananas, taro, sugarcane, and breadfruit to their diet of rice, chicken, and pigs. Within another 1,000 years, it spread to the coasts of Southeast Asia and the islands of Indonesia, from which Polynesian descendants colonized the Pacific Ocean as far east as Easter Island and as far west as the Indian Ocean and Madagascar, paving the way for the introduction of the yams, bananas, and other tropical fruits into Africa.

To summarize, the domestication of plants and animals gave certain peoples, though not always the original inventors, a leg up on the next global revolution—cities and state societies. The future would belong to those who, by accident of geography, could borrow, imitate, innovate, and interact with neighbors in a similar environment—and that often meant latitude.

*Agriculture and Language.* The first farmers may have spread their languages with their seeds. Whether farmers actually moved and displaced earlier hunting-gathering populations or passed on their words with their seeds and techniques, a map of the spread of languages follows the spread of agriculture. Each of the original nine places of domestication seems to have passed its language along to those who adopted its foods. Thus, the Indo-European language family, which extends from Ireland to India, covers a northern band of the territory that received the crops of the Fertile Crescent. The Afro-Asiatic family of languages, which includes ancient Egyptian and Semitic languages like Hebrew and Arabic, extends across a southern band of shared crops from Egypt or the Fertile Crescent. Chinese cultivators may have spread three language families: Sino-Tibetan, Tai, and Austroasiatic. From the latter in Taiwan came the Austronesian language group, which spread throughout the Pacific. Most of these language groups spread in an east–west direction. Where such movement was blocked, as in the Americas, languages and crops moved slower and not as far. In Africa, the Niger-Congo language family spread from West Africa eastward and then southward, never fully displacing the earlier click languages of the non-agricultural Khoisan people. In general, forager languages remained more localized.

Languages and crops could travel with people on the move or be exchanged in trade with foreigners. In the Americas, corn spread mainly through trade. Mexican corn moved gradually to the southwestern and southeastern United States in separate series of trading exchanges. In the Middle East, early farmers spread their crops and languages by moving to new areas and cultivating new lands. The process varied in speed and intensity. Early agriculture spread rapidly. One recent theory argues for a spur in a possible natural catastrophe: the displacement of early farmers by the overflow of the Mediterranean onto the shores of the Black Sea about 8,000 years ago.[32] Whether the early farmers of the Mediterranean were refugees from a rapidly flooding homeland or merely the descendants of earlier Middle Eastern farmers starting new families, the process was swift across the Mediterranean but very slow into northern Europe.

Agriculture, however, drove one of many waves of language change. In later centuries, pastoral peoples, most notably Arabs, Turks, and Mongols, spread their languages over vast areas of Eurasia. In the modern era, European colonizers substituted their languages for innumerable Native American, African, and Asian languages, a process that continues today with the use of English for certain computer and international purposes.

## The Long Agricultural Age: Places and Processes

From our vantage point as members of a city-based civilization, it may seem as though the domestication of plants and animals was merely a step on the way to cities, states, governments, complex societies, and often bronze metallurgy and writing. But agricultural village life, without cities or states, was the norm for most of humanity for most of the past 10,000 years. In this section, we survey the scope and length of the agricultural age by looking at a few specific sites at particular times. In addition to suggesting the enormous variety of agricultural societies before the formation of cities and states, these examples suggest how the transition to cities occurred.

*Jericho.* The remains of one of the earliest agricultural villages in human history lie beneath the modern town of Jericho in

Figure 1.7  Inside a model of a house in Catal Huyuk. Notice the ladder to the roof entrance.
*Photo by Stipich Béla.*

Palestine, on an oasis in the desert northwest of the Dead Sea. Archaeologists have unearthed signs of the conversion from gathering to farming dating more than 10,000 years ago. There are round huts indicating permanent settlement and a large wall circling the village. There is also evidence of pottery, baked brick, textiles, grinding stones, and the polished stone blades that became a hallmark of the Neolithic period, or New Stone Age. More than 2,000 people may have lived in the village at an early stage. Its permanence for them is attested by the recent discovery of decorated human skulls with seashells in the eye sockets, placed in a collective burial.

*Catal Huyuk.* One of the most intensely excavated sites of the early agricultural or Neolithic age is Catal Huyuk, in Turkey, dating from 9,000 years ago.[33] Spanning 32 acres, at its height it may have numbered 10,000 people. While earlier Jericho consisted of rounded dwellings and only later switched to rectangular houses, Catal Huyuk was composed from its beginning of rectangular dwellings, situated side by side and on top of each other like a layered field of bricks three or four stories high. Without streets to separate one row of buildings from another, the people of Catal Huyuk entered their dwellings by ladder from the roof.

Why did farming people deliberately live in such crowded quarters in what resembles a modern apartment complex? For over 1,000 years (10,500 to 9,000 years ago), the dwellings of people in places like Jericho were moving farther apart as foragers became full-time farmers. It seems that the introduction of agriculture pushed people apart by giving families independence from each other. But from the beginnings of Catal Huyuk, about 9,000 years ago, its

Figure 1.8   A statue from about 6000 BCE called by some "the great goddess of Catal Huyuk," sitting on a throne, flanked by large cats and giving birth: an echo of earlier "Venus figurines" and a precursor of the Middle Eastern agricultural goddess Cybele. *HIP/ Art Resource, NY.*

inhabitants clustered together like bees in a beehive. James Mellaart, the archaeologist who began excavations of the site in the 1950s, called it a "Neolithic city." But later excavations have revealed none of the elements of city life except for the clustered living. Archaeologists have found no public spaces, for instance. Even Jericho had public walls and a tower. Catal Huyuk also shows no sign of a division of labor, not even the distinction between farmers and other occupations, which is a basic characteristic of city life. Each family constructed its own home with a slightly different mix of materials for mud and plaster. Families also used the nearby deposits of obsidian for blades and mirrors, which they fashioned in their own homes.

In fact, the inhabitants of Catal Huyuk were not even full-time farmers. People lived on wild seeds, acorns, pistachio nuts, fruits, and grains as well as domesticated cereals (wheat and barley), lentils, and peas. Similarly, while they domesticated sheep, goats, and cattle, they also consumed wild horses, deer, boar, bears, foxes, wolves, dogs, birds, and fish. Catal Huyuk had other Neolithic characteristics, however. The people created ceramic pottery, wove cloth that they wore in addition to skins, and amassed a wide range of tools, containers (straw baskets as well as pots), weapons (bow and arrow), and objects for art or ritual.

Archaeologists also found early examples of an art form that is characteristic of Neolithic societies. There are numerous figurines of women, many of which show heavy breasts or protruding stomachs that might suggest pregnancy or fertility. One enthroned woman figurine, dubbed the "mother goddess" by Mellaart, evokes later myths of goddesses who suckled animals and of Earth Mothers who gave birth to vegetation each spring. But there are other images as well. There are sculptured heads of bulls and animal horns on walls. There are headless figures with arms and legs splayed outward, possibly giving birth. There are also images of vultures, apparently pecking at headless bodies.

What does all this mean? Archaeologists are excavating this huge site with painstaking care, and their work is expected to take another 20 years. But at this point, they can venture a couple of theories. One is that religion, whether or not it was related to goddess worship, was a central focus of daily life in Catal Huyuk. There are no freestanding temples. The sculptured clay and plaster images have been found in people's homes, usually in one room of a three-room house. This separateness within the house, in a place that was frequently swept clean, suggests a sacred space for each family: a family religion rather than a larger public worship.

Finally, the excavations reveal considerable attention to death, dying, and the dead. Like earlier farmers (e.g., Jericho), the people of Catal Huyuk buried their dead under the floor. Sometimes they decapitated the bodies and just buried the skulls. The images of vultures pecking at headless bodies may reveal what happened to the rest of the remains outside. In Jericho, whole rooms of skulls were found in addition to sculptured or cast figures of the heads of the deceased. In Catal Huyuk and some nearby sites, people did something else. At the end of a particular time frame, after a number of family skulls or bodies had been buried under the house, the whole house would be filled up and everything covered in dirt, including the images on the wall, the oven, and the possessions of the last person who died. Then it appears that the next generation of the same family would construct its house over the one that had just been buried, beginning the cycle again. This is why Catal Huyuk appeared to be a Neolithic apartment complex: people did not live on top of each other; rather, they lived on top of their ancestors. This may have been a form of ancestor worship or a way of making sense of the passing of previous generations. The fertility imagery might have added the important dimension of the future. In any case, art, religion, and daily life seem to have been closely related in Catal Huyuk in houses that were also temples to the ancestors.

*Banpo.* One of the oldest well-excavated Neolithic sites in China is Banpo, a village near the Yellow River and modern Xian, settled about 6,000 years ago. The inhabitants domesticated millet, pigs, and dogs and supplemented their diets with numerous fish and fowl. The dwellings at Banpo resembled Jericho more than Catal Huyuk; many were rounded dwellings of mud and thatch on a scaffold of wooden poles; they were scattered rather than clustered together. A trench encircled the village, like the wall of Jericho. Like Jericho, Banpo had public spaces that may have been meeting or ritual areas. But adults and children were buried whole, adults outside the trench, children inside the village and enclosed in pottery jars with open bottoms. Like both Catal Huyuk and Jericho, Banpo was a village of equals. There was little, if any, sign of political or religious leadership: no palaces, temples, or signs of differentiated status. Each house was the same size, constructed by its occupants.

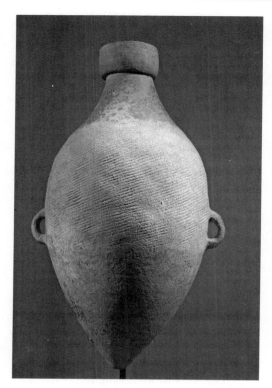

Figure 1.9   Chinese vase from early Neolithic village, Banpo, about 5000 BCE, marked with hemp cord. The agricultural revolution created pottery and advanced weaving, both likely women's work. © *DeA Picture Library/ Art Resource, NY.*

Figure 1.10   Writing was a later urban invention, but we see here some possible beginnings in pottery design from Banpo village 6,000 years ago.

As at Catal Huyuk, there is some evidence at other early Neolithic sites that women played an important role. At Banpo, a young female was buried with more possessions than others. This may be a sign that the society was matrilineal, that is, that inheritance was figured from mother to daughter. Matrilineal inheritance was common in Native American Neolithic societies and among some of the first Neolithic settlers in Europe, the Bandkeramik people, where female graves are also more ornate than those of males. In fact, the matrilineal clan may have been common in early Neolithic society. Excavations in Thailand at Khok Phanon Di (near modern Bangkok) have revealed evidence of early rice cultivation about 4,000 years ago along what was a shellfish-rich mangrove coast. Among many unexceptional burials, archaeologists have excavated the body of a woman elaborately clothed in a dress sewn with 120,000 beads whose arms were covered with decorative shell bracelets. Because she is buried with a treasure of pottery, archaeologists surmise that this "Princess" of Khok Phanon Di was an expert potter who may have traded her pottery for shell ornaments. More generally, the role of women in producing high-quality pottery at Khok Phanon Di may have raised their status.

If early Neolithic society was frequently matrilineal, it may have been related to women's role in the domestication of agriculture. As the gatherers of an earlier age, women were the first to cultivate plants. One can easily imagine an early association between women's capacity to produce life from their own bodies and their skill or rapport with Mother Earth. The worship of women's fertility might have been a key ingredient of Neolithic religion. Long after Catal Huyuk had been abandoned, farming communities worshipped goddesses of the earth, harvest, field, or hunt. One archaeologist, Marija Gimbutas, has reported excavating thousands of figurines that suggest the continuation of a worship of the mother goddess in southern Europe until about 4,000 years ago. Many later cultures captured in written myths and stories what must have been living legend in the early age of agriculture. The Sumerian goddess Inanna descends to the underworld, and the crops and animals die; she returns, and all life is reborn. The Greek goddess of the harvest, Demeter, allows the earth to turn green during the six months that her daughter Persephone is allowed to visit from the underworld. Later folk myths continued the identification of women and the fertility of the earth: women should plant corn because they know how to produce children, the sterile wife is injurious to a garden, seed grows best when planted by a pregnant woman, and only bare-breasted women should harvest the crops.[34] Until quite recently, it was common practice to throw rice at a bride to ensure her fertility.

*Ibo Culture.* In some places, Neolithic culture ended with the rise of cities 5,000 years ago. New urban ways replaced the culture of the village. But in most parts of the world, Neolithic culture continued or changed more gradually. The modern African novelist Chinua Achebe re-creates the Neolithic culture of his Ibo people in a series of novels set in West Africa at the end of the nineteenth and the beginning of the twentieth century. In *Things Fall Apart*, a story of the destruction of traditional Ibo culture by European missionaries and colonialists, as well as other historical novels, Achebe recalls a world of family-centered rural Africa in which individual households are relatively equal and individuals are distinguished by merit and ability rather than birth. Ibo men compete not for money, which barely exists, but for titles that recognize their good works or feats of strength. Some have more yams than others, some are more ambitious than others, but everyone is taken care of by family, clan, and village. In proverbial Ibo wisdom, individuals must remember their roots: "However tall a coconut tree, it originated in the ground."[35] And no one is entirely self-sufficient: "A bird with a very long beak does not peck out what is on its head."[36]

At the beginning of the previous century, Ibo culture was also one in which both men and women had important sources of power and status. Both had personal spiritual guides, called *chi*, which they challenged only at their peril. There was an earth goddess, Ani, who was the source of fertility, provider of the harvest, and arbiter of morality. There were other gods and goddesses, natural and ancestral, mediated through priests and priestesses, but in an agricultural society, the earth goddess was the most important in people's lives. Her power did not necessarily translate into female domination, however. Ani was interpreted through her priest.

In certain respects, Ibo culture favored men over women. Men but not women were allowed to have more than one spouse. Men were the heads of the household. A male-centered culture encouraged men to discipline women and demeaned weaker males by calling them women.

Was Ibo society more male-centered than early Neolithic societies like Catal Huyuk? Did inequality increase? How did Neolithic societies change? In some cases, of course, they became larger. Population pressure could lead to increased density in a single village like Catal Huyuk. Alternately, a growing population could send members away to settle new colonies. On a large scale, this is how Austronesian and Polynesian society colonized the Pacific. Population size affected government. Small villages often governed themselves. Typically, a group of elders would decide what was best for the village. From all indications, Catal Huyuk managed such self-government by elders despite its size. The slice of Ibo culture that Achebe re-creates in *Things Fall Apart* consists of nine villages. In this case, some decisions were made by the elders of the village and some by the larger clan or tribe that embraces all nine villages.

Not all societies become larger and larger. Some were able to reach a balance and remain the same size for generations. But when some Neolithic societies expanded beyond the size of self-governing villages, they often developed a more complex system of government. Some anthropologists call this a transition from a tribal structure to a chiefdom. Such a transition may have occurred for the first time in the Middle East as early as 7,500 years ago and in the Americas about 3,000 years ago. One example of an American chiefdom was the Taino people of the Caribbean at the time of the arrival of Columbus, 500 years ago.

*The Taino.* The Taino inhabited the Bahamas and the Caribbean, north of Guadeloupe, in 1492. The island of Hispaniola (Haiti and the Dominican Republic today) may have had as many as 500,000 inhabitants. Cuba, Puerto Rico, and Jamaica each had a population of a few hundred thousand. The Taino lived in villages of 100 to a few thousand in round wood and thatch dwellings around a plaza. In a slightly larger building on the plaza lived the *cacique*, or chief. A group of villages were ruled by a district chief, one of whom, the regional chief, was in charge of all districts. This hierarchical organization was reflected even on the small scale of the village, which distinguished between upper- and lower-class people.

Taino society was also more specialized than Catal Huyuk or later Ibo society. There were Tainos experienced in such crafts as woodworking, pottery, cotton weaving, and hammering gold nuggets into jewelry (but not smelting). There were Tainos who made the hammocks in which most people slept, the baskets that hung from every wall, the elaborate wooden stools on which the chief sat, and the individual and grand chiefly canoes that provided transportation.[37] Yet none of these were full-time specialists.

The basic work of Taino society, like less complex Neolithic societies, was agriculture. And the basic implements of agriculture were still the digging stick and the hoe. But Taino agriculture was more sophisticated than that of early Neolithic farmers. Those who lived in lush environments like the Taino often used a method of clearing land called swidden, or "slash and burn." By this method, they cleared land by cutting trees so that they would die and dry out. Then they burned off the dry biomass for ash that would provide nutrients for three or four plantings before becoming exhausted, but at that point they would have to move on to slash and burn another area of forest. The Taino developed a more sustainable agriculture with a unique method of irrigating and draining their crops. They constructed mounds of soil called *canuco* in which they planted their mainly root crops—yuca (manioc or cassava) and sweet potatoes. These mounds were self-irrigating and needed little weeding or care. Yuca and potatoes added carbohydrates to a rich protein diet that included fish, small animals, and beans.

Did the complexity of Taino society make it necessary to have a more hierarchical political structure? Or did the *caciques* and nobles create a more complex society for their own benefit? Two aspects of Taino culture may help answer that question: religion and sports.

Taino religion, like other Neolithic religions, had elements of ancestor and nature worship. Every individual had a special relationship to an ancestral deity called a *zemi*. While each Ibo had one *chi*, the Taino had many *zemis*; the term was applied to objects that contained the spiritual force of the ancestor as well as the ancestor. These objects—made of wood, bone, shell, pottery, or cotton cloth—were kept in special places in a Taino home. In this respect, they may have functioned much like the skulls, masks, figurines, and sculpture of ancient Catal Huyuk. But unlike Catal Huyuk and Ibo society, each Taino village also had a chief. And each chief had *zemis* in his home or in specially built temples that required the worship of the entire village. Once a year, the villagers would gather to pay homage to the chief's *zemi*. Women brought cassava bread as a gift. A priest would make sacrifices, and all would sing the praises of the *zemis* and feast and dance. Clearly, the centerpiece of Taino religion was the chief's *zemi*. The sacred ground was the plaza in front of the chief's house, where all rituals and festivals were carried out under the watchful eye of the most important *zemi*.

As the religion of the Taino chiefdom was both more centralized and more widespread than that of less complex societies, so was its leisure. The bounty of the natural environment, combined with *canuco* agriculture, gave the Taino a considerable amount of free time. One activity that filled that time was a kind of ball game that was played throughout the Americas. The ancestors of the Taino had brought the rubber ball from the Amazon. On the Taino court, two sides of about 10 players each tried to keep the ball in the air without using their hands or feet. Ball courts were located not only in villages but also at the border between villages. In Puerto Rico, the most elaborate ball courts have been found on what were the borders between chiefdoms, suggesting that they may have played a role in diplomacy or the settlement of disputes. In the Caribbean, the outcome of the ball game was benign, but in the more complex states of Central America at the same time, the losers (or sometimes winners) would forfeit their lives. Did shared competition and shared religious observance bring unity and commonality to a society spread out over hundreds or thousands of villages? Or did the controller of the game and the owner of the *zemi* use sport and religion to magnify and centralize power?

The changing role of women offers a clue. Tainos worshipped two supreme deities: a male god of cassava and the sea and his mother, the goddess of freshwater and human fertility. But in practice, it was the chief and his *zemi* who commanded obedience. Theoretically, women could be chiefs, but few were. Taino society was matrilineal; even the chief inherited the position through his mother's line. Nevertheless, at least by the end of the fifteenth century, male Taino chiefs and nobility seem to have garnered considerable power and privilege for their sex as well as their class. They commonly took a number of wives, and when a chief died, one or two of the wives might be buried with him. That was a hallmark of patriarchy that was to become more common in post-Neolithic kingdoms and imperial states.

### Neolithic Continuity and Change

In comparison with foraging societies, agricultural societies were larger, denser, and more complex. Neolithic life was settled life. Dozens of related families or clans lived in villages, and almost everyone tilled the soil or cared for animals. Neolithic villagers made and used far more tools, containers, clothing, and other objects than hunter-gatherers. They invented not only farming but also pottery, fermenting, and storage. Like their Paleolithic predecessors, Neolithic farmers were relatively equalitarian: no individual, group, or sex dominated. Women's work, although different from men's, was invaluable, and their deities were indispensable. Fear of famine or disaster mitigated greed, arrogance, and self-indulgence. Security lay in numbers and mutual aid.

In these respects, most agricultural societies were similar. But Neolithic societies also changed over the course of the past 10,000 years. From the time of ancient Jericho, agricultural societies evolved from family-centered villages to larger chiefdoms, in the process eroding early traditions of equality, goddess worship, and matrilineal descent. This process was gradual in some places, swift in others. Signs of inequality appeared in ancient Catal Huyuk, yet habits of mutual aid continued down to the present. But despite their many differences, Neolithic societies shared a lot of common ground. Unlike later cities and state societies, virtually all villages managed without money, writing, occupational specialization, or social classes but relied on a common fund of tradition and experience.

*Changes in a Mexican Valley.* Archaeologists have recently excavated the site of one of the earliest state societies in the Americas, the Zapotec state of Oaxaca in a valley of central Mexico.[38] By digging beneath the elaborate remains of the state society, they have been able to reconstruct some of the changes that occurred in the Oaxaca valley since about 7000 BCE, when it was occupied by foragers. At the lowest excavated level, they found a ritual earthen field surrounded by stones, dating from 6500 BCE. Here they believe that hunters and gatherers gathered at special times of the year for initiations and courtship. Like foragers today, they probably joined together in ritual dances to celebrate these meetings.

Around 1500 BCE, the people of the Oaxaca valley domesticated corn and began living in permanent settlements. The first villages were probably communities of equals like the equalitarian bands of hunters and gatherers. At a slightly later stage, there appeared men's houses apart from community field of dance, suggesting the development of a special religious or political role for leading males.

Figure 1.11  The great Mexican ceremonial center of Monte Alban, capital of Zapotec state, built after 500 BCE. *iStock/frentusha.*

By 1150 BCE, the Neolithic villages show signs of social inequality and the emergence of elites who lived in large houses, wore jade, and stretched the skulls of their children as a mark of their status. The men's houses were now large temples, destroyed and rebuilt every 52 years to conform to the calculations of two calendar systems of 260 and 365 day-years, which came together every 52 years. A world in which the natural rhythms of gathering and planting could be marked by the entire community had become a hierarchical chiefdom with secret knowledge preserved by privileged specialists.

Around 500 BCE, the Zapotecs wielded the chiefdoms of the Oaxaca valley into a military state centered on the crown of Monte Alban. There they constructed large pyramids around a central ceremonial plaza, where priests lived apart from the people, administering the rule of a king with religious rituals sanctioned by celestial calendars and the force of arms.

The history of Oaxaca from foraging to Neolithic villages to chiefdoms to state summarizes the history of much of the world over the course of the past 10,000 years. In the following chapters, we survey that pattern, its varieties, and its exceptions.

## Conclusion

The history of 99 percent of the past 14 billion years is hard to summarize. From the vantage point of seconds before midnight, however, certain conclusions leap out at us. Two are as obvious as they are contradictory: humans have taken over the world, and human history is a flash in the pan.

Each of these truths reflects a different time line. From the perspective of the past 10,000 years, even perhaps the past 300,000 years, the emergence, expansion, and increase of the human population is staggering. Its capacity for invention and adaptation marks the human animal as far and away the most successful of its age. And yet that age is only seconds on the solar calendar. Further, the fossil remains on which we walk so proudly are reminders of numerous species that thrived far longer than our brief 300,000 years, only to evaporate in a cosmic accident or fall prey to a new carnivore.

Are human chances any better than the dinosaurs'? Certainly, our tool kit is infinitely more subtle and diverse. But the tools that might intercept and destroy a small to middling meteor or even provide food for a population under an ashen sky are not unlike the tools used to kill other humans or those that extract ever-greater leverage from the mantle of nature that gives us life. The exploitation of nature did not begin with agriculture. In some ways, farmers were more attentive to nature's ways and needs than hunters and gatherers. But more than any other species, humans have sought and found ways of reaching nature's limits and surmounting its obstacles. There is both enormous hope and vulnerability in that achievement.

## Suggested Readings

Christian, David. *Maps of Time*. Berkeley: University of California Press, 2004. A "Big History" by the founder of the movement; full of charts and insights about the first 14 billion years.

Diamond, Jared. *Guns, Germs, and Steel: The Fates of Human Societies*. New York: Nor-ton, 1997. Award-winning best-seller offers a long-view answer to the question of why some countries became rich and others poor.

Fagan, Brian. *World Prehistory: A Brief Introduction*. 8th ed. Englewood Cliffs, NJ: Prentice Hall, 2010. A well-written short text by a master of the subject.

McNeill, J. R., and William H. McNeill. *The Human Web: A Bird's Eye View of World History*. New York: Norton, 2002. All of world history in a brief volume by two masters—the modern dean of the subject and his son.

Peregrine, Peter N. *World Prehistory: Two Million Years of Human Life*. Englewood Cliffs, NJ: Prentice Hall, 2003. Well-written and well-illustrated college-level text.

Ristvet, Lauren. *In the Beginning: World History from Human Evolution to the First States*. New York: McGraw-Hill, 2007. The story of this and the next chapter told engagingly and authoritatively.

## Notes

1. Robert F. Service, "Researchers may have solved origin-of-life conundrum," *Science*, Mar. 16, 2015. Also in http://www.sciencemag.org/news/2015/03/researchers-may-have-solved-origin-life-conundrum.

2. Kenneth Chang, "Meteor Seen as Causing Extinctions on Earth," *New York Times*, November 21, 2003, A28.

3. Peter Brannen, "When Life on Earth Nearly Vanished," *New York Times*, July 30, 2017, SR2.

4. On North America here and later in this section, I am indebted to Tim Flannery's *The Eternal Frontier: An Ecological History of North America and Its Peoples* (New York: Atlantic Monthly Press, 2001), a fascinating and highly readable account of North American prehistory. Recently, some scientists have argued that such collisions may have occurred far more often than previously thought: possibly every few thousand years rather than 500,000 to a million years. See Sandra Blakeslee, "Ancient

Crash, Epic Wave," *New York Times*, November 14, 2006, F1.

5. Elizabeth Kolbert, *The Sixth Extinction: An Unnatural History* (New York: Hentry Holt, 2014).

6. *Science*, May 29, 2014; and Christine Dell Amore, "Species Extinction Happening 1,000 Times Faster Because of Humans?" *National Geographic*, May 30, 2014. See http://news.nationalgeographic.com/news/2014/05/140529-conservation-science-animals-species-endangered-extinction/.

7. Peter Brannen, *op. cit.*

8. See Jamie Shreeve, "The Evolutionary Road," *National Geographic*, July 2010, 35–67.

9. Pallab Ghosh "'First human' discovered in Ethiopia," BBC News, March 4, 2015. http://www.bbc.com/news/science-environment-31718336.

10. Nicholas Wade, "Signs of Neanderthals Mating with Humans," *New York Times*, May 7, 2010, A10.

11. John Noble Wilford, "Bones in China Put New Light on Old Humans," *New York Times*, November 16, 1995, A8.

12. New DNA evidence has established that the crossing could not have been made more than 18,000 years ago, not, as previously thought, 30,000 years ago. Nicholas Wade and John Noble Wilford, "New World Ancestors Lose 12,000 Years," *New York Times*, July 25, 2003, A19.

13. The thesis of University of Arizona paleontologist Paul S. Martin—that it was mankind, not a change in climate, that caused the great extinctions at the end of the Pleistocene—might be modified slightly to emphasize the role of the post–13,000 BCE wave of "Clovis" or stone projectile point–wielding humans.

14. See Sally McBrearty and Allison Brooks, *Human Evolution*, November 2000. The entire issue of the journal is devoted to their thesis.

15. Hillary Mayell, "Oldest Jewelry? 'Beads' Discovered in African Cave," *National Geographic News*, April 15, 2004.

16. Mark Stoneking and his colleagues at the Max Planck Institute for Evolutionary Anthropology in Leipzig, Germany. See, for instance, John Travis, "The Naked Truth? Lice Hint at a Recent Origin of Clothing," *Science News* 164, August 23, 2003, 118.

17. Nicholas Wade, "Adventures in Recent Evolution," *New York Times*, July 20, 2010, D1.

18. Milford Wolpoff and Rachel Caspari, *Race and Human Evolution* (New York: Simon and Schuster, 1997).

19. Nicholas Wade, "DNA Study Yields Clues on First Migration of Early Humans," *New York Times*, May 13, 2005, A8.

20. Nicholas Wade, "New DNA Test Is Yielding Clues to Neanderthals," *New York Times*, November 16, 2006, F1.

21. Called the "Movius line" after the anthropologist Hallam Movius, who suggested it in 1944.

22. Mary C. Stiner, Natalie D. Munro, Todd A. Surovell, Eitan Tchernov, and Ofer Bar-Yosef, "Paleolithic Population Growth Pulses Evidenced by Small Animal Exploitation," *Science*, January 8, 1999, 190–94.

23. C. Schrire, ed., *Past and Present in Hunter-Gatherer Studies* (London: Academic Press, 1984).

24. Carl L. Hoffman, *The Punan: Hunters and Gatherers of Borneo* (Ann Arbor, MI: UMI Research Press, 1986).

25. Kathleen Gough, "The Origin of the Family," *Journal of Marriage and the Family* 33 (November 1971): 760–71. Reprinted in *Toward an Anthropology of Women*, ed. Rayna R. Reiter (New York: Monthly Review Press, 1975), 69–70.

26. Larry Rohter, "Brazil Moves to Protect Jungle Plants from Foreign Biopiracy," *New York Times*, December 23, 2001, A4.

27. Kyle Jarrard, "On the Origins of the Dentist (with a Stone-Age Drill)," *New York Times*, April 7, 2006, A15.

28. Scientists refer to this period as the Younger Dryas, or Big Freeze, and date it from 10,800 to 9,500 BCE.

29. Jared Diamond, *Guns, Germs, and Steel: The Fates of Human Societies* (New York: Norton, 1997), 132.

30. Steve LeVine, "The Eden of Apples Is in Kazakhstan: It May Be a Godsend," *Wall Street Journal*, July 3, 2003, 1.

31. Diamond, *Guns, Germs, and Steel.*

32. William Ryan and Walter Pittman, *Noah's Flood* (New York: Simon and Schuster, 1999).

33. The excavations at Catal Huyuk can be followed on the website maintained by the Cambridge University team under the direction of Ian Hodder. It can be accessed at http://www.catalhoyuk.com.

34. Robert Briffault, *The Mothers*, abridged by C. R. Taylor (London: Allen & Unwin, 1927, 1959), 363.

35. Chief Solomon Amadiume, *Ilu Ndi Igbo: A Study of Igbo Proverbs*, vol. 1 (Enugu, Nigeria: Fourth Dimension Publishing, 1994), 3, #14.

36. Chief Solomon Amadiume, *Ilu Ndi Igbo*, 4, #27.

37. The English words "tobacco," "hurricane," "barbecue," "canoe," and "hammock" originate from the Taino words *tobaco*, *huracan*, *barbacoa*, *canoa*, and *hamac*.

38. Nicholas Wade, "7,000 Years of Ritual Is Traced in Mexico," *New York Times*, December 21, 2004, F4.

# 2

## The Brave New World
## of City, State, and Pasture
### From 3000 BCE

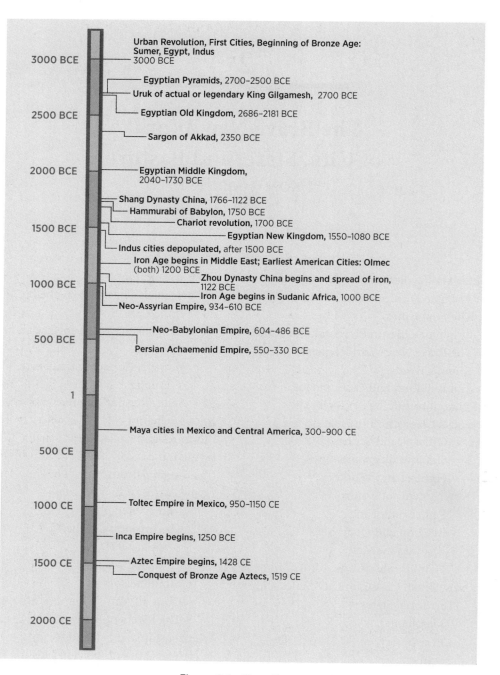

Figure 2.1   Time line.

# The Urban Revolution: Causes and Consequences

## The Epic of Gilgamesh

> Come then, Enkidu, to ramparted Uruk,
> Where fellows are resplendent in holiday clothing,
> Where every day is set for celebration,
> Where harps and drums are played.
> And the harlots too, they are fairest of form,
> Rich in beauty, full of delights,
> Even the great gods are kept from sleeping at night.[1]

*T*HE EPIC OF GILGAMESH, the world's earliest surviving written epic, tells the story of Gilgamesh, king of Uruk, one of the world's first cities, built along the Tigris and Euphrates rivers 5,000 years ago. According to the epic, King Gilgamesh, two-thirds god and one-third human, built the great ramparted wall of Uruk, enclosing three and a half square miles of the city and its gardens. But Gilgamesh was an overbearing and arrogant king, and so the people of Uruk called on the gods to bring them a strong man who might keep Gilgamesh in check. In answer

to their call, Aruru, the goddess who created the human race, created Enkidu, a wild man who roamed the pasture like a gazelle. Before Enkidu could tame Gilgamesh, he himself had to be tamed, a task carried out by Shamhat, the harlot, who seduced Enkidu and invited him to Uruk with the words quoted above.

To the modern ear, there is much that is foreign in *The Epic of Gilgamesh*: goddesses and sacred harlots, wild men who cavort in the fields with the gazelles, and kings who are descended from gods. But there is also much that is familiar—cities, walls, kings, holidays,

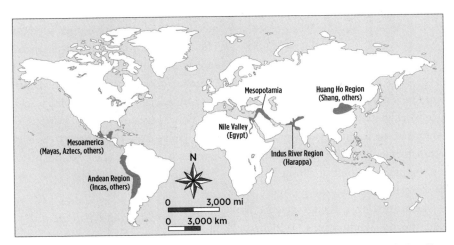

Map 2.1 The first urban civilizations arose in some of the areas of the first agricultural revolutions.

Figure 2.2 This early bronze (copper and tin) statue from Iran or Mesopotamia of a hero or a demon—a man of the hills, where they wore upturned boots and hunted wild prey not too different from themselves—evokes Enkidu, as imagined by the skilled metal worker of the city. Or maybe the royal beard and triple belt suggested Gilgamesh himself. Ca. 3000 B.C.E. *The Metropolitan Museum of Art/Purchase, Lila Acheson Wallace Gift, 2007.*

fine clothing, and nightlife (in the above passage alone).

## The First Cities

*The Urban Revolution.* We recognize elements of our own world here because *The Epic of Gilgamesh* stands at the beginning of a revolution that has transformed us all. We call that transformation the urban revolution. Some historians prefer to call it the beginning of complex societies, the formation of state societies, or the rise of the first civilizations. Whichever words we use, when we look at the Uruk of King Gilgamesh almost 5,000 years ago, we see

the beginning of these developments: cities, states (or organized territories with governments), and the whole range of activities and institutions that are summarized as "complex societies" or "civilizations" because they entered the world together.

Archaeologists of the Middle East first called the age of cities and states the Bronze Age because people of the region had learned to smelt bronze (copper and tin), which as weapons and tools replaced those of the stone age, specifically the polished stone tools of the Neolithic period, or New Stone Age. *The Epic of Gilgamesh* mentions the bronze work on Uruk's wall. Above all, the *Epic* speaks to us because it was written and we can read it. Some historians call the period before cities the preliterate or prehistoric age since there was no writing and therefore no written history before the creation of cities 5,000 years ago.

*First-City Firsts.* The first cities changed the world in countless ways. The number of firsts is staggering: defensive walls, writing, wheels, and wars; kings, priests, soldiers, officials, and numerous specialized occupations, crafts, arts, services, and manufactures; laws, literature, philosophy, astronomy, calendars, and science; and money, markets, merchants, metalworking, and monumental architecture. The first cities were the first places where everyone did not have to find or produce food. Cities introduced not only the division of labor but also social classes, the first world of rich and poor, private property, patriarchy, debts, taxes, treasures, treasuries, treaties, theater, temples, and (thank the city gods) textbooks.

## Origin of Cities in Plow and Irrigation

How did cities come about? One answer is that agricultural societies were able to feed

Figure 2.3 The origin of cities in the Middle East was a result of the marriage of agriculture and animal domestication: of farm and pasture. Animals first domesticated for meat were increasingly used for secondary products and purposes after 4,000 B.C.E. These included milk, cheese, leather, wool, and pulling plows. Plowed fields provided food for city societies, which invented writing-- like Egyptian hieroglyphics of pictures and symbols at top. This example is from an Egyptian tomb about 2,000 B.C.E *Wellcome Collection.*

larger populations, including increased numbers of people who could spend their time in ways other than farming or raising animals. Furthermore, agriculture became more productive as the use of animal-drawn plows and irrigation took hold.

The first farmers used simple tools like digging sticks and hoes. They planted seeds or placed roots in the soil in garden plots without turning over the soil. Some prepared the soil with a technique called swidden, or slash and burn. They would slash away a band of bark from large trees, thus killing them; cut down the rest of the underbrush; and then burn it

all off, producing a rich ash that fertilized the soil. Whether or not the soil was prepared with fire, this garden agriculture, sometimes called horticulture, required little more than cursory attention, occasional weeding, and some intensive labor at harvest time. Consequently, plots and populations remained small. People produced only what they needed, and very few people worked as nonfarming specialists. Horticulture was normally the work of women in family units that numbered a few to a few hundred in villages. While women gardened, men were often involved in the domestication and care of animals.

*Middle East.* In the Middle East, or Southwest Asia, the initial urban revolution was the marriage of village and pasture, the joining of women's gardens and men's animals, the bonding of Enkidu and Gilgamesh. Certainly, the use of animal-drawn plows to till large fields made agriculture much more productive. Oxen-drawn plows dug furrows into the soil for deeper planting over extensive areas for the first time about 5,600 years ago in the Middle East. A thousand years later, European farmers used oxen and plows to dig into the hard soils of northern Europe. But cities appeared in the Americas without plow or draft animals and in other parts of the world, especially in river valleys, where agriculture was intensified as much by irrigation.

Agriculture did not originate along rivers, but cities did. River agriculture in the Middle East, Egypt, China, and Southeast Asia was much more productive than the earlier oasis gardens of places like Jericho or the rain-watered hillsides and plains of places like Catal Huyuk. The farmers of the Euphrates could multiply the amount of food produced along the river banks with irrigation dikes channeling silt and flood waters precisely where it was needed. In addition, irrigation systems required constant attention, virtually demanding the concentrated labor, common purpose, and community decision making that distinguished cities from other farming communities. Irrigation systems did not just provide the greater numbers for city life—they *were* city life. This was especially true of the first cities along the Euphrates, cities like Ur and Uruk, each a state unto itself with its own gods, temples, laws, and identity.

*East Asia.* Great river irrigation systems also nourished the growth of cities in India, China, and Southeast Asia. The first cities of India grew from villages on the Indus River that runs through modern Pakistan. Chinese cities first sprouted along the northern Yellow River, where farmers grew millet, and later along the Yangtze River, farther south, where farmers cultivated rice. The earliest cities of Southeast Asia were similarly made possible by the irrigated rice paddies of the great deltas and marshlands of the Red River in northern Vietnam, the Mekong River in southern Vietnam and Cambodia, and the Chao Praya River of Thailand.

*Americas.* In the Americas, irrigated agriculture supported city populations on the large central plateau of Mexico, the Mayan areas of Mexico and Guatemala, on terraced mountainsides in the Andes, and along rivers on the Peruvian coast. The Mexica, or Aztecs, who settled on an island in the more-than-mile-high Lake Texcoco of central Mexico created a highly intensive agriculture by building stationery floating islands of fertile mud for planting. Modern tourists can still visit a few remaining cultivated *chinampas* at Xochimilco near modern Mexico City. Farmers tend their crops in canoes, paddling by raised strips of corn and other plants that seem to rise from the lake. In Aztec times, before the Spanish conquest in 1519, these strips of mud, constantly replenished and fertilized with human waste, supported four crops a year and a very high population density.

The Mayans, who lived in the tropical rain forests of southern Mexico and Guatemala, also used *chinampas* and irrigated fields. Combined with Taino-like terracing and slash-and-burn farming in forest areas, Mayan agriculture was as productive as that of the Mexica; each supported more than double the population density of ancient Egypt and Mesopotamia.

In South America, the development of cities in the Andes relied on both irrigation and terraces. Irrigation ditches trapped the sparse runoff of rainwater that cascaded down the desert-dry western cliffs of the Andes to the Pacific coast. The resulting irrigated coastal farms supplemented the dense fishing villages spawned by the rich anchovy fisheries of the Pacific coast south of the equator. In addition to subsistence crops, the irrigated fields of the lowland towns and cities grew the cotton used to fashion the fish nets used to catch anchovies.

High in the Andes, farmers built terraces to harvest the numerous varieties of potatoes that grew in the mountains. The Andes was the one area in the Americas that had domesticated large animals, but neither the llama nor the alpaca ever pulled a plow. Instead, Inca men pushed a foot plow along terraces while, behind them, their wives dropped seeds and potato cuttings into the ground.

Along the South American rivers that cascaded into the Pacific Ocean, cities appeared as early as in South Asia—beginning about 3100 BCE, according to recent excavations.[2] Without bronze or even pottery, dozens of cites of 25 to over 250 acres dotted the Peruvian coast by 2600 BCE.

## *The Brave New World: Squares and Crowds*

From a telescope on the moon, the effects of plow and irrigation agriculture would have seemed similar. Since oxen plowed long straight furrows, the dry and rain-watered agricultural lands would have appeared from a great distance as an expanding patchwork of rectangular fields, green or brown, depending on the season. Terraces would also appear as parallel lines running horizontally up the side of mountains. Irrigated fields, marshes, and deltas would look very much like plowed

fields that were more often blue than green. The overall impression would be of a world in which square shapes were increasingly replacing circular ones. This was especially the case near the expanding red/brown patches that had grown near each checkerboard of greens and blues. In fact, a very sharp telescope would have shown that those urban patches were growing very quickly. By 2500 BCE, about 80 percent of the people along the southern Euphrates lived in cities of at least 100 acres. To take one example, the city of Shuruppak (modern Fara), which did not exist in 3000 BCE, covered 250 acres by 2500 BCE, and the city wall enclosed 15,000 to 30,000 inhabitants.

The view from inside these new urban checkerboards was uniformly different from that of earlier villages. Not only had rectangular houses replaced round ones, but these new boxes, stacked side by side and soon on top of each other, marked off rectangular neighborhoods and straight streets instead of open fields and winding lanes.

China during the Shang dynasty (1766–1050 BCE) reflected the new checkerboard world. Fields were divided into nine squares so that peasants would receive the proceeds of eight, and the ninth would go to the lord. Shang city houses were rectangular, laid out on grid plans with palace grounds in the center. Each of seven palace cities duplicated the layout of the capital city. The tastes of emperors ran from the uniform large to the uniform extra large.

The great rivers like the Euphrates and Indus might meander or change their courses, but the cities that relied on their bounty were constructed along the straight and narrow. Even the probably more peaceful Indus cities of Harappa and Mohenjodaro (2500–1500 BCE)[3] follow the grid layout of military camps.

## Tall Buildings and Monumental Architecture

Even more noticeable to a visiting villager was the size and variety of buildings. Although ordinary workers lived in rows of small buildings that were no larger or more comfortable than village huts, there were also large buildings, 4 to 10 times the size of workers' homes, enclosed in high walls, barely accessible from the street, but open to large interior courtyards. And, more striking, there were palaces and temples: monumental buildings that no village could afford.

How could cities afford palaces, monuments, and large houses for some? By taxing the villages, the farmers, and the urban poor. Kings like Gilgamesh, noble friends like Enkidu, and the other "fellows . . . resplendent in holiday clothing" could afford to have "harps and drums played, and the harlots too" because of the new intensive agriculture. The king and the members of other wealthy and powerful families in the city taxed the farm and pasture a percentage of their produce so that they and those who supported them could eat without soiling their hands in the dirt.

## Social Classes and Inequality

Everywhere cities first sprang up, they grew only a small portion of the food they consumed and used their power to fleece their country cousins. The first city societies were class societies, and nowhere were the class differences greater than inside the city itself. The city pyramid was topped by kings, often kings like Gilgamesh who claimed some share of divinity. In Egypt, the pharaohs were literally gods and their pyramids their eternal resting homes. Just beneath the king were noble families, people related to the king or members of families who had previously been headed by

kings. The early cities of Peru display similar signs of hierarchy: huge pyramids and broad ceremonial plazas.

*Officials and Scribes.* Beneath the rulers was history's first middle class: a wide range of officials, priests, administrators, artists, and artisans who served the king, his court, and the nobility. To be a scribe, a writer, opened the world of officialdom, a middle-class paradise compared to the prospect of working with one's hands. In ancient Egypt more than 4,000 years ago, students were advised,

> Put writing in your heart that you may protect yourself from hard labor of any kind and be a magistrate of high repute. The scribe is released from manual tasks; it is he who commands . . .
>
> I have seen the metal-worker at his task at the mouth of his furnace, with fingers like a crocodile's. He stank worse than fish-spawn. . . . The stonemason finds his work in every kind of hard stone. When he has finished his labors his arms are worn out, and he sleeps all doubled up until sunrise. His knees and spine are broken. . . . The barber shaves from morning till night, he never sits down except to meals. He hurries from house to house looking for business. He wears out his arms to fill his stomach, like bees eating their own honey. . . . The farmer wears the same clothes for all times. His voice is as raucous as a crow's. His fingers are always busy; his arms are dried up by the wind. He takes his rest—when he gets any—in the mud. . . .
>
> Apply your heart to learning. In truth there is nothing that can compare with it. If you have profited by a single day at school it is a gain for eternity.[4]

*Slaves and Servants.* At the bottom of the city class system were slaves. In the beginning, slavery was not as pervasive as it later became, but slavery existed in virtually all ancient city societies. In Egypt, as in many other ancient societies, most slaves were war captives who were employed as domestic servants. Some were owned by wealthy families and others by the state, such as the women who were loaned to working families at tomb-building sites, for example, to grind the workmen's grain into flour.

Slaves were not the only underclass. Slightly above them in the social hierarchy was a wide range of servants. A pyramid-building site would require servants who were water carriers, woodcutters, fishermen, gardeners, and washermen.

*Farmers and Workers.* Most of the heavy lifting on public projects like Egyptian pyramids was done not by slaves or servants but by peasant farmers who owed a certain number of labor days in the off season. But they were hardly alone. All the classes of Egyptian society were marshaled to build the great pyramids along the lower Nile by the pharaohs of 4,700 to 4,500 years ago (2700–2500 BCE). Such projects required architects, scribes, stonemasons, carpenters, sculptors, and artists. Each new royal tomb involved the construction of an entire city of suppliers, bakers, physicians, ration providers, guards, and officials just for the period of construction.

## New Systems of Control

Why did villagers who lived in general equality accept the inequality of cities? The loss of equality was probably a gradual process. In the previous chapter, we noticed how villages turned into tribal societies and then chiefdoms as they became more complex. City societies were merely the next step in complexity and concentration of power. City societies created

Figure 2.4  Nikare was an Egyptian granary official around 2400 B.C.E. His wife stands to his right; his daughter kneels to his left. What does this tell you about the ancient Egyptian family? *The Metropolitan Museum of Art/ Rogers Fund, 1952.*

new institutions that led people to accept inequality as natural.

*Fathers and Kings.* One of these was an increased emphasis on the father's command of the family. Having already seized control of the agricultural surplus through plow and irrigation agriculture, men concentrated property in their own hands and sought to pass it on to their sons. In the cramped quarters of cities, men were eager to ensure that sons were their own, so they restricted their wives to the interior of the houses or demanded that they cover themselves outdoors. In the cities of the Middle East, women wore veils and covered their hair thousands of years before the Arabs brought Islam in the seventh century CE. Thus, the man's control of wife, children, and family modeled the king's control of city society. The words for father and king were

Figure 2.5   A reconstructed scene of the tomb of Queen Puabi at Ur before the slaughter of the animals and attendants. ©*The Trustees of the British Museum/Art Resource, NY*

interchangeable, and both meant power. Even religion changed to support men's claim. In the age of cities, sky fathers and sun gods replaced Earth Mothers and fertility goddesses, even those who had presided over planting, harvesting, and giving birth. One Egyptian myth even imagined the god Atum creating the world from his own body through masturbation.

*Religion and Queens.* Goddesses did not disappear in the early cities, but they did become subordinate to gods. Not all women lost power and influence in patriarchal states. With kings came queens, women whose privileged lives were another sign of one man's power. One of the earliest and most successful archaeological discoveries of ancient Mesopotamia was Leonard Woolley's discovery of the royal tombs of Ur in the 1920s. In one of these tombs, Woolley found the tomb of Queen Puabi (ca. 2600 BCE), buried with a crown of

golden leaves, silver bracelets, and hundreds of strings of precious stone beads—deep blue lapis lazuli from central Asia and bright red carnelian from western India. In addition, the queen was buried with golden sculptured gifts for the gods and a harp-sized lyre, decorated in gold and precious stones.

In death, Queen Puabi exerted wide dominion. To accompany her on her voyage to the netherworld, Queen Puabi was joined by more than 70 guards and attendants, including 12 young women dressed like the queen in beaded cloaks and golden diadems. One can only wonder what these young women understood about their service to Puabi. Did they realize that they were to be buried alive with their queen's corpse? If so, did their feelings about royal service or religious duty comfort them?

Human sacrifice became a city ruler's prerogative, not only in Mesopotamia and Egypt.

In China, too, the graves of Shang dynasty emperors reveal hundreds of attendants sent to accompany the king on his journey to heaven. In this regard and many others, India stands out as an exception. Excavations of Harappa, Mohenjodaro, and other cities along the Indus show no sign of human sacrifice in elite burials.

*Law and the State.* Neither kings nor queens, neither fathers nor gods, could ensure inequality without the other major innovations of city society: the law and the state. Unlike tribal chiefs, the first kings did not justify their power in arbitrary or personal terms. That is one of the lessons the people of ancient Mesopotamia read into *The Epic of Gilgamesh*. The *Epic* begins with King Gilgamesh terrorizing the people of Uruk, leaving no son or daughter safe from his lust. The plea of the nobles asking the goddess Aruru to counter Gilgamesh symbolized the beginnings of a state—the formation of a government more permanent and less arbitrary than the whim of a tribal chieftain. States were administered by officials and ruled by law.

Law promised predictability, a limit to vengeance, and a certain standard of fairness. But that did not mean village equality. In a class society, the ministers and scribes of kings wrote laws that protected the wealthy and powerful while still claiming the loyalty of lower-class commoners.

*Hammurabi's Code.* One of the earliest law codes, the Mesopotamian code of Hammurabi of Babylon, about 1750 BCE, balanced these two goals adroitly. The class bias of the code is obvious in the law on assault. The penalty for knocking out an eye of a noble was to have your own eye knocked out, no matter who you were. This, of course, was the origin of "an eye for an eye" as a legal principle, but it protected only the eyes of the upper class. If the eye of a common person was knocked out, the penalty was a small fine. The same Hammurabi's code, however, laid claim to protecting the common people with another set of laws on theft. A noble person who commits a theft must repay 30 times the cost of the stolen property; a common thief need pay only 10 times the cost. The principle here may be that the upper classes had a greater stake in the rule of law and a greater responsibility to society. But before we make too much of this charitable finger on the scales of justice, we should add the last part of the law: "if the thief cannot pay, he shall be put to death." Clearly, the state cared for some lower classes more than others.

In general, states achieved legitimacy with only the grudging support of the class of ordinary farmers by winning the more energetic approval of the nobility and middle class. The kind of middle class varied, however, depending on the nature of the state.

## New Urban Classes in City-States and Territorial States

The urban revolution actually created two kinds of states 5,000 years ago, and in many ways these two varieties have persisted down to the present day. One type, known as the city-state, consisted of the city, sometimes suburbs or a subordinate city, and the farm and pasture that were necessary to support the urban population. Uruk was one of these, as were the other first cities in the Tigris and Euphrates valley. City-states also sprung up along the Indus River in India and in Mexico though a bit later. The earliest city in central Mexico, Monte Alban, originated about 1000 BCE, but by about 300 BCE it reached the same population, 25,000 people, as Uruk had about 3000 BCE.

The other type of state, called the territorial state, was much larger in area and less urban. Cities mattered less, or there were fewer of them. Egypt was a territorial state. Its spine was the Nile River, dotted with villages and urban settlements, but it stretched into the desert on either side as far as the eye could see. The capital city of Egypt was the location of the pharaoh's court: Memphis near modern Cairo during the Old Kingdom in the third millennium BCE and Thebes, upriver near modern Luxor, during the New Kingdom after 1550 BCE. But the vast remains of the pharaoh Akhenaton's city of the middle 1300s BCE on a previously undeveloped location midway between the two earlier capitals shows how easy it was for a determined king to pick up everything and move when it suited his purpose. The *Gilgamesh* poet's pride in Uruk would have sounded strange to Egyptians, who felt no particular pride in any city. What mattered to each pharaoh was the design and construction of his final resting place, usually on the west bank, or sunset side, of the Nile. What mattered to the pharaoh's court was the location of the pharaoh. And what mattered to the more than 80 percent of Egyptians who were peasant farmers were their meager fields and ancestral villages.

*Merchants.* Markets were also more important in city-states than in territorial states. In large territorial states like Egypt, kings commanded and taxed all they needed. In the city-states of Mexico, farmers and merchants brought their products to market.

The Aztec city of the Mexica was a successor to many city-states that flourished in the valley of Mexico in the centuries before the Spanish conquest of 1519 CE. One of the Spanish conquistadors, Bernal Diaz, wrote of its great market:

We were astounded at the great number of people and the quantities of merchandise. . . .

Let us begin with the dealers in gold, silver, precious stones, feathers, cloaks, embroidered goods, and male and female slaves who were sold there. . . . Next there were those who sold coarser cloth, and cotton goods, and fabrics made of twisted thread, and there were chocolate merchants with their chocolate . . .

There were sellers of kidney beans and sage and other vegetables and herbs . . . and in another place they were selling fowls, birds, turkeys, rabbits, ducks, dogs, and other creatures. Then there were the fruiterers and the woman who sold cooked food, flour, and honey cake, and tripe. Then came pottery of all kinds, large and small. . . . Elsewhere they sold timber too, boards, cradles, beams, blocks, and benches, all in a quarter of its own. But why waste so many words on the goods in their great market? If I describe everything in detail I shall never be done. Paper, which in Mexico they call *amal*, and some reeds that smell of liquid amber, and are full of tobacco, and yellow ointments, and much cochineal [insects for red dye]. . . . I am forgetting the sellers of salt and the makers of flint knives . . . and the fisherwoman, and the men who sell small cakes made from a sort of weed that they get out of the great lake, which curdles and forms a kind of bread which tastes rather like cheese. They sell axes too, made of bronze and copper and tin; and gourds; and brightly painted wooden jars.[5]

Mayan society was also made up of various independent city-states, linked by markets in which the long-distance trade of obsidian was particularly important. Nevertheless, the importance of markets in city-states did not translate into the importance of merchants, who were only one group among many.

*Priests.* In the city-states of both Mesopotamia and Middle America, religious temples presided over central squares, and priests were more influential than merchants. In both areas, priests administered irrigation and the rhythms of agriculture. Priests were the interpreters of the calendar, the celebrants of religious rites. Even kings who claimed divinity relied on their priests. All Bronze Age states were theocracies: they did not distinguish between religious and secular matters. Religions were local, and the deities were very much involved in life within the city walls. Recall Aruru. Local deities were able to control larger natural forces: the winds, rain, sky, sun, and underworld. The *Epic of Gilgamesh* contains an early version of the biblical flood story, but the great flood in the epic occurs because the people are too noisy and the gods cannot sleep.

The well-being of the people, nature, and the gods were intimately bound together. Kings were descended from the gods or became gods. Gods often acted like people, displayed human emotions, or had relations with people. They had to be placated, appeased, or offered sacrifices. At times, the gods seemed to need the people as much as the people needed the gods. One ancient Mesopotamian poem has a slave advise his master to "teach the god to run after you like a dog" by withholding sacrifices.[6]

Numerous city societies offered human sacrifices to ensure the health and vitality of the god and natural forces. In Mexico, the Aztecs and the Mayans offered flesh to the sky and blood to the earth to ensure the continuance of the rains and fertility. Priests and rulers led their people in rituals of bloodletting from various parts of their bodies as offerings to the gods. The Aztec sun god, Huitzilopoctli, required regular human sacrifices just to ensure that the sun rose each day. Consequently, the Aztecs conquered the cities of central Mexico, making some of them allies while turning others into permanent enemies and suppliers of captive soldiers for sacrifice.

The sacrifice of palace attendants in the tombs of kings was a frequent practice in other city societies, especially territorial states where the power of the king was more like a god. The tombs of kings in Egypt, Inca Peru, and China contain such remains. In addition, defeated soldiers were sacrificed in ritual ceremonies in China and in other states.

*Soldiers.* After merchants and priests, the most important urban class was soldiers. Unlike in modern armies, they were normally conscripts rather than professionals, drawn from the farmers and urban working class and commanded by members of the nobility. In periods of war or expansion, however, soldiers were granted special privileges. The Aztec state, for instance, promoted soldiers to the nobility and gave them land after they had captured four enemy combatants. And as the ancient states expanded, they developed professional armies. They also used mercenary armies, often recruited from pastoral societies on the borders of their expanding empires.

*New Country People.* What sorts of people inhabited the countryside? Farmers, of course, but we would be mistaken if we thought of farmers as a single class, all alike. The class divisions of the city extended to the countryside. In fact, wealthy farmers often lived in the city, as in the following Egyptian account attributed to an official who contemplates a visit to his country estate, where the farming was done for him:

> You go down to your ship manned from bow to stern. You reach your beautiful villa, the one you have built for yourself. Your mouth is full of wine and beer, of bread, meat and cakes. Oxen are slaughtered and wine is opened, and melodious singing is before you. Your chief anointer

anoints you. Your manager of cultivated lands brings garlands. Your chief fowler brings ducks, your fisherman brings fish. Your ship has returned from Syria laden with every manner of good things. Your byre is full of calves, your weavers flourish.[7]

The countryside was full of people who were not farmers, as the city was full of people who owned or rented farmland. Nevertheless, the majority of people in the countryside worked the land. Many were free peasants, but there was also a vast number of semifree farmers, bound to work the lands of the state or of religious temples. In Egypt, they were called "royal workers," and in Mesopotamia they were officially "bringers of income." In Egypt, where the status was hereditary, men worked in the fields, while the women of the household spun cloth and sewed in special workshops. All classes of workers, dependent and free, participated in mammoth public work projects and the building of monuments.

Here is another clue to why social inequality was widely accepted. Beneath the king or pharaoh, people of all classes worked on public projects, and they were not generally distinguishable by appearance. Slaves were foreigners, drawn from conquered armies of various racial or ethnic backgrounds. In addition, foreign mercenary soldiers mirrored the diversity of slaves but were free.

## Change and "Civilization"

To ask how things change is a difficult but important question for historians. But to ask if the change was good or bad is a question most historians would rather avoid. "Good for whom?" they might ask. "We should be careful not to impose our values on the past." Yet as citizens, we make judgments about how the world is changing all the time. In fact, we would be ill equipped to shape our future without an understanding of how things were changing and without an ability to evaluate those changes.

*The Bias of "Civilization."* No change in human history is more loaded with value judgments than the development of cities and state societies. Traditionally, they are called "civilizations," a word related to "cities," "civic," and "civility," which implies urban sophistication, high culture, and great achievement. In addition, "civilized" has long had a special meaning of emotional control, maturity, and politeness.

The problem with all these associations is that they reflect the viewpoint of people in city-based societies. It is a self-congratulatory view that originated in the first cities themselves. *The Epic of Gilgamesh* presents such a perspective:

> . . . ramparted Uruk,
> Where fellows are resplendent in holiday
>     clothing,
> Where every day is set for celebration.

Moreover, it is the view that the upper class and literate class developed of itself. The ideas of civilization, progress, and perhaps even change were urban inventions, created to denigrate the people of farm and pasture as "uncivilized" or "barbaric." Thus, to ask if city society was an improvement is to open a huge can of worms.

Clearly, we are well advised to ask "good for whom?" The Egyptian official described above lived far better than his chief fowler; he, in turn, lived far more comfortably than the rowers in the master's ship. But did the rise of cities and state societies improve the lives of most people? Did it raise the level of living for future generations?

There are many reasons to say "no": increased inequality, suppression of women, slavery, organized warfare, conscription, heavy taxation, and forced labor, to name some of the most obvious. A list like this is enough to make one wonder if anything good came out of the first state societies. But we do not have to wonder long.

*Achievements of Ancient Civilizations.* Our museums are full of the art and artifacts of the ancient civilizations. The monuments of the ancient world, the pyramids of Egypt and of Mexico, and the ziggurats of Mesopotamia are among the wonders of the world. Does it matter that the great pyramids of Egypt were built from the forced labor of thousands to provide a resting place for a single person (and those who were entombed alive in order to serve him)? We can view them today as a remarkable achievement of engineering and organization while still condemning their manner of execution. We can admire the art in the tombs, thrill to the revealing detail of ancient Egyptian life, and marvel at the persistence of vivid colors mixed almost 5,000 years ago and still detest their purpose.

We can do this because these monuments have become something different for us than what they were for the ancients. They have become testaments to human achievement, regardless of the cost. These ancient city-based societies were the first in which humans produced abundant works of art and architecture that still astound us in their range, scope, and design.

The significance of the urban revolution is that it produced things that lasted beyond their utility or meaning—thanks to new techniques in stonecutting and hauling; baking brick, tile, and glass; and smelting tin, copper, and bronze—as a legacy for future generations. Even 3,000 years ago, Egyptian engineers studied the ancient pyramids to understand a very distant past, 1,500 years before, and to learn, adapt, revive, or revise ancient techniques. In short, the achievement of the urban revolution is that it made knowledge cumulative so that each generation could stand on the shoulders of its predecessors.

*Writing.* The invention of writing was the single most important step in the urban revolution. Almost all the ancient city societies created some form of writing. The techniques and symbols differed widely. The earliest system in Mesopotamia, called cuneiform, began with wedge markings in clay, sun-dried or oven-baked to form a permanent record. Egyptians and Mesoamericans developed hieroglyphic systems of pictures and symbols painted on a sort of paper that the Egyptians made from papyrus leaves and the Mexicans made from bark. The Inca of Peru devised one of the most unusual systems for recording information; they tied knots at particular intervals on strings of different colors and weaves and hung dozens of these strings from a horizontal belt called a *khipu*. The combination of knot placement and color and weave of string gave an Inca *khipu* maker 1,500 separate units of information, like digital bits according to a recent study,[8] a number equal to the approximately 1,500 Sumerian cuneiform signs.

Remarkably, writing was invented for different purposes in different societies, and creating literature was not one of them. The first writing in Mesopotamia registered economic information about temple workers, such as work schedules and ration payments. In Egypt, writing designated kinship relations and property ownership. Mayan writing related the ancestors and achievements of Mayan kings. The earliest examples of Chinese writing that we have are the inscriptions written on animal bones that were used in the Shang dynasty about 4,000 years ago. Priests would inscribe their questions on the bones and then put them in a fire until they cracked. The lines of the cracks were interpreted as answers to their questions.

*Control and Change.* In these and other ancient state societies, writing was invented as a means of social control and administration by the wealthy and powerful. In its origins, writing had nothing to do with self-expression or literature, and it served only the interests of a tiny portion of the population. But writing was too powerful an invention to be contained within a narrow class. Despite frequent efforts by priests and scribes to preserve their monopoly, they could not control the spread or use of reading and writing. By 1700 BCE, at the latest, the story of Gilgamesh had been written down, and Egyptian scribes were copying sample letters and descriptions of society to learn to write.

Writing was one of the most important forces for change in the Bronze Age. Even if it had been limited to the scribes, it would have inevitably led to innovation. Writing enabled a range of other crucial breakthroughs. Calendars were written representations of the changes in evening light (lunar) and the seasons (solar). At first an aid to determine the time of planting, especially in Egypt, where the river rose predictably, solar calendars became complex records of the movement of the stars and in Mayan society remarkably accurate measures of time. In conjunction with written observations about the movement of the stars and the natural rhythms of the earth, the beginnings of astronomy and earth science evolved.

There were other important forces of change in state societies. All technological

innovation takes on a certain momentum of its own as improvements are made and problems lead to new breakthroughs. In ancient societies, however, such improvements were by no means as rapid as they have become in modern times. The class divisions of the ancient world generally divided manual labor and technical knowledge on the one hand from science and the power to innovate on the other. Markets were a richer source of change in the Bronze Age, as was the meeting of traders in market areas, especially in city-states, where markets played a greater role than they did in territorial states. Before the invention of coinage in the seventh century BCE in Lydia (modern Turkey), however, the range of trade and markets was limited.

Not all forces of change in ancient society came from inside the society. Traders often came from distant lands, for example, and their very presence would encourage thoughts about different ways of doing things. In addition, there was a very powerful force of change restlessly looking on from the frontiers of ancient states. Perhaps the most important of these frontier societies consisted of the people of the pasture.

## Pasture and Empire

The urban revolution began with the transformation of some highly productive or well-placed agricultural villages into cities 5,000 years ago. While some prospered as city-states, others turned outward and created larger territorial states. Warfare punctuated the relations of them all.

Across Eurasia, an additional threat to the stability of city societies came from the grasslands, where people specialized in animal husbandry and traveled with their animals from one grazing land to another. In most of

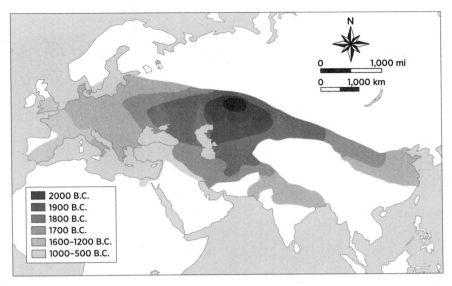

Map 2.2   The Chariot Revolution

Eurasia, a revolution that began with cities ended with empires that were made possible by changes outside the city walls in the pasture.

People domesticated animals almost everywhere they domesticated plants, beginning 10,000 years ago. Early communities like Catal Huyuk lived on both food sources. Village and later city settlements continued to keep chickens, goats, sheep, ducks, turkeys, and other domesticates within the city walls. The rooster's announcement of sunrise can still be heard in most cities of the world. But at some point, the raising of animals became a specialized activity, and the growth of herds required a continual search for grasslands instead of settlement. This was especially the case over the huge grasslands that run across Eurasia, from eastern Europe across Turkey, Russia, Mongolia, and China.

Agriculture and the settled life flourished especially in well-watered places and times. Pasture expanded across the dry, treeless grasslands of central Asia—and farther during times of drought. Most of the period between 3000 and 2200 BCE provided ample moisture to feed the agricultural settlements of the Middle East. From 2200 to 1900 BCE, however, low rainfall reduced the number and size of northern Mesopotamian settlements by about a third, turning many of the farmers who did not flee to the south into pastoral nomads. Similar conditions may have aided the spread of pastoral lands elsewhere.

*Nomads Put the Horse before the Cart.* A catalyst for this change to a migratory life in the central Asian steppe was the horse. Before the domestication of the horse about 3500 BCE in southern Russia, people in the grasslands of Eurasia lived along rivers, where they farmed and raised sheep, goats, and cattle. Near these settlements, archaeologists have even found the remains of domesticated pigs, which are never kept by nomads.

After 2000 BCE, horses gave the people of the Eurasian grasslands easy movement and a much greater range, allowing them to increase vastly the size of their herds. Evidence of bit marks on horses' teeth suggests the early use

Figure 2.6   Early chariots like this Hittite chariot were barely platforms, carrying driver, shield holder, and archer and often drawn by multiple horses. *Erich Lessing/Art Resource NY.*

of bridles and of horseback riding, but it was the invention of spoked wheels, carts, and chariots (see Map 2.2) that transformed the economy of the grasslands from mixed farming and grazing to nomadic animal raising. With horse-drawn carts, people could comfortably take themselves and their belongings over an almost endless supply of pasture. Sheep and goats remained the staples of their herds, supplying most of the peoples' needs for food, hides, wool, and even dung for fuel, but horses put their previously settled world in motion. The change was somewhat akin to fishermen who were used to casting their lines from the shore suddenly getting ships to fish the open seas.

Everyone took up the new nomadic life, from forest dwellers in Siberia to settled farmers along the southern border of the grasslands. A world of different isolated cultures became a single culture of nomadic pastoralism. The similar transformation of the North American plains when the Spanish introduced the horse after 1500 shows how rapid such a change could be. Within a century, widely differing tribal cultures all seized on the advantage of horseback riding for hunting bison, creating a "Plains Indian" culture that was entirely new.

*New Balance between City and Pasture.* The new nomads of Eurasia brought change to city societies in a number of important ways. Their mobility brought them physically closer to new cities. They entered a closer relationship of reciprocal wants and needs. The herdsmen desired the fine clothes, jewels, and precious products of the cities as well as wheat for bread. City rulers recognized the value of horses and horse-drawn vehicles. But the relationship between farm and pasture could verge from fraternal to fratricidal. Gilgamesh both battles and befriends the wild man Enkidu from the grasslands, and in the Bible, Cain the farmer slays his brother Abel the herdsmen.

As city societies built walls and trained armies to raid others, the nomadic peoples forged military formations of their own with horse-drawn chariots. In clashes with settled societies, charioteers with bows and arrows enjoyed the advantage of speed and surprise. Their forces transformed the balance of power from southern Europe to China. The settled communities closest to the Eurasian grasslands were the first to recognize the value of the new technology and make it their own.

*Nomads Conquer and Create Empires.* Tribal leaders and kings of border states in what is today Turkey, Iran, Afghanistan, and central Asia were instrumental in creating the new technology that melded horses and wheels into a powerful force for change. In some cases, as in India, the new technology gave an edge to Indo-Aryan–speaking nomadic peoples who already lived in the subcontinent. In other cases, the combination of horses and wheels created a devastating war machine of trained archers and chariot drivers that overcame the cities of Egypt and Mesopotamia.

Indo-Aryan nomads probably lived among the Indus cities long before they were abandoned around 1500 BCE. These people introduced camels before 1500 BCE, but horses and chariots did not come until later when the center of urban life had shifted east toward the area of the Ganges River.

Since the writing of Harappa, Mohenjo-daro, and the other Indus cities has not been translated, we do not know how similar or different their culture was from the Indo-Aryan Sanskrit culture that emerged after 1500 BCE. Nevertheless, the great Indian epic *Mahabharata* tells stories of battles between archers on chariots. In one famous passage, the god Krishna, incarnated as a charioteer, explains that members of the military caste must not shirk their obligation to wage war. Similarly, the oldest extant Sanskrit document of Hinduism, the *Rig Veda*, laid out the prayers and sacrifices of tribes skilled in horsemanship whose leaders were charioteers. In fact, the spoked wheel of the chariot became an enduring symbol of India, transformed into a symbol of eternal return in Hindu and Buddhist imagery and displayed on the modern flag of India after independence in 1947.

The conquest of Mesopotamia by the charioteers of the Kassite kingdom of Iran was more of a military affair. While the Kassites were still able to defeat the cities of the Tigris and Euphrates valley, they could not or chose not to impose their culture on the more sophisticated one they conquered. Instead, they learned Akkadian (the educated language of Mesopotamia), copied the stories of gods like Marduk and heroes like Gilgamesh, and revived the law codes of Hammurabi. As the Kassites became like Babylonians, new kingdoms arose to take advantage of the chariot military technology, like the Hittites and the Assyrians.

The Egyptians were conquered by a chariot-based military kingdom called the Hyksos, who came from the area of Syria and Palestine. The Hyksos imposed a regime that was partly foreign and partly respectful of Egyptian traditions. They moved the capital from Thebes to Avaris and partnered with the Nubian kingdom of Kush, south of Egypt. In response, a prince of Thebes led a successful Egyptian rebellion against the Hyksos and established an Egyptian New Kingdom that reconquered Nubia and used Nubian gold to pay for the best horses, chariots, and charioteers that money could buy. Horses do not breed easily close to the equator because their estrous cycle is triggered by changing hours of sunlight, so the Egyptians got their horses from the Hittite kingdom in Anatolia (present-day Turkey). A letter from the period reveals that, for Nubian gold, the Hittites supplied not only the horses but the equivalent number of chariots as well. It was today's equivalent of getting a fleet of jet planes, complete with trained pilots and spare parts.

*States Regain Empires with Chariots.* In Egypt and then in Mesopotamia, native chariot-based states created empires larger than any that had ever existed before. Earlier ancient Egypt had looked inward, protected by miles of desert. By contrast, the Egyptian New Kingdom after 1600 BCE created an empire that extended from Nubia to Syria. Similarly, the Kassites, Hittites, and Assyrians controlled all of Turkey and the northern Middle East. Horse-drawn chariots vastly increased the range of military conquest and administration. It was an international age. Akkadian became the first transnational language, used in diplomatic correspondence from Egypt to Iran.

Chariots gave the Bronze Age states of Eurasia a new lease on life. By increasing the size of states and turning them into empires, chariots vastly expanded the number and size of dependent villages, cities, and kingdoms that the great states could tax and exploit. The Egyptian New Kingdom (1570–1085 BCE) was marked by some of the greatest cultural achievements (though the period of the pyramids was long past): Queen Hatshepsut established trade relations with Punt in East Africa

Figure 2.7  The face of the sphinx shows the Egyptian queen Hatshepsut with the beard that testified to her kingship, fifteenth century BCE. © *The Metropolitan Museum of Art. Image source: Art Resource, NY.*

in 1493, Akhetaton initiated the monotheistic worship of Aten around 1362, and Ramesis II carried Egyptian armies to their widest boundaries by 1283.

The success of these empires was temporary, however. The imbalances that characterized Bronze Age states remained. In fact, in some important ways, they increased. Kings became richer and more remote from their subjects. Farming communities were exploited more and more. Military occupations became more brutal and slavery more pervasive. The greatest of the new empires, the Assyrian, prided itself on the brutality of its armies. At some point, the farmers and other producing classes of Bronze Age society were squeezed beyond the point of return. Between 1200 BCE and 1000 BCE, many of these empires declined. By 1000, many in the eastern Mediterranean were in a state of collapse.

## Empires and Collapse

Ruined cities are evocative sights. The barest of them evokes the life of a distant time far more persuasively than the most thorough Disneyesque re-creation. But one question they usually leave unanswered is "why?" Why did they decline? Why were they abandoned? A frequent answer is "earthquake," and often the stones of ancient ruins seem to have been tossed by a careless Earth. But earthquakes were often final indignities that followed curable catastrophes.

The Bronze Age city of Ugarit, a rich kingdom at the northeastern corner of the Mediterranean, was destroyed by an earthquake, fire, and tidal wave around 1300 BCE. The entire port and half the city laid in ruins. But not for long. With the help of the wealthy merchant families and possibly its Hittite overlord, Ugarit was rebuilt and prospered anew. But then around 1200 BCE, Ugarit suffered pirate raids, and the declining Hittite Empire was in no position to help. A poem suggests the mood of the times:

> The ephemeral joy of a single beautiful
>      day
> is followed by the sadness of 36,000
>      years.
> May the divine coffin, my son,
> be your desire in affliction!
> Such is the lot of humanity.[9]

Shortly after this was written, another earthquake destroyed Ugarit, and it was never rebuilt. At about the same time, the once powerful Hittite Empire also disappeared.

In many cases, earthquakes were the last indignities suffered by the cities of the Bronze Age. When the earth shook well-placed stones into their final resting place, most of these cities had long since lost their vitality and their people. Disease, sometimes plague, had reduced their numbers and their capacity to endure. Crops had failed and animals died; famine had set up the weakened survivors for disease. The crisis of late Bronze Age empires was broad based, especially in the eastern Mediterranean and the Middle East. Like a hot desert wind blown into an expanding balloon, chariots had stretched the capacity of Bronze Age empires. But the resource base that was the flesh and blood of these empires was still agricultural, and the increasing wealth needed to sustain the rulers, aristocracy, army, and officials was drawn from the same tax base. The result was an eventual breakdown that was systemic. Farmers left the land they could no longer afford to work. Cities became overburdened and underfed, and people abandoned them. Everywhere, people were displaced and on the move. City and countryside were threatened by pirates, bandits, and what contemporary Egyptian inscriptions called a horde of looting vandals. Looking back, slightly less than 3,000 years ago, a later Assyrian king recalled, "I brought back the exhausted people of Assyria who had abandoned their cities and houses in the face of want, hunger, and famine, and had gone up to other lands."[10] One Egyptian illustration of the period shows refugees carrying their children and belongings on oxen-drawn carts with solid wooden discs for wheels—a far cry from the wildfire of horses and spoke-wheeled chariots that once froze hearts in fear.

Of course, not all ancient states collapsed. Bronze Age Shang China was overrun but without a long crisis. Egypt was conquered, but, like China, elements of the old culture continued into a new age.

In the Americas, where there was no pastoral challenge or wide use of metals,[11] some ancient state societies collapsed early, most notably the Mayan and pre-Aztec Mexican. The Inca, by 1500 CE the last of a long series of state societies in the Andes, was wracked by a civil war that aided Spanish conquest. The Aztecs were conquered by a much later horse culture, one that progressed from chariots to iron armored cavalry to gunpowder. But that is a later story.

More to the point, perhaps, the urban revolution was permanent. Today on the island where the Aztecs chose to create their city stands the capital city of modern Mexico. In the central square of Mexico City on the site of the ancient Aztec pyramid Major Temple stands the Roman Catholic Cathedral, constructed in part with stones from the Aztec pyramid.

## Iron Age Eurasia

Not all cities were permanent, but the urban revolution itself was permanent. One of the features that gave it permanence was the capacity of urban institutions to maintain continuity yet change, even when change involved substantial transformation. One of the more profound transformations in the second and third millennium of urban societies in Eurasia was the substitution of iron for bronze as the material for tools and weapons.

### Iron versus Bronze

Even before there were cities, some people had learned to work soft metals like gold and copper, but we date the urban revolution, or Bronze Age, with the use of the harder metal

formed by smelting a combination of tin and copper. Bronze was an expensive alloy, however, since tin and copper were not widely available in the same areas. Consequently, bronze was accessible only to a wealthy few.[12] It was a fitting adornment for the limited aristocracy of early civilization. In Shang China, bronze was intentionally barred from peasants lest they become too powerful.

By 1000 BCE, many ancient civilizations had discovered iron, which was more abundant in nature, easier to shape, stronger, and less brittle than bronze. The technique of smelting or heating iron to be shaped and then hardened originated in the Hittite Empire in what is today northern Turkey and the Caucasus Mountains between 1900 and 1500 BCE. From there, ironworking spread throughout Eurasia and North Africa, although there may have been additional discoveries.[13] The technique seems to have been discovered independently, for example, around the Great Lakes of Central Africa (modern Rwanda) about 1000 BCE and in the area of Cameroon in West Africa about 800 BCE.[14] From these centers, ironworking spread throughout sub-Saharan Africa. In fact, the Bantu-speaking people of the Cameroon region migrated throughout Africa over the past 2,000 years, spreading their skills, their superior iron tools and weapons, their languages, and their genes.

Iron tools and weapons were stronger and sharper than bronze. Iron plows turned over harder soils, enabling farmers to expand their fields and the size of their harvests. The main advantage of iron, however, was that it was more widely available in nature and therefore much cheaper than bronze. It could supply a far greater number of farmers and soldiers, increasing their yields and giving commoners more leverage in the new massed

Figure 2.8 The Neo-Assyrian Empire dominated the Middle East in the seventh century BCE with its cavalry archers. *DeA Picture Library/ Art Resource, NY*

infantries that replaced Bronze Age charioteers. If bronze was the fitting adornment of an aristocratic age, iron was the metal of the common person.[15]

The Iron Age did not abolish social classes. In fact, as empires grew ever larger, emperors and ruling classes enriched themselves from a greater world of plunder and taxation. During the first millennium BCE, the gap between the very rich and the very poor increased, and slavery became more pervasive. The long-term impact of iron was as double-edged as its finest blades. Iron enabled empires to grow by fielding larger armies, but it also increased the raw power of common people, who had access to iron weapons and tools.

## New Forms of Inclusiveness: Words and God for All

*Iron as Metaphor.* During the first millennium BCE, iron became available to people throughout Eurasia and Africa, but in the area of the eastern Mediterranean and the Middle East, the variety of civilizations and the degree of interaction among them stimulated a series of innovations that were far more important than the use of a new metal. Yet if we think of the Iron Age as a period in which people became both more powerful and also part of a larger political world, then iron is at least an apt metaphor. It suggests not only the iron tools of farmers and weapons of soldiers but also a society in which many people participated in new ways.

The new participatory society took many forms. The development of a phonetic alphabet in the Middle East made writing and reading easier, but even those who could not read participated in public religious and cultural activities to a greater degree than before. The Iron Age was the period in which the great global religious traditions were born and prospered. These traditions were based on books: holy books and sacred words, even for those who could not read them.

The Iron Age cultivated independent populations and institutions to a far greater extent than Bronze Age societies. Merchants and manufacturers were more numerous, prosperous, and powerful. While state-supported priests still played an important role in some societies, so did new groups of more independent cultural leaders: missionaries, educators, and public intellectuals. Indeed, the Iron Age societies of the Eurasian crossroads created the idea and reality of "the public": public space, the republic, and, in some societies, civic identity and citizenship. Not incidentally, the first democracy developed in Iron Age Greece. In addition, not incidentally, it developed in the Greek Empire, where citizens enjoyed the labor of slaves.

The eastern Mediterranean and the Middle East after 1000 BCE constituted a patchwork of states of different sizes. The largest power by far was the Assyrian Empire, which had re-created itself after the upheavals at the end of the Bronze Age. This New Assyrian Empire (934–610 BCE) controlled the entire Tigris and Euphrates valley, southeastern Turkey, and the eastern Mediterranean coast. It was the largest, richest, and most powerful empire of this pivotal region or any other up to this time. Yet the powerful Assyrians sometimes allowed a certain degree of independence to the city-states and kingdoms on the Mediterranean coast. Among these were the Phoenician cities, most of which paid tribute to Assyria between 877 and 635 BCE, and the Hebrew states of Judah and Israel.

*The Invention of the Alphabet.* The Phoenicians are remembered for the Phoenician, or Phonetic alphabet, which is the system of symbols for sounds that is the basis of our 26 letters. The idea of using symbols for sounds (which are relatively few) as opposed to symbols for things and ideas (which are almost infinite) was not unknown before the Phoenicians invented the alphabet. Egyptologists recently discovered earlier alphabetic writing in Egypt's Western Desert dating from about 2000 BCE, but that system never challenged the established Egyptian hieroglyphs. Still, Egyptian writing included some symbols for sounds, as did Sumerian and Akkadian, the languages of ancient Mesopotamia. Nevertheless, a writing code that used only symbols for sounds was a significant departure. It meant that anything could be written with about a couple dozen symbols for sounds, in any language, and with very little training. The Phoenician alphabet was so useful that it was adopted by people who spoke Aramaic, the most widely spoken language of the Middle East until the spread of Arabic in the seventh century AD, and by speakers of Greek, Etruscan, and Latin, which became the root of many European languages.

*"T" Is for Trade.* Why would a system of city-states, like Phoenicia, rather than a great empire, like Assyria, invent a system that made writing accessible to more people? We have only to ask the question to know the answer. In great empires, written communication was the secret preserve of the priests or scribes. An Egyptian priest or a Chinese scholar had to learn 50,000 symbols, knowledge that one did not share lightly. But the cities of the eastern

| | | | | | Corresponding letter in | | | | |
|---|---|---|---|---|---|---|---|---|---|
| **Letter** | | **Name** | **Meaning** | **Transliteration** | **Hebrew** | **Arabic** | **Greek** | **Latin** | **Cyrillic** |
| 𐤀 | 𐤀 | 'āleph | ox | ' | א | ا | Αα | Aa | Aa |
| 𐤁 | 𐤁 | bēth | house | b | ב | ب | Ββ | Bb | Бб, Вв |
| 𐤂 | 𐤂 | gīmel | camel | g | ג | ج | Γγ | Cc, Gg | Гг |
| 𐤃 | 𐤃 | dāleth | door | d | ד | د | Δδ | Dd | Дд |
| 𐤄 | 𐤄 | hē | window | h | ה | ه | Εε | Ee | Ee, Єє |
| 𐤅 | 𐤅 | wāw | hook | w | ו | و | (Ϝϝ), Υυ | Ff, Uu, Vv, Ww, Yy | Уу |
| 𐤆 | 𐤆 | zayin | weapon | z | ז | ز | Ζζ | Zz | Зз |
| 𐤇 | 𐤇 | ḥēth | fence | ḥ | ח | ح | Ηη | Hh | Ии |
| 𐤈 | 𐤈 | ṭēth | wheel | ṭ | ט | ط | Θθ | | Фф |
| 𐤉 | 𐤉 | yōdh | arm | y | י | ي | Ιι | Ii, Jj | Ii |
| 𐤊 | 𐤊 | kaph | palm | k | כ | ك | Κκ | Kk | Кк |
| 𐤋 | 𐤋 | lāmedh | goad | l | ל | ل | Λλ | Ll | Лл |
| 𐤌 | 𐤌 | mēm | water | m | מ | م | Μμ | Mm | Мм |
| 𐤍 | 𐤍 | nun | fish | n | נ | ن | Νν | Nn | Нн |
| 𐤎 | 𐤎 | sāmekh | fish | s | ס | س | Ξξ, Χχ | Xx | Xx |
| 𐤏 | 𐤏 | 'ayin | eye | ' | ע | ع | Οο | Oo | Oo |
| 𐤐 | 𐤐 | pē | mouth | p | פ | ف | Ππ | Pp | Пп |
| 𐤑 | 𐤑 | ṣādē | papyrus plant | ṣ | צ | ص | Ͳͳ | | Цц, Чч |
| 𐤒 | 𐤒 | qōph | monkey | q | ק | ق | Ϙϙ | Qq | |
| 𐤓 | 𐤓 | rēš | head | r | ר | ر | Ρρ | Rr | Рр |
| 𐤔 | 𐤔 | šin | tooth | š | ש | ش | Σσ | Ss | Cc, Шш |
| 𐤕 | 𐤕 | tāw | mark | t | ת | ت | Ττ | Tt | Тт |

Figure 2.9 Which Phoenician letters look like the objects they describe? What does this resemblance suggest about the origin of alphabets? Notice also how the sound of the Phoenician name became the sound of the letter.

Mediterranean coast had a different agenda. The Phoenician agenda was trade, and its trading partners ranged far and wide. The biblical poet Ezekiel praised the Phoenician city of Tyre for its wide range of trading partners:

> Tarsus was a source of your commerce, from its abundant resources offering silver and iron, tin and lead as your staple wares. Cities of Turkey offered you slaves and vessels of bronze. Nomads offered you horses, mares, and mules. The people of the islands, like Rhodes, traded ivory and ebony [from Africa].

Ezekiel continues with a long list of Tyre's numerous imports and trading partners: wine and wool from Edom (modern Jordan); wheat, oil, and balsam from Israel and Judah; cloth from Damascus; lambs and goats from Arabia; spices and precious stones from Sheba (Yemen); and "gorgeous stuffs, violet cloths and brocades from Ashur [Assyria] and Media [Iran]."[16]

Trade was the lifeblood of Phoenician city states like Tyre. Its trading operations were organized by merchant companies that were independent of local rulers, though even the kings of Assyria were sometimes prominent investors. The need of Assyrian kings for the products and profits of these city-states also ensured their relative independence. Like modern Hong Kong for China, Tyre and the other Phoenician cities were valuable to Assyria even when independent.

*Monotheism.* Monotheism, the idea of one God, emerged from the same network of competing states, each committed to its own god but each aware that its enemies did the same. In that combination of global awareness and local loyalty, some people came to believe that their own god was the only god.

Bronze Age states like Uruk and Egypt had many gods. Political loyalty had little to do with worship. The temples of ancient Mesopotamian cities were politically and economically important, but only the priests ever entered them. Egyptian kings had to be obeyed and gods placated but not because there was an intense bond between god and people.

The Hebrew Bible tells of the development of such a bond between the people of Israel and their god, Yahweh. He is a jealous god, he tells them, and abhors their worship of other gods. But in return for their loyalty, Yahweh battles their enemies. Around 900 BCE, David, the warrior king, conquered neighboring states with the aid of Yahweh. A typical account of David's battles against the Philistines tells how Yahweh not only encouraged, indeed commanded, the attack but even suggested a winning battle plan: "Do not go straight up, but circle around behind them and attack them in front of the balsam trees" (2 Samuel 5:23). The ancient Hebrews believed that God acted on behalf of his people, but in a monarchy the king was God's anointed. When the Bible tells of King David's Judean war against the northern kingdom of Israel, his armies massacring the relatives of his predecessor, King Saul, the moral of the story is that Yahweh serves his people even when he seems to abandon them. Many of the biblical books of prophecy take on the explicit task of accounting for the defeat of the northern kingdom of Israel by the Assyrians in 721 BCE and of the southern kingdom of Judah by the Babylonians in 587 BCE. Nothing, not even the people's defeat, happens without the consent of their god. The prophets find a ready explanation in the failure of Yahweh's people to live up to their responsibilities.

*Gods at War.* Similar ideas developed on the other side of these battlefields. An Assyrian history tells of an occasion when King Ashurbanipal chose to attend a festival for the goddess Ishtar in her city Arbella rather than lead his forces in battle. In Arbella, he learns that the Elamites have attacked his troops, and he pleads for help from Ishtar. The goddess appears before him: "her face fire flamed, with raging anger; she marched forth against Teumman, the king of Elam,"[17] telling Ashurbanipal to remain, drink her beer, and praise her divinity. She will take care of the rest.

Before battles, on both sides, militant kings invoked their gods, prophets foretold the outcome, and gods saved or abandoned their people. In most cases, people assumed that their own gods were more effective among their own people than among others, and wars became a test of whose god was more powerful. Rarely did people expect conquered foreigners to switch loyalties to the winning god.

At some point, however, the people of Israel believed that Yahweh was not only their god but also the only god that people anywhere should worship. The Hebrew Bible is full of stories of backsliders among Yahweh's people, tempted by Baal, the god of the neighboring Cananites, or the great goddess Asherah. The transition to monotheism must have been gradual and long incomplete.

What could have prompted the spread of monotheism—such a departure from the traditional idea of competing states under competing warlike gods? Ironically, it was probably not military success since the greatest military victories were achieved under David and his son Solomon in a brief 40 years around 900 BCE. After that, Yahweh's people suffered a series of reversals, including the split between Judah and Israel, civil war, and the conquest of Israel by the Assyrians and of Judah by the Babylonians.

*The Rivers of Babylon.* Strangely, defeat may have been more of a spur to monotheism than victory. It was common practice in this period for victorious empires to resettle conquered people, often exchanging populations to keep them divided. The Assyrians and Babylonians were masters of this tactic and spread the people of Israel and Judah far and wide. Yahweh worship, like that of Ishtar and other deities, had been very much based on location. Solomon built a temple to Yahweh in Jerusalem (albeit with Phoenician workers and artisans from Tyre) that became the focal point of the religion. Devastated by exile, the Judeans who were taken captive to Babylon asked how they could worship away from their temple, in a strange land:

> By the rivers of Babylon,
> There we sat down, yea, we wept,
> When we remembered Zion. . . .
> How shall we sing the Lord's song
> In a strange land?
> If I forget thee, O Jerusalem,
> Let my right hand forget her cunning.
> If I do not remember thee,
> Let my tongue cleave to the roof of my
>     mouth; (Psalms 137)

In fact, the experience of exile did much to turn a national religion into a universal one. Away from Jerusalem, Yahweh's reach extended far beyond temple priests and local concerns. A god who was everywhere required neither image nor temple. Daniel received the Lord's protection far away in a lion's den in Babylon, a city that provided him a global vantage point on God's universal plan. In exile, refugees from Jerusalem felt more acutely the need to keep their traditions alive. As a consequence, much of what became the Hebrew Bible was remembered and put to writing by and for generations raised in exile.

When Cyrus, king of Persia, conquered Babylon and restored the Jews to Jerusalem, it was clear to the prophet Isaiah that the god of Abraham, the creator of the world, and the god of Cyrus and his vast empire must be all one and the same:

> This is what the LORD says—
>     your Redeemer, who formed you in
>     the womb:
> I am the LORD,
> who has made all things,
> who alone stretched out the heavens,
> who spread out the earth by myself,
> [25] who foils the signs of false prophets
> and makes fools of diviners,
> who overthrows the learning of the wise
> and turns it into nonsense,
> [26] who carries out the words of his
>     servants
> and fulfills the predictions of his
>     messengers,
> who says of Jerusalem, "It shall be
>     inhabited,"
> of the towns of Judah, "They shall be
>     rebuilt,"
>  and of their ruins, "I will restore them,"
> [27] who says to the watery deep, "Be dry,
> and I will dry up your streams,"
> [28] who says of Cyrus, 'He is my shepherd
> and will accomplish all that I please;
> he will say of Jerusalem, "Let it be
>     rebuilt,"
> and of the temple, "Let its foundations be
>     laid." (Isaiah 44)

The belief in a single god of all nations and the use of one alphabet for all languages were two important ways in which the Iron Age Middle East and Mediterranean turned local knowledge into universal truths. In both cases, the creation of universals occurred in the struggle between small independent city-states and large empires.

The area from the Fertile Crescent to the eastern Mediterranean was unusual in the abundance of city-states. City-states had been the first Bronze Age societies on the Tigris and Euphrates, and they sustained themselves along jagged coastlines of the Mediterranean Sea as merchant cities and as colonies from North Africa to southern Spain. But the Middle East was also dominated by increasingly large empires in the early Iron Age. After the Assyrians came the Babylonians (sixth to fifth centuries BCE), followed by the Persians (later sixth to fifth centuries BCE) and Alexander the Great and his successors (fourth to first centuries BCE). Throughout the first millennium BCE, the conflict between city-states and large empires contributed to the increasing universalism of people in Middle Eastern and Mediterranean Iron Age societies.

Iron, alphabets, and monotheism were not the only marks and makers of a more inclusive society in the first millennium BCE. One might also think of money or, more precisely, coinage minted in Lydia from the beginning of the seventh century.[18] Lydia was an empire, not a city-state, but situated in what is today eastern Turkey, it was as mindful of the power of the Assyrian Empire as were the Phoenicians and Israelites. The creation of coins, worth their weight in metal but also backed by the king whose face was engraved on them, was another local invention that quickly won universal acceptance. Not only did the idea of coinage quickly pass to other states, but the actual coins circulated throughout the region and beyond.

## Citizenship and Salvation: Leveling in Life and Death

Two other ideas of the Iron Age gave the people of the Middle East and Mediterranean a sense of equal participation between 600 BCE

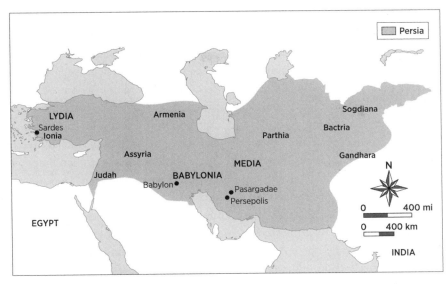

Map 2.3  Persia in the sixth century BCE was a huge cosmopolitan empire that united the lands between Greece and India, including what had been Judah, Israel, Phoenicia, and Lydia.

and 200 CE. One was the idea of citizenship: the equality of the citizens and their common stake in their city. The other was the idea of salvation: a kind of equality beyond life and beyond death. We associate the idea of citizenship with the cities of ancient Greece, especially Athenian democracy, and the idea of an afterlife with the rise of Christianity, notably the idea of heaven, but these two examples were neither the only cases nor the first.

*The Cities of Babylon.* The cities of the Neo-Babylonian Empire (626–539 BCE) may have originated the idea of citizenship. The inhabitants of Babylon and other Babylonian cities claimed special privileges from the monarch. When Babylonian cities were conquered by foreign kings (the Assyrians before and the Persians after this period), the conquerors contacted delegations of urban inhabitants and agreed to respect elements of city law and tradition. The root of this idea, called "divine protection," was probably laid in the Bronze Age cities of the Tigris and Euphrates, where

each local temple was dedicated to a city god, but the concept was expressed frequently in the Neo-Babylonian period after 600 BCE.

*The Persian Paradise.* If the idea of citizenship sprang from the local interests of city-states and independent cities in empires, the idea of salvation came from the opposite direction—from the large empires that suppressed local initiative. The largest of these in the ancient world was the Achaemenid Persian Empire[19] (ca. 550–330 BCE), created by Cyrus the Great (559–530 BCE), who conquered Babylonia in 539 and by the time of his death had extended Persian power from Asia Minor to India and Egypt to central Asia. An empire of such global scale, with its variety of peoples and traditions, sought universal explanations of its power. Like the Hebrew refugees in Babylon, Persian kings and soldiers needed a deity who was not limited by geography or language. The Persians called that god Ahura Mazda. An inscription above the tomb of King Darius (522–486 BCE) proclaimed, "A great god is

Ahura Mazda, who created this earth, who created yonder sky, who created man, who created happiness for man, who made Darius King, one king over many, one lord over many."

The idea of a single god, creator of heaven and earth, creator of mankind and anointer of kings, does not necessarily imply the idea of life after death, heaven, or eternal salvation, certainly not on an individual level. The monotheism of ancient Jews, many of whom were returned to Jerusalem by Cyrus, was a belief in a creator god who protected his people collectively in this world. Many Jews do not believe in a life after death. But under the influence of Persian thought, some Jews began to envision a last judgment and an individual immortality that inspired the prophet Daniel in the second century BCE. In fact, the driving force behind the Persian idea of a last judgment was not monotheism but the idea of two gods—Ahura Mazda and Angra Mainyu, the good, creative god and the evil, destructive deity, described by the Persian prophet Zoroaster. Zoroastrians believed that there would be a final conflict between Ahura Mazda and Angra Mainyu in which the force of evil would be defeated. In the end of days, there would be a last judgment, the passage of souls to heaven or hell, a resurrection of the dead, and paradise on Earth. These ideas filtered into Judaism and became core beliefs of Christianity.

## Imperial Size and Reach

Zoroastrianism spread with the Persian armies across an empire that extended from Egypt and Greece in the west to the Indus Valley in the east, an area of 2 million square miles with 10 million people, representing 70 different ethnic groups. The empire was five times larger than the previous largest, the Assyrian, only 200 years before. Traditionally, the size

of empires depended on the ability of soldiers to get from the center to the farthest reaches. That, in turn, depended on the speed and carrying capacity of their transportation technology. The invention of the horse-drawn chariot around 1700 BCE made possible the late Bronze Age empires of Shang dynasty China, central Asian migration to India, the Hittite Empire of Turkey, and the New Egyptian Empire of Egypt and the Levant. The Iron Age cavalry revolution gave the Assyrians the capacity to cover an area of 375,000 square miles with considerable speed. The Persians also made good use of cavalry, but the weapon that stretched their reach far beyond the Assyrians was the warship.

*Ships and Satraps.* The Persian navy sent galleys from the Persian Gulf to the Indus, across the Mediterranean, and down the Red Sea. In one sense, it was not a Persian fleet at all but rather the ships and sailors of countries and cities that the Persians had conquered or brought into their empire. The most effective of these were the fleets of the Phoenician cities, including Tyre, and the Greek cities on the coast of modern Turkey and throughout the Mediterranean. These fleets included both mercenaries (sailors who fought for pay) and the sailors of subject cities and states.

Persian ability to rule such a vast empire depended in part on an innovation in organization carried out by Darius soon after he came to power in 522 BCE. He divided his empire into districts, called satrapies, each governed by an appointed governor, or satrap. Depending on size, wealth, and population, each satrapy was assessed taxes and troops: infantry soldiers, cavalry and horses, and sailors and ships. Mercenaries and ethnic Persian forces rounded out the huge Persian force, estimated to number 300,000. "Of all the troops in the Persian army," the Greek historian Herodotus wrote, "the native Persians were not only the best but also the most magnificently equipped."[20] He was referring probably to the elite palace guard of 1,000, which the Greeks called the Immortals because of the Persian practice of immediately replacing the fallen to keep the force at full strength.

That the Persians could govern the largest empire in the world from 522 BCE until 330 BCE testifies to their organizational ingenuity and military power. That the entire empire could be lost in just under four years—as the 23-year-old Alexander of Macedon forced one satrap after another to change sides—shows how fragile the system could become.

## Conclusion

### *The Legacy of Gilgamesh's Wall*

What, then, is the legacy of the urban revolution? The great ramparted wall of Uruk was meant to magnify the power of the king and to keep out his enemies: to mark the boundaries of the civilized from the barbarian. The walls inside the city served a similar function within the urban community. The walls of temple, palace, and fort separated the new divisions of class, function, power, and wealth. These divisions increased throughout the course of the urban revolution. As cities grew in size and number, so did the power of kings and the numbers of soldiers and slaves.

Farmers, herders, and other food producers vastly increased their output and efficiency with irrigation, terraces, plowing new fields, adding new crops, and improving yields. The raw measure is the number of people who could be fed. World population grew slowly from about 6 million at the beginning of agriculture around 8000 BCE to about 7 million by 4000 BCE. But from there, it doubled every 1,000 years: 14 million by 3000 BCE, 27

million by 2000 BCE, and 50 million by 1000 BCE. Iron Age food producers doubled the pace again—to 100 million by 500 BCE.

The growth of cities meant a faster increase in the number of those who did not have to farm, herd, hunt, or gather. Cities popped up like mushrooms after a spring rain from 3000 BCE to 2000 BCE. From populations of a few thousand, they reached about 80,000 in Uruk by 2600 BCE. The Iron Age forged new cities again after 1000 BCE, and the new imperial capitals attained sizes never seen before: Babylon probably numbered 200,000 in 612 BCE.

Quantity of life is not the same as quality, and quality went to the few. The finest arts and treasures of the first civilizations were buried in the tombs of pharaohs and princesses. The work of the most accomplished astronomers and mathematicians enabled rulers to predict eclipses, improve calendars, and increase taxes. The scribes wrote for the eyes of the lords only.

Cities could not keep up their walls indefinitely, however. Gilgamesh needed Enkidu. Cities needed pastures: their meat, milk, horses, hides, and chariots. Iron Age empires needed soldiers, taxpayers, farmers, herders, artisans, merchants, and specialists. Some cities needed citizens.

Words leapt the walls of sacred precincts. The secret symbols of scribes and priests, initially used to collect taxes and communicate with the gods, became more versatile as they became simplified and more accessible. Epics, stories, and poetry could not be contained like secret formulas. Written laws could teach one to read. Literature could tempt one to dream.

### *The Promise of Pharaoh's Dream*

The pharaohs of Old Kingdom Egypt monopolized the resources of their realm to provide for their own afterlives. Immortality was reserved for kings, their accommodations prepared by the backbreaking work of Egyptian peasants, especially in the period of pyramid building between 2700 BCE and 2500 BCE. By 2000 BCE, Egyptian peasants were drawn to cults of the god Osiris, who himself had been restored to life by his loving wife Isis after being dismembered by his wicked brother Seth. As the god of the underworld, Osiris weighed the souls of all deceased Egyptians against the feather symbol of justice. Immortality was opened to those beyond the family of the pharaoh, and a person's worth could no longer be measured only by wealth and social position. Osiris worship became so common in the Egyptian New Kingdom that the priests attempted to regain control by devising fees and duties that would ensure a light heart (or a heavy feather). Cults of Osiris and Isis spread to the occupiers of Egypt in the Iron Age, filtering idea of judgment, rebirth, and immortality to Assyrians, Babylonians, Jews, and Persians. Persian Zoroastrianism recirculated the promises of Egyptian mysteries throughout South Asia and the Mediterranean in the fifth and sixth centuries CE.

The urban revolution was too big to remain the preserve of the few. The city released too many genies that could not be rebottled. They would be granting wishes for centuries to come.

## Suggested Readings

Chadwick, Robert. *First Civilizations: Ancient Mesopotamia and Ancient Egypt*. London: Equinox Publishing, 2005. Introductory survey from the agricultural revolution to the rise of Persia.

Foster, Benjamin R., trans. and ed. *The Epic of Gilgamesh*. New York: Norton, 2001. Well worth reading in full; a classic for thousands of years.

Ristvet, Lauren. *In the Beginning: World History from Human Evolution to the First States*. New York: McGraw-Hill, 2007. As thoughtful and well informed here as for the previous chapter.

Scarre, Christopher, and Brian Fagan. *Ancient Civilizations*. Englewood Cliffs, NJ: Prentice Hall, 2003. Very good textbook; includes the Americas.

Trigger, Bruce G. *Early Civilizations: Ancient Egypt in Context*. Cairo: American University of Cairo Press, 1993. Interesting effort by an anthropologist to compare Egypt with other ancient civilizations, including African and American.

## Notes

1. Benjamin R. Foster, trans. and ed., *The Epic of Gilgamesh* (New York: Norton, 2001), p. 10, tablet I, 226–32.

2. John Noble Wilford, "Evidence of Ancient Civilization is Found in Peruvian Countryside," *New York Times*, December 28, 2004, F3.

3. Jonathan Mark Kenoyer, *Ancient Cities of the Indus Valley Civilization* (Oxford: Oxford University Press, 1998), 42.

4. There are many ancient Egyptian documents like this, copied by student scribes for writing practice. This selection is adapted from two: "Teaching of Khety, Son of Duaf," quoted in Sir Leonard Woolley, *The Beginnings of Civilization*, vol. 1, pt. 2, of *UNESCO History of Mankind: Cultural and Scientific Development* (New York: Mentor, 1963), 170, and V. Gordon Childe, *Man Makes Himself* (New York: Mentor, 1951), 149.

5. Adapted from Bernal Diaz, *The Conquest of New Spain*, trans. J. M Cohen (London: Penguin, 1963), 232–33.

6. James B. Pritchard, *Ancient Near Eastern Texts relating to the Old Testament* (Princeton, NJ: Princeton University Press, 1955), 438–40, cited in William H. McNeill, *The Rise of the West* (Chicago: University of Chicago Press), 138, n. 31.

7. P. Anastasi IV, cited in R. A. Caminos, *Late-Egyptian Miscellanies* (London, 1954), 137–38. Adapted from Barry J. Kemp, *Ancient Egypt* (London: Routledge, 1989), 310.

8. John Noble Wilford, "String and Knot, Theory of Inca Writing," *New York Times*, August 12, 2003, F1.

9. Quoted in Amelie Kuhrt, *The Ancient Near East c.3000–330 B.C.*, vol. 1 (London: Routledge, 1995), 316–17.

10. E. Weidner quoted in Kuhrt, *The Ancient Near East c. 3000-330 B.C.*, vol. 2 (London: Routledge, 1995), 396.

11. Bronze was used for tools in Peru in addition to gold and copper. The Aztecs fashioned objects of gold and silver, but the Mayans lacked an indigenous metal industry.

12. Again, the Americas are an exception. In Peru, bronze tools were available widely, but there was no iron anywhere in the Americas. Highland Mexican societies received bronze from South America, but the lowland Maya did not.

13. There may have been other, possibly even earlier sites. For the claim of a separate Indian discovery as early as 1800 BCE, see Tawari Rakesh, "The Origins of Iron-Working in India: New Evidence from the Central Ganga Plain and the Eastern Vindhyas Antiquity," *Antiquity* **77** (297, 2003): 536–44. For China, see Donald B. Wagner, *Iron and Steel in Ancient China* (London: Brill, 1996).

14. A book published by the Iron Roads Project of UNESCO, *Les Routes du Fer en Afrique* (Paris: UNESCO, 2000), argues that African iron production in central Africa may be as much as 5,000 years old and that there is evidence of iron production in Niger dating to at least 1500 BCE.

15. See William H. McNeill, *The Rise of the West* (Chicago: University of Chicago Press, 1963), 117–18.

16. Ezekiel 27:12–25, adapted from *New English Bible*.

17. Quoted by Kuhrt, *The Ancient Near East*, vol. 2, 511.

18. Coinage also originated in India and China toward the end of the seventh century CE.

19. "Achaemenid" refers to the name of the founder of the Persian dynasty. This was the first great and largest Persian Empire. It was followed by the other Persian empires after the interruption of Alexander the Great and his Seleucid successors.

20. Aubrey de Selincourt, trans., Herodotus, *Histories* 7.83.

# 3

## Eurasian Classical Cultures and Empires
### 600 BCE–200 CE

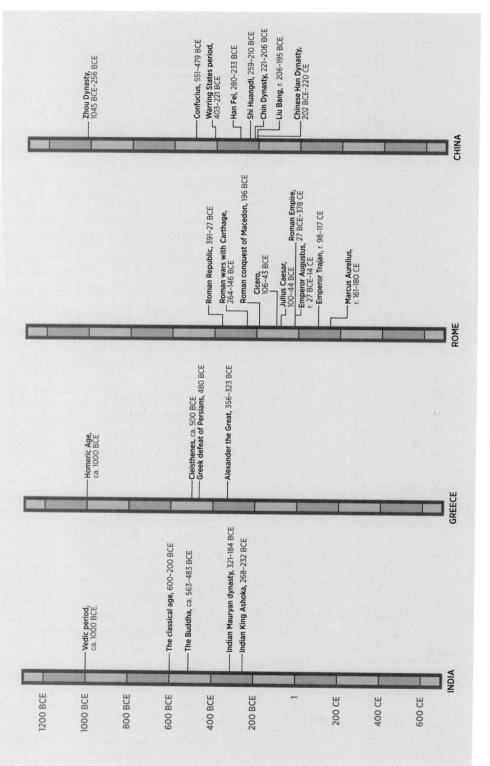

Figure 3.1  Time line.

# The Great Traditions of the Classical Age

## *The Classical Age*

WHAT IS a classic? The great American humorist Mark Twain once quipped that a classic was a book that everyone praised but no one read. There is much truth in that. Classic books, read or not, are often praised for what they symbolize as sources of a people's culture or civilization. What is interesting is that many of the world's people find their classics in the same historical period. That period spans no more than the few hundred years from about 600 BCE to 200 CE. In that brief period of 800 years, one could date the great Chinese classics of Confucius and Laozi (Lao Tze); the sacred books of Indian Hinduism and Buddhism; the work of the Persians Zoroaster and Mani; the Hebrew Bible and the Christian New Testament; the classics of Greek philosophy, theater, and science; and the literature of ancient Rome.

Why do so many of the world's cultures see their classical ages in the same period about 2,000 years ago? The Eurasian Iron Age brought far more people into public participation than had the Bronze Age. Iron, the widely available metal, gave ordinary farmers and soldiers the tools to claim a stake in the world. The larger states of the Iron Age, united by fast cavalries and administered by laws, required masses of people from varying backgrounds to share some common culture, sufficient at least to accept and obey. Writing was the glue of the new order.

Scribes and people newly exposed to writing often thought that words were sacred. They cultivated writing as an act of devotion and cultural identification. These were book people, or, rather, the writers inscribed the beliefs and values of the ruling classes—the priests, kings, and aristocrats—and propagated those values by writing. Most people could not read, but everyone could be read to. In India, the priests could read the holy books and practice the sacrifices on behalf of the people. In Greece, where public literacy was greater, even the illiterate could understand the language and message of the theater. No wonder so many cultures trace their origins back to the writings of their formative era. But the similarities among these cultures end there. Their writings are actually quite different, so different in fact that we can use them to distinguish the styles of some of the great cultures of the world.

## *The Great Divergence*

It is likely that the world's people took different paths long before the age of iron, alphabets, and mass migrations. But without the record of written works, we cannot know how those paths might have diverged. The writings of the Bronze Age are generally too limited, beyond Mesopotamia and Egypt, to show cultural differences. The Bronze Age writings of India have not even been deciphered. The writings of the classical Iron Age are the first to allow us to see in some detail how the cultures of India, Greece, Rome, and China differed. But a couple of provisos are in order.

*Interpreting Literature.* We have to be very careful in using literary writings as a tool to understanding a people's beliefs and behavior. There is always the question of who a particular author speaks for or represents. By using works that are considered classics, we at least can assume that the ideas have some general relevance or resonance. But classics are often such because they are used by the elite to indoctrinate others, and the illiterate of a society may not be easily indoctrinated by books. Further, we may not be aware of the meaning or purpose of a writing that has since become a classic. Many holy books, for instance, were memorized and recited by rote so that the words became frozen in time, divorced from the changing world in which they were spoken.

*Differences Not Permanent.* Some people find the discovery of cultural differences distasteful, as if cultural differences implied racial differences or disparagement. Nothing like that is implied here. In fact, since culture is entirely learned, cultural differences cannot be biologically based. Nor are cultural differences permanent. They are changing all the time. The variety of human cultures is a testament to human variability and possibility: the opposite of a stereotype. As we try to understand the differences between Indian, Greek, Roman, and Chinese acculturation more than 2,000 years ago, we should not assume that these same differences operate today. Some may; many will not.

## The Ways of India and Greece

The classical civilizations of both Iron Age India and Greece supplanted earlier Bronze Age civilizations that collapsed in the first half of the second millennium (about 1700 BCE). The earliest Indian and Greek civilizations, the Harappan on the Indus River (in modern Pakistan) and the Minoan on the island of Crete in the eastern Mediterranean, evolved in similar ways after 3000 BCE. Both seem to have lacked city walls, major fortifications, or evidence of large armies. The remains of the Indus cities even suggest the absence of kings or imperial palaces—a feature that the excavated Minoan

city of Knossos displays prominently. If both Indus and Minoan societies enjoyed relative peace, it may be because their prosperity was based on trade rather than conquest. We are unable as yet to translate the early writing of either society, but the artistic representations of both (e.g., dancing figures) suggest a grace and lightness that we do not find in their successors.

Knossos and much of the Cretan shipping fleet was probably destroyed by a volcanic eruption around 1628 BCE. Soon afterward, Crete was conquered by the Mycenaean civilization that had grown up on the Greek mainland in its shadow. Mycenae was also a port city that prospered through trade and shipping, but the high fortifications of its cities and the stories of its epic battles, told later in Homer's *Iliad* and *Odyssey*, indicate a more militarized society or less peaceful times.

Historians used to believe that the Indus civilization of India and the Mycenaean civilization of Greece were suddenly overrun by invaders from central Asia, usually referred to as Aryans or Indo-Europeans, who were credited with bringing Iron Age and classical ideas from afar. This theory has been largely rejected by current historical research in favor of a view that sees greater continuity between the peoples of the Bronze Age and the classical age. Nevertheless, there was a significant lapse of time between the effective collapse of the Bronze Age Indus River cities and the Mycenaean civilization, all by around 1600 BCE, and the stirrings of Indian and Greek classical civilization around 700 BCE. This "dark age" was enough time for the populations to be enhanced by peoples from central Asia as well.

The new peoples were descended from or influenced by nomadic horse breeders who originated in the grasslands of central Asia. During the second millennium (2000–1000

BCE), these Indo European horse people spread their ways, genes, and language across southern Europe and Asia with the aid of chariots. We can trace their influence by the way in which the earliest Indo-European language appeared, displaced earlier languages, and eventually broke up into separate languages. In northern Syria, we have a document that tells part of this story. It is a treaty between the Hittites and the Mittani, dated 1380 BCE, that uses the names of gods that are ancestral to what they became in Persian and Indian Sanscrit. Another document from this period shows the same common names of horses, charioteers, and numbers. Therefore, it is sometime after 1380 that ancestral Persian and Indian developed into separate Indo-European languages. Greek and Sanscrit also went their separate ways, but the movement of languages is not the same as the migration of people. Languages travel in many ways. Think of the global spread of modern English through the Internet or the influence of American culture. Similarly, in the ancient world, people who borrowed plants or inventions would often borrow their names and sometimes eventually learn a new language. We cannot say that Indians and Greeks were descended from the same people; we can say only that their languages descended from a common proto Indo-European. But we might also wonder what elements of that ancestral culture—with its horses, chariots, and deities—continued among the speakers of Greek and Sanscrit.

We do know that Greek and Indian societies developed different social structures and different cultures. Indian society based itself on groupings of families and occupations that have come to be known as castes. Beginning in the sixth century BCE, Greece changed from a mainly tribal society to one organized by territory. From the Indian choice came occupational and religious institutions, guilds, and monasteries that quickened seemingly opposite impulses toward economic development and spiritual transcendence. They prospered without state intervention because Indian culture shunned politics and provided a sanctioned place for princes and kings. From the Greek organization by territory came city-states, intense political participation, civic identity, and ideals of patriotism. The idea that one was subject to the rule of the law of the land rather than the tribe encouraged the development of a culture of political debate, intellectual competition, individual speculation, philosophy, and natural science.

## India

*Vedic Civilization.* Classical Indian civilization is sometimes called "Vedic" because of the centrality of the religious writings called vedas. These were written in Sanscrit and serve as the foundation of Indian religion. In addition, a Sanscrit epic called the *Mahabharata* celebrates the stories and traditions of warring families of horsemen and charioteers, possibly in reflection of their history in India.

Beyond these books we know very little of the people who composed them or their lives. We know little of their relationship to the remaining inhabitants of Harappa, Mohenjo-daro, and the other Indus cities. We do know, however, that they engaged in frequent cattle raids (probably mostly among themselves), preyed on settled farmers, took some captives as slaves, and forced a darker-skinned people, called Dravidians, to move farther south.

*Four* Varnas. If like other Indo-Europeans these Vedic Indians initially thought of themselves as three kinds of people—priests, protectors, and providers—they added a fourth group to account for the Dravidians or other

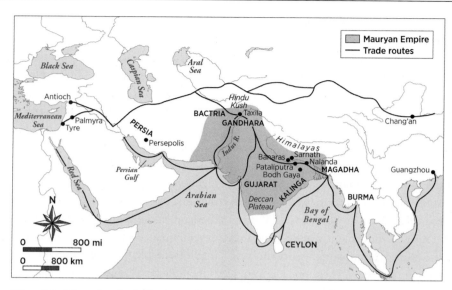

Map 3.1 The classical Mauryan Empire of India, 321–185 BCE, almost 1,000 years after the collapse of the ancient Indus cities, was the first empire to rule most of the Indian subcontinent (and beyond).

local coerced laborers. They theorized this social scheme as the four *varnas* (literally, "colors"): *Brahmin* priests, *Rajana* (later *Kshatriya*) warriors, *Vaishya* producers, and *Sudra* dependent laborers. The Brahmin priests, who lived on offerings from the other groups, enshrined this distinction with a passage from the earliest of the *Vedas*. The *Rig Veda* told of the primeval sacrifice of the god Purusha, from which all things were created: the sacred hymns, horses, cattle, as well as human beings. And so that no one could doubt their place in the world, it declared that the Brahmin came from the god's mouth, the Rajana from the arms, the Vaishya from the thighs, and the Sudra from the feet.

*Karma and Reincarnation.* The importance of *varna* was also stressed by the *vedic* doctrine of *karma*, the idea that one gained merit from doing the duties of one's station. Combined with the doctrine of reincarnation, Brahmins could argue that those who fully followed the obligations of their particular *varna* would be reborn to a higher state in the next life. Even a lowly Sudra might, through proper obedience and hard work, become one of the higher orders but only in the next life and only by accepting one's fate in this life. This Brahmin religion came to be known as Hinduism.

A section of the *Mahabharata*, known as the *Bhagavad Gita*, tells the story of the conflict between two great lineages. The leader of one is the young Kshatriya, Arjuna, who is faced with the predicament of war. He knows that the enemy forces include many friends, former teachers, and people he respects. Why should he fight and kill them? he asks himself. His question is answered by none other than the god Krishna, who has taken the form of Arjuna's charioteer. Krishna's answer is that the dead will be reincarnated as the living and that, in any case, it is the duty of a Kshatriya to wage war:

Death is certain for anyone born
and birth is certain for the dead;
since the cycle is inevitable,
you have no cause to grieve. . . .
Look to your own duty;
do not tremble before it;
nothing is better for a warrior
than a battle of sacred duty[1]

*Farmers and* Jatis. By the middle of the
first millennium BCE, the descendants of these
pastoralists had settled in the upper Ganges
plain, cleared forests, and become farmers,
planting wheat and barley and, increasingly,
rice. Their pastoral traditions never disappeared. Horses and cows remained especially
valuable to them: 100 horses figured as the
worth of a man's life.

Society was becoming more complex and
in one way simpler than a world of four
*varnas*. The complexity came from the appearance of new groups: products of mixed
marriages, strangers, and assimilated people.
The members of these new groups, called *jatis*
because they did not fit in to one of the *varnas*,
were expected to keep to themselves when
sharing food or arranging marriages. Eventually, every occupation or group of relatives
who shared food and intermarried constituted
a new *jati*. Today in India, there are thousands
of *jatis*, subgroups of *varnas* and what are also
called (after the Portuguese word) *castes*.

The way in which the new agricultural
world was becoming simpler was that it was
becoming a peasant society; the four *varnas* mattered less as some Vaishyas became
wealthy, bought land, and hired others, regardless of *varna*, to work the land. Increasingly after 500 BCE, the India of the Ganges
plain became like other agricultural societies
where the private ownership of land created a
world of two classes.

*Cities, States, and Buddhism.* After 500
BCE, some agricultural settlements became
important trading cities, and different lineages
merged into states, with particularly powerful
lineage chiefs as kings. Sometimes, the new
kings were Vaishyas or even Sudras.

The commercialization of Indian cities
and the rise of cities and states owed much
to the rise of Buddhism. The Buddha (ca.
563–483 BCE) was born a prince, the son of a
Kshatriya. But, according to legend, the young
Gautama Siddhartha's temperament was more
philosophical than political. It was said that he
was consumed at an early age by the problem
of suffering and increasingly drawn to a life of
meditation and withdrawal.

The Buddha's preaching was radically
equalitarian since the enlightenment he prized
was unrestricted by birth or status. The early
Buddhists felt Brahmin Hinduism to be rigidly
hierarchical. In addition to the ranking of *varna*
and *jati*, Brahmins taught a religion in which
any action was governed by rules of purity and
pollution, and the greatest pollution was spread
by a class of people lower than Sudras, who
were called "untouchables." An early Buddhist
work complained that an upper-caste woman
washes her eyes on seeing an untouchable, and
"a *brahman* is worried that a breeze that blows
past [the untouchable] will blow on him as
well."[2] To underscore the Buddhist distaste for
such prejudice, the Buddhist author suggests
that the untouchable in the story might be the
Buddha himself in a previous incarnation.

In cities, wealth mattered more than birth,
a fact that bothered Brahmins but appealed to
Buddhists. The Vedas disparaged mercantile
activity and forbade usury, while Buddhism favored commerce and investment. The Buddha
advised his followers to avoid expenditures on
ritual (Brahminical expenses) and devote only
a quarter of their income to daily expenses.

Figure 3.2 The "Great Stupa" at Sanchi in north-central India was built by King Ashoka to cover the relics of the Buddha. Pilgrims came to honor the Buddha by walking around the brick-hemisphere monument. *Scala/Art Resource, NY. Great Stupa, Sanchi, Madhya Pradesh, India.*

Another quarter was to be saved and the remaining half invested.[3]

*Mauryan Dynasty.* Buddhism both reflected and encouraged the new urban state society of the Mauryan dynasty (321–184 BCE). Trade and artisan guilds (*shreni*) administered their members and gathered considerable resources to their workshops despite their *varna* status as Sudras. A Greek ambassador to Mauryan India in 302 BCE, Megasthenes, said that Pataliputra, the capital city, was governed by a committee of 30. Its six subcommittees were involved with economic matters: industry, trade, manufactures, taxes, the welfare of foreigners, and recording births and deaths.

*Ashoka.* In fact, Mauryan cities were governed by the kings of the dynasty: first the founder, Chandragupta Maurya (321–297 BCE), and then his descendants. Perhaps the most famous of these was the king Ashoka (268–232 BCE), who united all of northern India (including modern Afghanistan and Pakistan) into a single empire. But Ashoka's fame does not rest on the fact that he ruled more of the subcontinent than anyone before modern times. Nor does it stem from his brutal defeat of the Kalingas, the last unconquered people north of central India. Rather, the memory of Ashoka is honored for what he did after the victory over the Kalingas. Remorseful of the human cost of his victory, Ashoka converted to Buddhism and renounced warfare. Instead of soldiers, he sent out ministers of *dharma* (goodness) to administer the kingdom.

*Buddhism, Politics, and Commerce.* Ashoka's benevolence may not have been as effective as his grandfather Chandragupta's reliance on almost a million soldiers, thousands of spies, and the advice of his aide, Kautilya, on the uses of deceit and treachery. The empire fell apart after Ashoka's death, and Hinduism replaced Buddhism in India. Hindu ideas of divinely endowed kingship were more useful to kings and Kshatriyas throughout South Asia. Buddhists preferred the quiet and direct dharma of monasteries to the messiness of politics. But Buddhists gave ascent to Hindu rulers in return for a free hand in their religious endeavors. It was a good compromise. Hinduism was a tolerant system that took no interest in people's beliefs as long as rulers were obeyed and priests were compensated. Buddhist monasteries, hospitals, and schools were jewels of the kingdom that performed needed services. The Buddhist embrace of poverty was oddly a route to general prosperity. Monks and scholars worked hard for little return, investing their energies in the needs of the community, even encouraging production and trade. It was a recipe for economic growth and indifference to politics.

Neither Hindus nor Buddhists sought political identities. People identified themselves by lineage, *varna*, *jati*, or religious community but not city, state, or territory. Religious communities could function isolated in the forest or in a monastery within the city, but these were separate communities. Buddhist holy sites attracted pilgrims or worshippers but rarely settlers, and they did not become reasons for building a city. Indian cities lacked public squares and neighborhood meeting

places. In these respects, Indian culture was different from that of Greek culture, with its public market (or agora), acropolis with religious temples, and public theaters, walks, and monuments.

## Greece

*The Hellenes.* Whether the Bronze Age Mycenean palaces were overrun by starving peasants, northern invaders, or the Sea People who destroyed Ugarit around 1200 BCE, there followed a century of cooler temperatures and a longer period of population decline sometimes called "the dark ages." From 1100 BCE to about 700 BCE, even writing may have been lost. The tribes that revived or reinvigorated writing in the seventh century did so with the aid of a borrowed alphabet and in one of the earliest examples of their new self-identity called themselves "Hellenes."

The settlement of Iron Age Greece was probably much like that of India. People settled into villages; towns became cities. But in Greece, lineage identities did not hold as strongly as they did in India. The impact of strangers and foreigners took a greater toll. Eventually, territorial sovereignty, the authority of the state, or the law of the land replaced the authority of the tribe or lineage group.

*Clans into Citizens.* In some sense, all of world history may be summarized as the process of turning clans into citizens, families into friends, and relatives into residents. And urbanization—the need to share an environment with strangers—is a long-term cause of that transformation. But it did not happen everywhere or at the same pace; indeed, it has still not happened fully even today. India today is a territorial state in which everyone must obey the laws of the land. But in India throughout the classical age, territorial sovereignty was

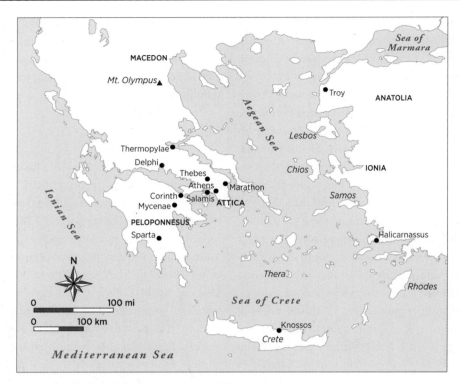

Map 3.2    Classical Greece, 500–350 BCE

constrained. The growth of cities weakened lineage attachments, but because people also thought of themselves in terms of *varna, jati,* guild, and religious affiliation, Indian cities did not create new identities as anonymous subjects, neighbors, or public-spirited citizens.

Greek cities created citizens. Sumerian cities had begun the process but were then conquered by Akkadian and Babylonian empires. Later Babylonians under Assyrian rule developed a particular civic identity in the seventh century. But for the first time, at least since the Sumerians, an entire nation of people—the speakers of Greek—developed a system in which civic identity was the core identity. In *The Constitution of Athens,* Aristotle tells us how the Athenians accomplished this about 500 BCE. He tells us that the tribal

leader Cleisthenes ended a system of alternating rule by the heads of the leading tribes by creating artificial tribes that were groups of neighbors rather than relatives and by making these artificial tribes the basic political units of Athens. Further, each of the 10 new tribes was composed of city, country, and coastal people so that each tribe would have an identity not only with its particular neighborhood but also with the larger Athenian city-state. Finally, all were to take on these new affiliations as their new names, to be passed on to their children and descendants. Aristotle's description was probably more ideal than reality, but it underscores how complete the transition from kinship to citizenship was to become.

*The Polis and Greek Religion.* The Greek system of territorial sovereignty was based on

Figure 3.3  Athenians walked up to the Acropolis to pay homage to Athena, the goddess of war, wisdom, and their city. *Hulton Archive/Getty Images.*

the polis, which we translate as "city-state." But the polis was much more than a city surrounded by enough farm and pasture to constitute a self-governing state. The polis meant raising politics above all else: not above the people but above the tribes, above kings, and even above the gods.

The Greeks were not irreligious. They worshipped the gods. But Greek cities paid homage to their particular patron deities, whose statue was placed high above the city on the hill of the Acropolis and adorned on special feast days for all to see. The temple of Aphrodite looked over Corinth, Zeus and Athena over Argos, and Athena over Athens. Many cities also had sanctuaries to the nurturing of Demeter or sanatoriums to the healing of Asclepius, and Greeks from all cities came together to listen to the Oracle at Delphi, honor Apollo at Delos, or pay homage to Zeus at Olympia.

*Public Spaces and Public Dramas.* Each city crowded around a large public meeting place, the agora, part market, part public square, and part promenade, where one came as much for gossip and amusement as for buying and selling. Around the agora were temples, covered markets, a gymnasium, shrines, public buildings, and perhaps a law court or theater. Every city of any size had a theater, a large concave, rock-inlaid tier of seats carved out of a hillside, facing a stage. There they saw the great dramas of Aeschylus, Euripides, and Sophocles and the comedies of Aristophanes. There they recalled the patriotism of their fathers in the war with Persia in 480 BCE as depicted in Aeschylus's *The Persians*:

> Come, O ye sons of Greeks,
> Make free your country; make your children free,
> Your wives, and fanes of your ancestral gods,
> And your sires' tombs! For all we now contend![4]

On other occasions, they gathered in these or similar assemblies to discuss the business of their polis or debate matters as weighty as war.

*Freedom and Law.* Freedom for these Greeks meant self-government and the rule of law, not individual liberty. The historian Herodotus imagined a dialogue between the Spartan Demaratus and Xerxes, the king of Persia, on the eve of the battle memorialized by Aeschylus above. The circumstances were extraordinary. Demaratus, a former king of the Spartans spurned by his people, had gone over to the Persian enemy, becoming a trusted confidant of Xerxes. When the Persian king asked if the Greeks, outnumbered a thousand to one, would surrender, Demaratus said they would fight until the last man because "they will not under any circumstances accept terms from you that

will mean slavery for Greece; . . . They are free—yes—but not entirely free; for they have a master, and that master is Law, which they fear much more than your subjects fear you."[5]

Greeks defined themselves as free men under the rule of law. Their self-government, they believed, separated themselves from all the empires around them. Herodotus also tells us that one of Xerxes' most trusted and fearless allies, Artemisia, advised the Persian king that all his vast armies from Mesopotamia, Egypt, Syria, and the Mediterranean were inferior to the Greeks because the Greeks were their own masters. "Good masters have poor servants,"[6] Artemisia told Xerxes. And since Xerxes was "the best master in the world," he had a "miserable lot" of allies.

Greek success against the Persians, the largest empire in the world at the end of the sixth century BCE, lay with the organization of the polis and the citizen militias that trained continually and enlisted every citizen in time of war. The classical Greek military formation, the phalanx, in which each soldier moved in unison, protected each neighbor with a large shield, and taught discipline, coordination, and mutual responsibility. Citizens who could not afford the expense of arms for the phalanx learned to fight in unison as rowers on the naval battering rams called *triremes*, where 170 oars touched the sea simultaneously to the beat of a shrill pipe.

*Law and War between States.* In the decades after the Greek defeat of the Persians in 480 BCE, the Athenians created a navy of hundreds of such ships that they allied with the smaller navies of other Greek city-states in the Delian League. At first, each city-state had a vote in the league council that met in neutral territory at the temple of Apollo on the island of Delos. After the Persian threat seemed to wane, some Athenian allies sought to withdraw from the league. But the alliance was too important to Athens as the dominant power. Gradually, Athens turned the league into an instrument of the Athenian Empire, building the membership to more than 100 while preventing withdrawals, moving the treasury and council to Athens, and directing the league into the coming struggle with Sparta and its allies in the Peloponnesian War (431–404 BCE).

Sparta was a very different city-state from Athens. While Athens was a commercial and maritime democracy, Sparta was a land-based, aristocratic, militarized city-state. The Spartan ruling class consisted of full-time soldiers, enlisted until the age of 60, living a hard, physical "Spartan" life made affordable by a class of conquered "helots" who grew their daily bread. When the Spartan Demaratus told the Persian Xerxes that Greeks would die for freedom and the law, he did not mean personal freedom but the freedom of the Greek state, and he did not mean the rights of citizens but the rule of law. In that regard, the Spartans were not that different from most Athenians.

The Peloponnesian War between Athens and Sparta was provoked by Sparta, but the longer-term cause, according to Thucydides, the Athenian participant and historian, was "the power of Athens" and the fear that such power engendered among the Spartans. The long war raged not only in the Peloponnese Peninsula, the home of Sparta, and throughout the rest of Greece but also in the waters of the Mediterranean and the Bosporus and in the cities of Sicily, North Africa, and what is today eastern Turkey. Both Athenians and Spartans had numerous opportunities to accept a peace, but the democratic forces of Athens and the proud ruling fathers of Sparta would have none of it. Finally, the end came for Athens in 404 BCE, when its navy was annihilated by Persian ships sailing for Sparta.

*Laws of Nature.* The idea of the rule of law may have guided the development of Greek science as much as politics. Greek philosophers looked for laws of nature that regulated the natural world in the same way that human laws regulated the social world. This idea of nature as a separate realm that could be understood by human reason was probably new in history. Earlier civilizations had solved particular scientific problems. The Mesopotamians recorded enough information about the positions of the sun, moon, and stars that they were able to predict new moons and possibly eclipses. The Egyptians recorded the daily movements of the star Sirius, which seemed to predict the rise of the Nile River. But this was pattern recognition from endless lists, a systematic activity undertaken by priests or scribes on behalf of the king.

The Greeks were the first to pose and attempt to answer questions about nature and the universe. Without regard to a particular problem and without the prodding of political authority, individuals like Thales as early as the sixth century tried to answer such questions as the basic ingredients of all matter. Some, like Thales, thought that it was water; others believed that everything was made of tiny particles, which they called atoms. The earliest such thinkers were Ionian Greeks. In the sixth century, Ionians had long lived on the Asian mainland in what is today eastern Turkey but was then part of the Persian Empire, and some had already migrated to Athens. As the richest city-state in the fifth century, Athens drew the best minds of the Mediterranean, but Athens did not always provide the best environment for speculative thought.

In some respects, the Persians were more supportive of free inquiry. The Persian Empire may have been the first in world history to accept the different religions and cultures of its many subject peoples. Consequently, the empire did not repress the speculative thought of Thales and the Ionian natural philosophers. By contrast, when Anaxagoras, an Ionian mathematician and astronomer, brought Ionian scientific ideas to Athens about 480 BCE, he was imprisoned for declaring that the sun and moon were not gods but only rocks like the earth. Even the great Athenian philosophers, Socrates and Plato, preferred to think of the basic ingredient of things in ethical rather than material terms. Eventually, however, the work of the Ionians prevailed in Athens. They developed logical formulas, laws of geometry, trigonometry, and higher mathematics. Astronomers understood that the earth and moon revolved around the sun, computed accurate sizes and distances for these bodies, and not only predicted eclipses but also understood why they occurred.[7] Hippocrates, the founder of modern medicine, speculated about arteries and veins, practiced dissections, diagnosed illnesses, and bequeathed the "Hippocratic oath" of physicians to do no harm. A modern historian of science suggests that the Greek struggle to discover truths of nature was a by-product of the intense debates in the law courts and assembly. In the competitive give-and-take of Greek public life, "it was dissatisfaction with merely persuasive arguments used there that led some philosophers and mathematicians to develop their alternative, to capture the high ground," with incontrovertible truths "that would silence the opposition once and for all."[8]

*Athenian Democracy.* Most of the Greek city-states were self-governing territorial states ruled by law, though some were ruled by kings, aristocrats, or even tyrants periodically. Few, however, were democracies, and Athens was the most democratic of all: in some ways more democratic than modern democracies. Some Greeks feared that democracy might lead to mob rule. Socrates and his student Plato, whose dialogues are our only written record of the thoughts of Socrates, believed that only philosophers should rule. In a famous passage in Plato's *Republic*, the Philosopher suggests that most people are like denizens in a cave who take the reflected light on the wall for the only reality. Most Athenians, however, prided themselves on their democracy.

The level of participation of citizens in government decision making was far higher than it is today. Citizens participated in a number of ways. First they came together in the Assembly to discuss public issues, debate proposals, and pass laws. The Assembly was therefore the equivalent of our Congress, and all citizens were legislators. Second, as members of one of the 10 tribes, citizens were chosen by lot to serve on the Athenian Council of 500, 50 members of which were again chosen by lot each month to administer the departments of government. From those 50, one citizen was chosen by lot each day to be Athenian president and chair of the Assembly. The turnover—and the resulting level of participation—was staggering by modern standards. One wonders how they got anything done and where they found so many able people. Since they accomplished a great deal and kept a relatively constant course, the answer must be that citizenship was a constant preparation. The prospect of being suddenly selected by lot to lead the country ensured their readiness, and the knowledge that they would be "president" for only a day ensured their commitment to the continuing interests of the larger community.

In addition to choosing their governors by lot, the Athenians also had elective offices. As the statesman Pericles put it,

> It is true that we are called a democracy, because the administration is in the hands

of the many and not of the few. But while there exists equal justice to all and alike in their private disputes, the claim of excellence is also recognized; and when a citizen is in any way distinguished, he is preferred to the public service, not as a matter of privilege, but as the reward of merit. Neither is poverty an obstacle, but a man may benefit his country whatever the obscurity of his condition.

We might find it strange, however, that one of the most prestigious offices that Athenians chose to elect was that of general. Each tribe elected a general each year, and the group formed a College of Generals who were responsible for military strategy in time of war. Perhaps in a world of citizen soldiers, military leadership was considered a widely available civic talent rather than a specialized skill. Pericles, the most famous statesman of Athens in the mid-fifth century, was able to exert enormous influence by virtue of his election as general 15 years in a row, including the early years of the Peloponnesian War with Sparta.

*Athens City Limits.* Citizenship in the ancient world was severely limited by modern standards. Even in Athens, women, foreigners, slaves, and former slaves were excluded from citizenship. Although estimates vary, slavery may have been pervasive, especially within the city. Many poorer Athenians were also sent to the numerous city-state colonies that Athenians settled throughout the Mediterranean. The resulting Athenian Empire put Athenians on an almost constant war footing. In a famous funeral oration marking the death of Athenian young men early in the Peloponnesian War, Pericles urged his listeners to be proud of their sacrifice:

> I would have you day by day fix your eyes upon the greatness of Athens, until you become filled with the love of her; and when you are impressed by the spectacle of her glory, reflect that this empire has been acquired by men who knew their duty and had the courage to do it, who in the hour of conflict had the fear of dishonor always present to them, and who, if ever they failed in an enterprise, would not allow their virtues to be lost to their country, but freely gave their lives to her as the fairest offering which they could present at her feast.

The rhetoric of patriotic sacrifice, familiar to the modern ear if generally limited to wartime and Memorial Day, was first voiced in classical Greece. One of its roots was, oddly, democracy—at least a democracy that required slaves and colonies. But another root may have been the city-state itself: so numerous in the ancient Mediterranean that they were bound to rub up against each other, even if there were no Persian Empire to settle disputes. And on a deeper level, patriotic sacrifice may have been the logical conclusion of territorial sovereignty. What greater power could the state command over the tribal patriarch or the mother of a family than the power to take away their sons forever? What greater defeat over the lineage system than to not only gain the acceptance of the grieving parents but also win their pride?

No society has existed very long without a means for turning some people into soldiers. The Persian Empire raised armies from the provincial governors, satraps, who received crown lands in return for troops. Classical India designated a hereditary population for military service and governance. The classical Hinduism of the *Bhagavad Gita* justified the sacrifice and killing by those whose *varna* was fighting. All ancient (and modern) societies purchased allies and used mercenaries. But the territorial state, especially as epitomized by fifth-century Athens, made the citizen army a source of new life as well as a new source of death.

## The Worlds of Rome and China

The differences between classical Rome and China were far greater than the differences between India and Greece. China was much older, having created a Bronze Age culture at least 1,000 years before the legendary foundation of Rome, with little or no contact with the Bronze Age societies of the Middle East, Africa, and India. Chinese language families were different from the Indo-European and Afro-Asiatic. Chinese written characters, which signified words, were not primarily phonetic or sound based, and Chinese foods, housing, and religion developed independently of the other great civilizations.

There were similarities between these great empires, however. Both were large territorial states in which a central government controlled numerous subject peoples. The unification of China and the expansion of Rome occurred simultaneously during the classical Iron Age, between 200 BCE and 200 CE. Each empire ruled at least 50 million people in an area of over 12 million square miles. The Chinese Han dynasty (202 BCE–220 CE) probably supported a larger population, partly because Chinese agriculture was more intensive than Roman. Both regimes managed to fund and field enormous armies, tax and control competitors for power in their own aristocracies, and convert millions to their cultural ideas. After the second century CE, however, both became increasingly vulnerable to the nomadic people of the steppe whom both called "barbarians."

### *Rome*

*Greco-Roman Society and Hellenism.* In its early centuries, from the fourth to the first century BCE, Roman society followed many of the

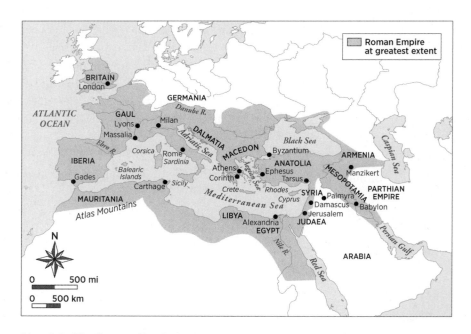

Map 3.3   The Roman Empire at its greatest extent, around 117 CE.

Figure 3.4 The Roman Capitol Temple of Jupiter, Juno, and Minerva dominated the Roman Forum from one of the city's seven hills. The architecture of this most important of Roman temples was modeled on the Greek Parthenon. Inside were three chambers. The central one contained a large statue of Jupiter. *The Granger Collection, New York.*

ways of Greece. Romans imbibed Greek culture, imitated its literature and art, and prided themselves on their institutions of self-government. Citizenship was even more widespread in Rome during the Roman republic (fourth to first century BCE) than it had been in Greece.

Greece, in turn, had both defeated itself and converted its neighbors. The Peloponnesian War, in which Sparta defeated Athens, exhausted the Greek city-states and made them easy prey to the armies of Philip of Macedon and his son, Alexander the Great. Alexander, trained by Aristotle, brought Greek culture as far as India before he died in Babylon in 323 BCE. The huge empire of Greek learning that Alexander forged and left to his generals after his death has been called *Hellenistic* to describe the continuing importance of Greek political and cultural models.

Rome expanded in the third and second centuries BCE in the shadow of that Hellenistic

world. Initially a city-state, Rome annexed other city-states in Italy, many former Greek colonies, so that it controlled the whole Italian peninsula by 235 BCE, thus confronting Carthage in Sicily, North Africa, and Spain. In three wars (264–146 BCE) Rome defeated Carthage, securing important silver mines in Spain and a western Mediterranean empire. The conquest of the Hellenistic kingdoms of Greece and Asia followed. But with the conquest of Macedonia in 196 BCE, the Roman Senate presented Roman troops as liberators, bringing the "freedom of the Greeks" against Asian kings and tyrants, a propaganda move that reflected Roman identification with Greek ideas of freedom, constitutionalism, and the rule of law.

*Republic Not a Democracy.* The Roman republic (which lasted until 27 BCE) was not a democracy, however. Although citizenship was widespread since all citizens bore arms, political power was shared by a class of self-selected nobility who governed as senators. The senatorial class was an exclusive club of men from large landowning families who devoted their time to public affairs and were not involved in business. The Romans prided themselves on their constitution, an unwritten tradition of governmental institutions and procedures.

*Armies, Lands, and Citizens.* Like Greece, the strength of Roman society was in its citizen army of independent landowners. In 391 BCE, when Rome was not much more than the city, an army of aristocrats was defeated by a force of nomadic Gauls who proceeded to burn down the city. When the Gauls left, ruling patricians called for vast constitutional changes in Rome. They extended citizenship and accompanying military service to small landowners (plebeians), distributed land to landless farmers (proletarians) so that they too could become citizen-soldiers, and granted the plebian assembly the power to pass laws. Plebeians could become consuls, the "presidents" and future senators of the republic, and plebian leaders, called tribunes, were granted extraordinary veto powers. The new constitution gave an extensive Roman citizenry a sense of common purpose and a common dedication to defend the state with their lives.

In time, patrician commitment to commonality waned as memories of the crisis dimmed. And as Roman armies spent more planting seasons conquering Italy and invading Carthage (in the First Punic War, 264–241 BCE), many Romans were forced to choose between farming and fighting. But even in the Second Punic War against Carthage (218–202 BCE) the threat of Hannibal's armies approaching Rome was enough to revive the old sense of common responsibility. In arguing the need of patrician women to give up some of their luxuries for the war effort, the historian Livy tells us that many of the men had already done so.

*Praetors and Publicans.* Romans applied their republican traditions of self-government to others as well as themselves. Greeks, as well as some conservative Romans, were shocked to hear the announcement at the Isthmian Games in 168 BCE, after the quick Roman defeat of Macedon, that Romans had come not to conquer but to liberate Greek cities. "Freedom for the Greeks" echoed Greco-Roman values. The conquered kingdoms of Greece and Asia (Turkey, Egypt, and Syria) were incorporated as Roman provinces and largely left to their own traditions although administered by Roman magistrates drawn from the city government of Rome.

Roman administration would have struck even a twenty-first-century American as highly privatized. All public economic functions, including tax collecting, were subcontracted by the Roman Senate to private entrepreneurs called *publicani*. These businessmen (later companies) bought the right to collect taxes in conquered provinces. To the modern eye, even in a society that has privatized some prisons, schools, postal services, and military functions, the possibilities of corruption in private tax collecting (in addition to all of these) would seem enormous. But the Romans at the top, the senatorial class, thought of themselves (almost like Indian Brahmins) as a class apart from the world of business. *Publicani* were excluded from political office and professed no interest in politics. Senators did not socialize with *publicani*. When the Senate sent out a provincial governor or praetor, he was expected to ensure that business was carried out honestly and without favoritism.

*Cicero on Provincial Government.* In 60 BCE, the great Roman orator and statesman

Cicero wrote a letter to his brother Quintus, governor of Asia, that conveys both the noble ideal and the array of temptations awaiting a provincial governor:

> It is a splendid thing to have been three years in supreme power in Asia without allowing statue, picture, [silver] plate, napery, slave, anyone's good looks, or any offer of money—all of which are plentiful in your province—to cause you to swerve from the most absolute honesty and purity of life.[9]

The job of a governor, Cicero reminded his brother, might routinely involve suppressing "some fraudulent banker or some rather over-extortionate tax-collector." These tax collectors were the publicans. You could not do without them, but you had to watch them like a hawk.

*Civil War and Empire.* Cicero's era was disappearing as he wrote. A series of civil wars in the second and first centuries BCE had already undermined the independence of the Roman citizen-soldier. By Cicero's time, standing armies of camp followers and paid professionals followed the ambitions of their generals. Most could no longer afford family farms and seasons of peace. Full-time soldiers needed full-time wars. A new breed of generals built careers on imperial campaigns. Rich men purchased armies: no one was truly wealthy unless he could afford to pay for a legion, the truly wealthy Marcus Crassus advised. After a victory in Asia or Gaul, a victorious general could make any claim, holding his loyal troops as collateral. Pompey returned victorious from his Asian campaign as the richest and most powerful person in Rome. His arrangements with Asian kings and Roman friends in senatorial and business classes made him for all practical purposes the "owner" of the Roman

provinces in Asia. The verdict of a modern historian reads, "No administration in history has ever devoted itself so whole-heartedly to fleecing its subjects for the private benefit of the ruling class as Rome of the last ages of the Republic."[10]

By the 50s and 40s BCE, it had become possible for a particularly ambitious Roman aristocrat, like Julius Caesar, to initiate a foreign and a civil war for his own glory and profit. In his triumphal celebration of 46 BCE, after conquering Gaul, defeating the Roman armies of his rival Pompey, and capturing Egypt, Caesar distributed a huge bonus to his soldiers, paraded captured treasures and 10 tons of gold crowns in a victory procession, and put on the largest gladiatorial games anyone had ever seen.

Caesar's death in 44 BCE plunged Rome into a civil war between his adopted son and great nephew, Octavian, and Mark Anthony, respectively. It completely erased any boundaries between private interest and res publica. One case in point: in 36 BCE, Mark Anthony gave Cleopatra, his lover and ally as queen of Egypt, the island of Cyprus, the Cilician coast (of Turkey), Phoenicia, Western Syria, Judea, and Arabia. Whole countries were no longer provinces of the Roman people; they were the personal possessions of those who ruled.

*Empire and Law.* Octavian defeated Mark Anthony in 31 BCE and became the most powerful Roman ever. Then, in 27 BCE, as "Augustus," he presented the new political order as a restoration of the republic. He later wrote, "I was in absolute control of everything, I transferred the *res publica* from my own charge to the Senate and the Roman people. For this I was given the title Augustus by the decree of the Senate."[11] He styled himself Princeps, merely first man, of the Roman state. There would be nothing like the title of permanent dictator that Julius Caesar had secured just before his death.

All the powers of Augustus were sanctioned by law. He simply put together more titles and offices than had any single individual before the decades of civil war. From the Senate and people, he received military command (*imperium*) over certain recently conquered provinces (Gaul, Spain, Syria, and Egypt) that contained the bulk of the Roman armies. In addition, he had himself repeatedly elected consul or tribune of the people, offices traditionally limited to a year but also frequently extended in the age of Pompey and Caesar.

Certainly, Augustus did not intend to restore the republic, and in that he probably had the support of most Romans, whose principal desire was peace and order after years of anarchy. Yet Augustus, like many Romans, was schooled in a 500-year tradition of rule by law stemming from the city-states of Greece. Therefore, if new powers were necessary, they had to be tailored to tradition and legal precedent. Augustus attempted, without success, to reduce the size of the Senate in order to make it a more effective body. He refused titles of divinity and "master" of the Senate and people. Nevertheless, he eventually accepted lifetime offices, superior powers and the building of temples to the "divine Augustus" in Roman provinces like Egypt, where divine rulers were traditional.

Romans did not lose the idea of the rule of law. Whether it was a guide or an unattainable ideal, it was always part of Roman expectations, even when least realized. Later emperors looked back to the principate of Augustus as their model. In 54 CE, the young emperor Nero declared his desire to return to Augustan principals: "Nothing in his household would be bought by money or open to intrigue; his private self and public self would be kept quite separate from each other. The Senate would keep its traditional prerogatives."[12] Such ideals were often far from the realities of rule, not least in the case of Nero, but even among the most autocratic of emperors, the rule of law reared its head. When, for instance, the emperor Claudius wanted to marry his niece despite the fact that it was specifically prohibited by law, he did not assume that he was above the law; rather, he went to the trouble of having the law changed.

*Administering the Roman Empire.* Augustus reformed the administration of the empire, making the provinces more uniform and government supervision more regular, but Roman rule remained indirect, decentralized, and entrepreneurial for another 200 years. In Italy and Greece, the empire was a federation of city-states, each of which enjoyed considerable local autonomy except in foreign policy. In Asia, the empire consisted of cities and kingdoms, most of which were ruled by local royalty and nobility with minimum Roman oversight. The brunt of imperial power—the Roman legions—was felt in recently conquered areas and on the borders where Roman power was still challenged. In the middle of the second century, 10 of 28 Roman legions were stationed in England and northern Europe, controlling recently subjected tribes, as well as those across the border. Another 10 legions controlled the new imperial provinces of Egypt and Spain.

Augustus also reformed the military system in a way that lasted until the third century. In addition to the regular army of citizen soldiers commanded by senatorial officers, he created an auxiliary army of foreigners who received Roman citizenship when discharged. They were commanded by middle-class Romans who were eager to climb the Roman social and political ladder. In this way, the Romans retained the model of citizen-soldiers and spread their

Figure 3.5 To declare military victory, Roman soldiers, like the Greeks before them, erected a trophy pole to which they tied prisoners and hung captured shields and weapons. This scene is a detail from a cameo carved from onyx stone probably to commemorate a victory of the emperor Augustus. *Erich Lessing/Art Resource, NY. Kunsthistorisches Museum, Vienna, Austria.*

culture and values to new citizens, but the military had become a full-time job. No longer could a farmer like the legendary Cincinnatus leave his field for emergency public service. The new legions were settled in distant areas of the empire where they were conscripted for numerous peacetime chores as well as soldiering. They spent their military years in forts, camps, and border towns where their presence was often harshly felt by civilians. "Don't bother to call the authorities if a soldier beats you up,"[13] Juvenal advised. Soldiers were subject only to military courts, which, according to the poet, always took their side.

*No Bureaucracy.* For all this, the Roman Empire was remarkably unbureaucratic. Compared to modern political administrations or, as we shall see, the Chinese Empire of the same period, Roman administration seemed spontaneous, haphazard, and arbitrary. In part, the reason was the tradition of local urban autonomy. Each city in the empire, like a miniature Roman republic, was ruled by the leading local noble families. Whether or not they held an office, these families tripped over each other to build public monuments, baths, arenas, theaters, and temples to honor their ancestors and their city. The cities of the Roman Empire devoted abundant space to public life as a result. City fathers competed for the acclaim of the lower classes with gifts of gladiatorial games, festivals, zoos, and even free bath oil. In return, the city would celebrate the generosity of the donor with a title that the "patron of the city" or "glorious benefactor" could take to his tombstone.

The empire was run for profit, although the publicans of the republic were no longer a separate class under the empire. Nobles, consuls, senators, and even emperors bought shares in the new corporate contractors who collected taxes, built aqueducts and roads, and administered whole countries. Bribes, kickbacks, and payoffs greased the machinery of empire without a Ciceronian raised eyebrow.

Laws still mattered to the Romans, but the growing body of Roman law regulated property and civil disputes, which were largely private matters. Matters of administration were mainly local, and they varied from one jurisdiction to another. Roman law was more judge made than legislative since magistrates were the leading officials of most cities. For imperial administration, the Romans preferred roads to laws, *publicani* to praetors, and business to bureaucracy.

Army, local notables, and corporate *publicani* created an ad hoc empire, making it up as they went along. As a result, emperors often found themselves involved in the minute detail of administration. In a series of letters between Pliny, governor of Bithnia in modern Turkey, and the emperor Trajan, Pliny asks the emperor about such minor matters of administration as how to treat accused Christians and whether he could form a firefighting brigade in the town of Nicomedia. There was evidently no official policy, department of state, or administrative handbook—at least none that worked as well as a letter to the emperor. Nor

does policy emerge from individual cases. One suspects that the next governor concerned about Christians or the need for a fire brigade would also have to write to the emperor.

*The Pax Romana.* The emperor Trajan (r. 98–117 CE) streamlined Roman administration and created a new "Augustan Age" of peace and cultural flowering in the second century. Edward Gibbon, the great eighteenth-century historian of Rome, wrote that if one were to pick the most happy and prosperous time in the history of the world, it would clearly be the period from 96 to 180 CE. The second-century emperors rebuilt the city of Rome in a new cosmopolitan splendor, and many provincial notables followed suit. The boundaries of the empire reached their furthest limits under Trajan and his successor, Hadrian (117–138 CE).

The Pax Romana that began with Augustus continued, despite interruptions, through the age of the "Good Emperors" until the reign of Marcus Aurelius (r. 161–180 CE), the "philosopher-emperor" whose philosophical Stoicism expressed both the vulnerabilities and the detachment of the new age. After a series of wars in Europe and Asia and a virulent plague spread by his returning legions, Marcus Aurelius wrote in his notebook *The Meditations,*

> He who fears death either fears the loss of sensation or a different kind of sensation. But if you lose sensation, you feel no pain; and if you feel a different sensation, at least you are alive.

*The Third Century.* The end of the Roman peace and the increased incidence of war in the third century led to the militarization of Roman society. Describing the third century, a modern historian writes, "There came a time when scribes were soldiers, bishops were soldiers, local governors were soldiers, the Emperor was a soldier. At that point the end of the ancient world was in sight."[14]

## China

*Similarities and Differences.* At first glance, classical China was very much like classical Rome: same time period, roughly the same size and population, and both based on agriculture and run by large noble families and a monarch. Both used large armies of horsemen and commoners to create empires over subject populations. Both developed Iron Age book-based cultures that shaped common identity and provided a sense of cultural superiority over nomadic "barbarians."

China had certain natural advantages. The light soil called loess[15] that clung to the hillsides of the Yellow River valley was unusually rich in nutrients. Chinese farmers could grow millet, an ideal cereal grain for dry climates,

without fertilizers (normally animal manure in India, Greece, and Rome), and they could plant continually without having to leave the land fallow half the time. In addition, compared to wheat, the chief Roman grain, millet, yielded twice as many grains at each planting. Consequently, Chinese millet agriculture on loess soil was four times as productive as Roman wheat. The state of Qin (pronounced "chin"), which conquered other states and gave its name and direction to the first unified China, was raised on loess-grown millet. As China expanded south of the Yangtze River, it added rice-producing areas that vastly increased agricultural productivity. In addition, the Chinese state grew expert at various forms of water management, introducing irrigation in the north and "wet rice" paddy agriculture in the south. Both of these multiplied yields.

The Chinese Empire encompassed more desert and low-rainfall areas than the Roman Empire. However, the productivity of Chinese

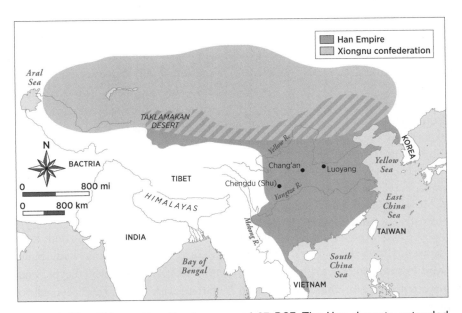

Map 3.4 The Chinese Han Empire, around 87 BCE. The Han dynasty extended the boundaries of the previous Qin (Ch'in) Empire into Vietnam in the south and deep into what had been the nomadic Xiongnu territory in the north and west.

agriculture compensated for this with a vastly greater population density in prime growing areas. One consequence was that Chinese agriculture precluded mixed farming and herding. While China had all the animals that Romans raised—and any Chinese farm of substance found room for pigs and ducks—the Chinese devoted much less land than Rome to raising animals, especially cattle. Animal manure was not necessary for raising crops, and cattle were expensive since they consumed 90 percent of the grain that would otherwise be available to humans. One consequence was that the Chinese diet, compared to the Roman diet, was lower in meat, especially beef, and virtually devoid of milk and cheese. The high-vegetarian, low animal–fat diet still distinguishes Chinese from most European cuisines today.

China had one considerable physical disadvantage compared to Rome: it was much more of a continental empire. This had enormous implications for transportation and communications within the Chinese Empire. One historian evokes the Roman fixation on gladiatorial games to suggest that the entire Roman Empire took the shape of an amphitheater bank of seats around the Mediterranean Sea. He adds,

> Like the [Persian] Achaemenid Empire, Han China was a road state on a plateau, and this in itself ensured inferiority in spatial integration to a Mediterranean empire, since in pre-modern conditions land transport was twenty to forty times more expensive than water transport.[16]

Of course, China had rivers, running mainly west to east, and eventually the Grand Canal to connect them, but compared to an empire surrounding a sea, the point still stands. Rome also developed the advantage of road networks to move troops and transport goods. Rome had 27 miles of road per 1,000 square miles, almost double China's 14. On the other side of the ledger, paved roads were necessary only for wheeled transport since paving kept roads from turning into ruts in rain. Horses and camels were far cheaper and more efficient than wheeled carts. On balance, however, the physical integration of the Chinese Empire was not as great as that of the Roman Empire.

*Lineages, Cities, and States.* The creation of the Chinese state—by unifying various warring states and kingdoms into a single China—was the work of the Qin which, like Rome, gave its name to the new empire it governed. Unlike Rome, however, Qin was not the name of a city but the name of a lineage or family. This is an important difference between the Roman and Chinese paths to state formation and empire. All states, traced back far enough, descend from tribal chiefdoms or societies made up of extended families called lineages. In the section on Greece, we followed Aristotle's description of the reforms of Cleisthenes around 500 BCE, and we suggested that this might stand as a model for the general transformation from family-based societies to public societies—cities and states. The difference between Greece and China, however, is that the Greeks created city-based states, city-states, before larger states or empires, and the Chinese created a state directly, without the intermediate step of cities or city-states. Greek and Roman state formation was in the tradition of the Middle East and Mediterranean, where cities were important power centers since the urban revolution. Chinese state building was more like that of ancient Egypt, where cities mattered less than royal dynastic families. We might consider the Indian route a third variant. There, lineages remained important as cities were created, but cities did not create states. Indian cities housed many independent cells but were themselves governed, often loosely, by monarchs. A city-state is a much easier thing to create than a lineage state. The smaller scale of a city ensures some degree of familiarity and participation by the residents. Even an empire builder of a territory that includes many city-states can take advantage, as the Romans did, of their existing institutions. By contrast, the creation of a state over other lineages and vast territories requires the pacification or replacement of other lineage heads and often involves the deployment of large (and expensive) occupation armies. On the other hand, once firmly established, a lineage state might have fewer pockets of political or cultural resistance to a uniform, centralized administration. Concentrated power at the top might endure longer, and if the reins fall out of the hands of one, they might easily be picked up by another.

The earliest Chinese state, the Xia (2200–1800 BCE), centered on the lower Yellow River, may have established a signature Chinese political system in which a centralized benevolent kingship ruled the state through law and harsh punishment, but most local decisions were made by clans and families. Such a system was evident in the Shang dynasty state (1766–1122 BCE), which circled the territory of the Xia, doubling its size and extending to the coast across the northern Chinese Yellow River but not as far as the Yangtze River in the south. The Zhou (pronounced "joe") dynasty (1045–256 BCE) circled the Shang, doubling the size again. In later centuries of the Zhou dynasty, called the Warring States period (403–221 BCE), the state was vastly reduced and seriously challenged. Across China, powerful lineages and warrior armies replaced organized state structures. Feudal lords, lineage powers, personal relationships,

and family ties were the only political reality. In this period, many Chinese thinkers looked back to the early Zhou centuries as a golden age of political stability and sought lessons for the re-creation of a Chinese state. Out of many competing schools of thought, two became particularly influential in this period, one associated with Confucius and the other with a group of thinkers called "legalists."

*Confucius.* Kong Fuzi (551–479 BCE), "Master Kong" to his followers and "Confucius" in the Latinized version, was a teacher and philosopher who sought employment as a public official. Like his Greek contemporaries, Socrates and Plato, Confucius was too independent a thinker (though he insisted he was not), maybe even a bit too cantankerous, to gain the approval of those in power. In any case, he did not rise beyond the level of a minor official in his native state of Lu in northern China. In search of a ruler who would give him broader authority, he roamed the feudal states of northern China but without success. Eventually, he returned home and devoted his life to teaching others.

Like many founders of classical traditions—Socrates, the Buddha, Jesus, and Muhammad—Confucius was a talker rather than a writer and left no writings in his own hand. According to tradition, he did gather classical Zhou texts that he used in his teaching, but the closest thing we have to his own words are the "sayings" known as the *Lun Yu*, or *Analects*, which were collected by generations of students. If these sayings are more reliable than most modern classroom notes, they show a moral philosopher interested in proper behavior and good government. In this respect, he is more like the Greeks than religious leaders. In fact, Confucius professed little interest in spiritual matters. When asked how to serve ghosts and spirits, he is reported to have replied that it was difficult enough to understand the living. But where the Greeks sought abstract truths like "the meaning of justice," the *Analects* taught practical lessons, such as the proper observance of tradition.

Learning, decorum, and propriety were the conservative values of Confucius. He favored those who showed respect for tradition, ritual, and order. He believed that people were basically good but that humanity consisted of natural inferiors and superiors and that society functioned best when people accepted their place. In these respects, Confucius would have received nodding agreement from Socrates and Plato. Confucius, however, would not have agreed with the Greek and Roman idea of politics as a separate realm of activity or thought. For Confucius, the model for a successful state was the family. A good ruler is like a good father. He sets an example that his dependents will seek to emulate. "The relation between superiors and inferiors is like that between the wind and the grass. The grass must bend when the wind blows across it."

The wind does not trample the grass, however. The most important possession of a good ruler is the trust of the people, more important than arms, even more important than food. The ruler should be a gentleman; his guiding principles should be benevolence and humanity. In return, the people will be like good children. The linchpin of the Chinese state was filial piety—the respect, even devotion, that a son owes his father. Filial piety was a prototype for all proper relationships: wife to husband, sister to brother, younger to older, servant to master, and commoner to king.

The idea that the state was only a larger family was an idea that made sense to many in the late Zhou period. That analogy and the belief that moral example could bind a society like honey might explain some of Confucius's

following. But there were other voices in the age of the Warring States, some of which argued the exact opposite: that to be successful, the state had to eradicate the influence of lineage and family, not celebrate it.

*Legalism and the Unification of China.* Confucianism eventually became a guiding orthodoxy in China, but it was, ironically, an anti-Confucian philosophy that established the single Chinese state. That philosophy was called "legalism." As the name implies, the legalists called for the rule of law, but they meant something very different from their contemporary Greeks and Romans. Legalist philosophers like Shang Yang (who became a powerful minister of the state of Qin in 359 BCE) and Han Fei (280–233 BCE) believed that people were not good enough to be swayed by moral example or controlled by rituals. Rather, human nature was such that only laws would keep people in line. Legalism in China was a strategy for organizing society, not a philosophy of human equality. Legalists believed that the laws should be applied equally to all subjects, but no one imagined that the king would be bound by human law.

More important, laws would undercut the authority of lineage chiefs and family elders, making it possible for the king to rule people directly. In its attempt to reorganize society in new units, legalist state creation was similar to that of ancient Athens around 500 BCE. Just as Cleisthenese created 10 artificial "tribes" out of four old clan networks, Shang Yang "commanded that the people be divided into tens and fives," the historian Sima Qian wrote. These new units of society, 5 to 10 households each, were smaller than the powerful extended families or lineages. When a family had two adult sons, it was to break apart into separate households. Each member of the new group was responsible for the actions of the others. In this way, neither clan leaders nor fathers stood between the state and its subjects.

Shang Yang used the new organization to increase the size and effectiveness of the Qin army in its conflict with the other "warring states." The state kept lists of each of the groups and tied farming to military service. All men were expected to serve in the army once they were 16 or 17 and reached the height of five feet. On completion of military service, they were assured farms and were expected to pay taxes. To further minimize lineage ties, all of Qin society was organized into 20 ranks based on their productivity, military effectiveness, or general utility to the state. All hereditary titles were replaced by these ranks, which also determined the amount of land and housing available as well as the clothing one could wear.

Like the contemporary Greek state of Sparta, the Qin state was organized as a fighting machine. After 316 BCE, it began to conquer the other states, some of which were attempting similar reforms a little too slowly and too late. In 237 BCE, the 22-year-old King Zheng (259–210 BCE) initiated a series of wars that lasted 15 years but ended in 221 BCE with the unification of China and his assumption of a new title, Shi Huangdi ("First August Emperor").

*Qin Creates China.* Shi Huangdi immediately set about creating a China on the model of the Qin state. First, he required all the kings and nobility of the defeated states (some 120,000 people) to take up residence under his watchful eye at the Qin capital, Xianyang. Then he reorganized all of China into 36 "commanderies" and appointed three commanders of each to direct military, tax-collecting, and administrative duties. Each commandery was divided into counties where the three functions were duplicated on a local level. In keeping with legalist thought, the new

emperor attempted to choose political officials by merit and ensure their compliance with the law. Candidates were tested in examinations, and attempts were made to avoid conflicts of interest, such as having a senior official govern in his own locality.

In creating a uniform empire, the emperor also sought to eliminate regional variations. He standardized weights and measures and introduced a system of coinage—strings of copper coins with square holes—that lasted until modern times. He also required that all parts of the empire use the same writing system—newly unified to make communication easier. In addition, Shi Huangdi is credited with massive public works projects, including the construction of 4,000 miles of roads, numerous irrigation canals, and the beginnings of a system of imperial defensive walls that came to be known, after 1,000 years of further building, as the Great Wall of China.

Like an Egyptian pharaoh, Shi Huangdi made his own tomb one of his crowning achievements. The historian Sima Qian wrote that 700,000 people were employed in the construction of the tomb, deep below sealed-off rivers. If the historian exaggerated, the recent discovery of the tomb overpowered archaeologists—not by the bronze arrows triggered to kill intruders but by its sheer scale and the image of the thousands of lifelike clay soldiers guarding the still enclosed vault that contained the emperor's last remains.

Such massive mobilization of human labor must have taken its toll. Sima Qian said that all who worked on the tomb were buried alive in order to conceal its location—a story we hear often of history's megalomaniacs. Opposition fed on itself. In 213 BCE, a group of scholars were assembled to offer advice to the emperor. One scholar called for a return to feudalism and Confucian values. Enraged, the emperor

Figure 3.6  These soldiers and horses represented the first Chinese emperor's army, protecting him against intruders in his tomb after his death. Compare this image to the royal tomb of Ur in Figure 2.5. *HIP/Art Resource, NY. Spectrum Colour Library, London, Great Britain.*

ordered the burning of all feudal books (which were written on silk and bamboo since paper had not yet been invented). A few years later, he had hundreds of scholars executed or exiled. For whatever reasons, the Qin emperor proved better at constructing lasting tombs than creating a lasting dynasty. Within three years of the first emperor's death, a series of revolts brought to power a commoner whose success on an exam had given him a minor office but whose speeches against Qin practices had gained a wide following.

*The Solution of Han.* The common birth of Liu Bang (r. 206–195 BCE) might make him seem an unlikely founder of a dynasty, especially one as storied as the Han (although, in fact, the great Ming dynasty was founded by a poor and even lower commoner). Maybe it was his face. One of the stories told by Sima Qian, the grand historian of the Han and earlier dynasties, is that when Liu Bang met his future wife, the future empress Lu, he was so poor that he could not hope to persuade her father to let them marry. Lu's father, however, was a fortune-teller who read faces, and Liu Bang's face was so unusual that Lu's father immediately consented to accept the young man as his son-in-law. A voice and a mind no doubt helped too. Liu Bang won followers by his vigorous denunciations of Qin brutality. As his forces took the Qin capital, Liu Bang promised three things: murderers would be executed, thieves would be punished, and all other Qin laws would be abolished.

Figure 3.7   Whether or not each soldier was modeled on an actual member of the emperor's army, individual features were carefully portrayed. *Rue des Archives/The Granger Collection, New York.*

In victory Liu Bang faced many of the same problems as had Shi Huangdi. The kings and nobles who had been uprooted by the Qin looked to regain their old estates, privileges, and powers. Liu Bang did not bother to install his feudal opponents in his new capital at Chang'an. (His armies had burned down the old Qin capital.) Instead, he created his own regional rulers and noble families from his own family and supporters. Nine brothers and sons became kings, 150 important followers received the titles and lands of nobility, and Liu Bang kept only the western third of the empire, centered at his capital. But the emperor wanted to retain the centralized administration of the Qin. He continued the Qin administrative structure with its commanderies (now numbering 100) and counties (numbering 1,500) and its threefold division of military, taxing, and administrative departments. While some of these positions were given to former Qin families who supported him, Liu Bang also looked for sons of new families and newly schooled advisers. His relationship with scholars was ambiguous, at one time urinating in a scholar's hat to show his disdain and later in life seeking to recruit them.

The Han Empire was considerably larger than its predecessor. Yet in the northwest, Liu Bang had to accept a stalemate with the Xiongnu nomads of the grasslands. Like the Roman standoff with the tribes of its north, the Han Empire had to continually negotiate its relationship with the peoples of the steppe, sometimes supplying them with wives and tribute and sometimes gaining horses, captives, new technologies, and foreign ideas.

*Empire and Dynastic Succession.* Like the firing of a diviner's tortoise shell, the death of Liu Bang revealed the cracks in an emperor's best-laid plans. How to institute a system of succession over an empire? Once the Romans abandoned the system of election and senatorial selection, they also had to find a way of ensuring continuity. Succession in Rome sometimes depended on adopted heirs, and some dynasties died out for want of an heir. Chinese emperors, who kept concubines and allowed multiple marriages, had the opposite problem: too many potential heirs. Liu Bang designated a son by his wife Lu as his successor, assuming that she would protect the youth until he reached maturity. But such a plan worked only as long as the designated son lived, the mother-protector desired no power for herself or others, and there were no other ambitious sons or mothers who could make a claim to the crown. Rarely did all these ducks line up in a row. In the case of Liu Bang, his chosen successor died early. The empress Lu continued to govern as guardian of another son, an infant, and then another. Before she herself died in 180 BCE, however, she had appointed many of her own family members to important positions and, it is said, assassinated four of Liu Bang's sons who had stronger claims to the throne but were children of other mothers. When the empress Lu died, imperial officials removed her family members from office and raised one of Liu Bang's sons of a courtesan as the next Han emperor.

The continuation of the Han dynasty in some form for 400 years must be considered quite an accomplishment given the push and pull of innumerable wives, courtesans, their families, old landed nobles, court officials, and military leaders. By comparison, the first 200 years of the Roman Empire saw five dynasties, and the last 200 years saw many more. What

made the Chinese Empire more stable than the Roman? Indeed, what made it possible for the Chinese Empire to continue into the twentieth century, almost 2,000 years after the Western Roman Empire had disappeared?

*The Mandate of Heaven.* One reason Chinese dynasties enjoyed such longevity was the acceptance of the idea that the emperor, his family, and his entire administration served with the "mandate" or approval of heaven. According to this idea, which originated in the efforts of the early unifiers of the Zhou dynasty (1100–256 BCE) to establish their legitimacy and was enshrined in Confucian philosophy, everything in the world was part of the moral and physical order ordained by heaven. This conviction, less demanding than a belief in a providential God, offered more direction than a Roman belief in quarreling deities. In one sense, the idea was a version of the traditional conservative: "what is, ought to be." In practice, however, it provided a framework for counseling obedience in good times and change in times of crisis. That is because the indicator of heaven's mandate was the general peace and security of the realm. Times of military defeat, natural crisis, or bad government signaled that the mandate had been lifted and would be conferred on another family.

*A Government of Experts.* Another reason for the staying power of the Chinese state was the creation of a permanent government—the court officials who helped an emperor govern and remained to ensure his succession and a bureaucracy that implemented the law and the wishes of the emperor from the palace grounds to the smallest county seat or municipality.

The Chinese invention of the world's first civil service system more than 2,000 years ago—and about 2,000 years before it was borrowed by European and North American state builders—can be viewed in different ways. Western eyes glaze over at the idea of bureaucracy. Eyebrows arch at the mention of a permanent government. But the idea of "a government of experts" throws a rosier light. Nevertheless, expertise took on a very different meaning for the Han Chinese than the word evokes today. In modern technological society, expertise is technical and practical. That view was not unknown in Han China; in fact, we have noticed the practical bent of Han legalists. But under the stewardship of the Han emperor Wu (r. 140–87 BCE), the legalists were routed, and Confucian learning became the source of learning for civil service and state administration.

The Confucian idea of expertise was closer to that of Plato—and to that of the nineteenth-century Western leaders trained in the Greek and Latin classics—than to today's idea of technical training. In a word, the Confucian idea of expertise was gentlemanly behavior: humanity, righteousness, benevolence, and morality. If these were not qualities likely to create a state from feuding families, they were qualities that might ensure honest and fair governance once the forces of disintegration had been overcome. A modern technocrat (or Qin legalist) might be excused for thinking that gentlemanly behavior could not be taught. The emperor Wu understood, as did Confucius himself, that humanity and fair-mindedness were habits of mind nurtured by the study of the past and the canon of classical literature. He also, no doubt, recognized that any classical tradition would ground his government with a set of shared principles and a common vocabulary.

In 136 BCE, shortly after he came to power at the age of 15, Emperor Wu reserved all academic appointments for specialists in the five great Zhou era books thought to be edited by Confucius. These books—*The Book*

*of Changes, The Book of Documents, The Book of Songs, The Book of Rites*, and *The Spring and Autumn Annals*—became the basis of a Confucian education and the core reading list of the developing civil service exams that came into widespread use in later centuries. In 124 BCE, the emperor appointed students to study with Confucian scholars and established an imperial academy to train future government officials. Then he established similar schools at the county and local levels to staff the lower levels of government workers.

The academy and examination system produced a more practical and professional class of officials. Before the classic texts were emphasized by Emperor Wu, Confucian officials behaved more like priests than scholars. In 208 BCE, a group of Confucian scholars who traveled to seek work in the camp of a Qin rebel dressed in their long robes and carried the ritual vessels of the Confucian family for their job interviews. Some two centuries later, an observer remarked about a similar group of Confucian job seekers that "there were none who did not carry in their arms or on their backs stacks of texts, when they gathered like clouds in the capital."[17]

Many trainees were still accepted on the recommendation of patrons from important families (and took the exam only to determine their placement), but the impact of the civil service system was to deprive the great families of much of their influence. Emperor Wu undermined the role of the large families in other ways as well. In 127 BCE, he ended the practice of elder sons inheriting entire estates, forcing them to be broken down and inherited equally. Like his predecessors, he also required the leaders of some families to live near the capital and required the members of some families to move apart from each other. He also broke with the practice of appointing the heads of noble families as important officials, choosing instead to make his own appointments.

*Salt and Iron.* The debate between Confucians and legalists did not end with a Confucian victory under Emperor Wu. Rather, it simmered beneath the surface throughout the Han dynasty, rising to the surface most famously in the "Salt and Iron Debates" of 81 BCE. Salt and iron were government monopolies under the Han. The mining and production of salt and iron, especially salt, provided the government with a considerable income to supplement variable tax returns, which had declined from one-fifteenth to one-thirtieth of agricultural produce.

Confucians generally opposed state monopolies, while legalists supported them. Despite the role the Confucian bureaucracy played in strengthening the state, Confucian scholars remained suspicious of economic activity, whether private or government sponsored, and they were particularly critical of strong governments. Ultimately, the faith of Confucians in moral example and gentlemanly behavior made them more sympathetic to the interests of feudalism than of centralized government.

Both sides in the debate posed as the defender of the poor against the large landowners. The government minister argued the legalist view that government regulations protected the less powerful:

> When the magistrates set up standard weights and measures, the people obtain what they desire. Even a lad only five feet tall may be sent to the market and no one could cheat him. If now the monopolies be removed, then aggressive persons would control the use and engross the profits. . . . This would serve to nourish the powerful and depress the weak, and the nation's wealth would be hoarded by thieves.

The Confucian scholars argued that monopolies destroyed the well-being of the average farmer:

> Life and death for the farmers lie in their implements of iron. . . . But when the magistrates establish monopolies and standardize, then iron implements lose their availability, . . . the farmer is exhausted in the fields, and grass and weeds are not kept down. . . . As I see it, a single magistrate damages a thousand hamlets.[18]

In the end, the Han dynasty kept the salt and iron monopolies and passed them on to later dynasties as part of a tradition in China of strong, centralized government directed by an autocratic emperor and administered by a trained civil service. Confucianism became a ruling orthodoxy, its classics cribbed for exams and mined for political solutions, but its ideas often were ignored by those whose main goal was to strengthen the state. In this respect, the fate of Confucianism was not unlike that of Christianity and Buddhism in later states: its principles were ignored, while it was enshrined as the official religion.

Did China benefit from state monopolies in salt and iron? Government sponsorship of mining supported an advanced technology of drilling and iron smelting. Han dynasty ironworkers learned to smelt iron at such high temperatures that they could remove almost all the carbon, in effect creating steel, a breakthrough not reached in Europe until the eighteenth century. Whether private initiative (the Roman model) or government sponsorship (as in China) supported greater innovation or increased revenues is still debated today. Government direction had the disadvantage of sometimes stifling new approaches but the advantage of state financing and institutional memory. Government ownership provided more income than taxation of private companies—as long as the government companies were run efficiently and honestly. In general, thanks to Confucian training, Chinese standards of government administration were almost Ciceronian.

*Palace, Consort Families, and Taxes.* The underlying weakness of the Chinese Empire—like the Roman—was the independent wealth and power of noble families and the growth of the large estates. Both empires faced a continuing struggle to assert central authority over potential opponents. Chinese emperors, we have seen, relied on periodic reshuffling of the nobility, a civil service system, and government monopolies. The central government, even an emperor, could not function without taxes, and as noble families flexed their muscles, they found ways of avoiding taxes. The upkeep of the imperial court, the expense of the army, and keeping the peace with the Xiongnu in the north all put a constant drain on the state treasury.

The institution of the emperor was stronger, his rule more absolute, in China than in Rome. As a consequence, it was sometimes possible for the emperor to readjust the balance between large landowners and the poor. In 7 BCE, the emperor proposed to limit all large estates to 500 acres and 200 slaves. The effort did not succeed, however. Instead, the noble families were able to depose the emperor, but a revolt in 9 CE brought the popular leader Wang Mang to establish, briefly it turned out, a new dynasty on behalf of the poor. Wang Mang divided the large estates, distributed land to the poor, and ended slavery. It was the sort of radical redistribution that populist leaders in Rome had attempted without success. In Rome, the principate of Augustus and the subsequent

empire were established to ensure the continued dominance of the senatorial nobility. In China, there were times when a powerful emperor could shake up the nobility, but the era of Wang Mang was short lived. The aggrieved families regrouped, killed Wang Mang in 23 CE, and placed an heir of Han on the throne two years later. For the next 200 years, a renewed Han dynasty, called now the "Eastern Han" because it moved its capital east from Chang'an to Luoyang, ruled under the watchful eye of the great families.

While the institution of the emperor remained strong in China, individual emperors were not. The palace was manipulated by the in-laws of the harem, the great families who competed to place their daughters as consorts of the emperor so that they could become mothers of future emperors. Like the empress Lu, these dowager empresses could supervise the reigns of their minor children, appointing family members to lucrative positions throughout the realm. The families were able to undercut the civil service examination system, which did not revive until another strong dynasty came along 500 years later. But another force manipulated the throne, often pulling in the opposite direction from the great consort families. These were the castrated captives made palace officials, protectors of the harem, and loyal advisers to the emperor. In Luoyang, there were probably 10,000 harem women and eunuchs at the palace out of a city population approaching half a million.

Rome, by contrast, numbered about a million in the city, but the palace—like the bureaucracy—was a much smaller affair. The two competing forces of Chinese administration—palace eunuchs versus the civil service—were virtually absent in Rome. Some Roman emperors bought eunuchs for their personal company, and at least one contemporary observer charged that these companions ran the empire, but the Romans never castrated young men for political service. Both harems and eunuchs were viewed by the Romans as examples of Persian or Oriental decadence. Instead, the Roman Empire relied to an unusual degree on slaves and soldiers. Slavery was much more pervasive in Rome than it was in China. By some estimates, slaves constituted only 1 percent of the population of Luoyang but 40 percent of the population of Rome. Both empires relied on soldiers, of course, but the military played a far greater political role in Rome than it did in China. Romans traditions of citizen-soldiers continued long beyond the actual practice in the prestige of soldiering, an occupation later despised in China. From the end of the Roman republic, the military was the training ground for citizenship, politics, and imperial rule—the equivalent almost of the Chinese civil service.

*Strains of Empire.* From the third century BCE to the third century CE, the Roman and Chinese empires faced the same external and internal strains. Externally, there were the nomadic pastoral peoples that each "civilization" termed "barbarians." In general, the Chinese were more successful at turning the threat of the Xiongnu into a trading relationship, allowing them to deploy troops elsewhere. By contrast, the Romans became increasingly anchored on military posts and garrison cities along its borders.

The internal strain between the emperor and wealthy noble families was also similar in both Rome and China. In both empires, the rich got richer and paid less in taxes. Roman agriculture became a world of huge estates worked by armies of slaves. Chinese estates became counties of dependent laborers.

In both Rome and China, these problems were linked by the need of the agriculturalists

to supply soldiers. In Rome, the solution was to extend citizenship since it traditionally required military service. In China, soldiers were conscripted from independent cultivators. Thus, periodically Roman emperors extended citizenship, and Chinese emperors redistributed land. But few emperors were strong enough to make such changes conclusive and permanent. In the end, both empires lost out to the families and the "barbarians."

The breakdown of state control was far more thorough and long lasting in the Western Roman Empire than it was in China. The period of disunity lasted about 350 years in China until 589 CE, when a general for the northern Zhou reconquered the south. In western Europe, efforts at reestablishing the Roman Empire by the Catholic Church or by kings like Charlemagne in 800 CE proved short lived. Indeed, despite the best efforts of European kings, a single European or Mediterranean empire was never revived. The Chinese Empire, however, was restored by Sui Wendi (r. 581–604 CE), and the Eastern Roman, or Byzantine, Empire was reorganized by Justinian (r. 527–565 CE).

## Conclusion

Such is the power of a classical culture. A Chinese tradition of government bureaucracy, centralized administration, and a highly trained and tested civil service, enabling a new leader to pick up the baton, continues today. Rituals of ancestor worship, respect for the family, filial piety, and Confucian principles of morality, passed on from generations of parents to children, inform Chinese film and television in the twenty-first century.

The European and Western inheritance of Greece and Rome continues as well. The autonomy of cities, the rule of law, the citizen-soldier, patriotism, the primacy of the individual and the state over the family and tribe, faith in reason and science over ritual and superstition, and the conviction that people are equal and life should be fair despite all evidence to the contrary—these are the legacies of a Greco-Roman classical age. So perhaps are military heroes, generals as presidents, private entrepreneurialism as a religion, limited governments, and universal ambitions.

Hindu spiritualism, transcendent yet anchored in communities defined by birth, affinity, occupation, and association, still pervades modern India. The law of the land has long superseded the dharma of caste, but Indians still define themselves by subcaste and religious community. India is a whirlwind of separate and independent cells of activity, an explosion of differences. No Indian government has the power to unite the people more than a weekly television production of the *Mahabharata* or *Ramayana*, which can empty the streets faster than a monsoon downpour.

The classical texts still shape our lives. In fact, the classical cultures we have surveyed actually influence a larger portion of the world's population—and far more people—than they did 2,000 years ago. Since the end of the classical age, Chinese culture spread to Korea, Japan, Vietnam, and communities throughout the world. Indian Hinduism spread across Southeast Asia; Buddhism converted millions throughout Asia. In the past 500 years, Europeans spread their culture and peoples across the Western Hemisphere and to the four corners of the planet.

Still, nothing remains the same. As the great classical traditions traveled, they took on local dress and dialects. The story of the past 2,000 years is not only the story of three or four classical traditions. It is also the story of borrowing, adapting, and blending: the story

of the earth becoming one. We turn next to that chapter in our history.

## Suggested Readings

Adshead, S. A. M. *China in World History*. New York: St. Martin's Press, 2000. Sophisticated comparisons, especially of Rome and China. Difficult but very rewarding.

Basham, A. L. *The Wonder That Was India*. 3rd. ed. London: South Asia Books, 2000. Rich interpretive survey of Indian culture. Joy to read.

*Bhagavad Gita*. Translated by Barbara Stoler Miller. New York: Bantam Books, 1986. An excellent translation of the classic.

Lloyd, G. E. R. *The Ambitions of Curiosity: Understanding the World in Ancient Greece and China*. Cambridge: Cambridge University Press, 2002. Challenging comparison of philosophical assumptions of Chinese and Greco-Roman cultural traditions.

## Notes

1. *Bhagavad Gita*, trans. Barbara Stoler Miller (New York: Bantam Books, 1986), 33–34.

2. Setaketu Jataka, no. 377, cited in Romila Thapar, *From Lineage to State* (Delhi: Oxford University Press, 1990), 108.

3. Setaketu Jataka, no. 377, 109.

4. *The Persians*. This English translation, by William Cranston Lawton, of "The Battle of Salamis," is reprinted from William Hyde Appleton, ed., *Greek Poets in English Verse* (Cambridge: Riverside Press, 1893). Fanes are ancestral protective spirits or their temples.

5. Herodotus, *The Histories*, trans. Aubrey de Selincourt (Baltimore: Penguin, 1954), 448–49.

6. Herodotus, *The Histories*, 521.

7. "Computing" may not be an exaggeration. On a second-century BCE Greek primitive computer to predict planetary motions and phases of the moon, see John Noble Wilford, "Early Astronomical

'Computer' Found to Be Technically Complex," *New York Times*, November 30, 2006, A7.

8. G. E. R. Lloyd, *The Ambitions of Curiosity: Understanding the World in Ancient Greece and China* (Cambridge: Cambridge University Press, 2002), 65–66.

9. Cic.Q.fr.1.1.2. All of Cicero's letters are available online at http://www.perseus.tufts.edu. The December 60 BCE letter to Quintus in Asia on provincial government runs from 1.1.1–1.1.16.

10. E. Badian, *Roman Imperialism in the Late Republic* (Ithaca, NY: Cornell University Press, 1968), 87.

11. *Res Gestae* 34.

12. Tacitus, *Annals* 13.4.

13. Juvenal, *Satires* 16:10.

14. Nicholas Purcell, "The Arts of Government," in *The Roman World*, ed. John Boardman, Jasper Griffin, and Oswyn Murray (Oxford: Oxford University Press, 1988), 180–81.

15. German for "loose," pronounced "luss" (rhymes with "bus").

16. S. A. M. Adshead, *China in World History* (New York: St. Martin's Press, 2000), 16.

17. Michael Nylan, *The Five "Confucian" Classics* (New Haven, CT: Yale University Press, 2001), 32.

18. Esson M. Gale, trans., *Discourses on salt and iron: A debate on state control of commerce and industry in ancient China*. Taipei: Ch'eng-wen, 1967.

# 4

## The Spread of New Ways in Eurasia
### 200 CE–1000 CE

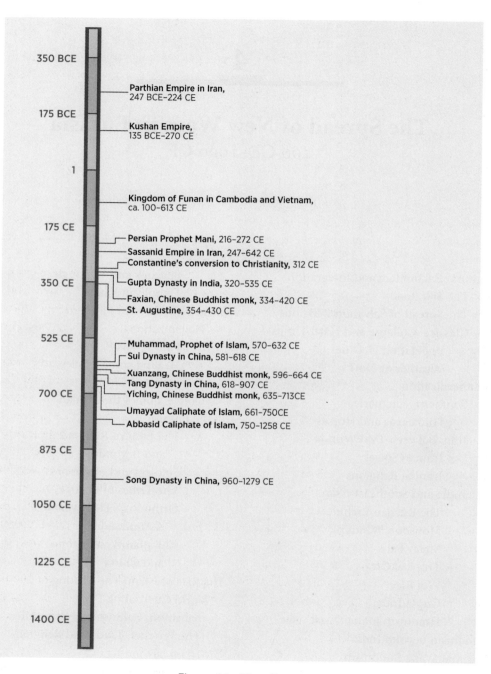

Figure 4.1   Time line.

## Cultural Encounters
## and Integration

ZHANG QIAN (pronounced "jang chee-an") must have known it was a mission impossible. Han Emperor Wu in 139 BCE needed someone to find the nomadic Yuezhi ("you-way-juh") and try to negotiate an alliance between them and the Chinese Han dynasty. The emperor needed an ally against an even more troublesome nomadic people, the Xiongnu ("shee-ong-new") also called Huns, a traditional enemy. It was the old Chinese policy of pitting "barbarians against barbarians." Everyone at the Chinese court knew it would be an extremely dangerous journey since virtually nothing was known of the lands west of the Great Wall. Consequently, none of the high-ranking officials came forward. Zhang Qian was only a low-level official, but he volunteered, and so he was chosen.

Almost as soon as he left the protection of Chinese territory, he was captured by the Xiongnu. Unaware of his assignment but treating him like a captive, the Xiongnu forced Zhang Qian to join their campaigns against the Yuezhi. Zhang remained in Xiongnu custody for 10 years, eventually taking a Xiongnu wife and raising a family. He never lost sight of his mission, however. In 129 BCE, he escaped a Xiongnu camp and found his way to the Yuezhi court in Fergana (in modern-day Uzbekistan). During the 10 years of fighting, the Yuezhi had been dispersed, their chief lay dead, and the survivors had migrated west to Bactria (near modern Afghanistan), where Zhang finally found them and the chief's son. Zhang spent the next year trying to convince the new Yuezhi chief to join China in an alliance against the Xiongnu, but he did not succeed and began his return trip empty handed.

On the way home, he was again captured by the Xiongnu and held as prisoner for another year. Finally, when the Xiongnu chief died, a civil war broke out, and Zhang Qian was able to escape with his wife and family. He returned to China 13 years after he left to a warm reception by the emperor.

### The Silk Road

When Zhang Qian finally made his way back to China in 126 BCE, he had a lot of stories to tell. Emperor Wu was particularly interested in Zhang's tales of "blood-sweating horses." For almost 1,000 years, Chinese prosperity depended on their ability to learn from and protect themselves from sudden storms of nomadic horseback-riding archers who could blight the countryside faster than a cloud of locusts. The earliest Chinese states protected themselves with high stone walls that horses could not jump, but an effective defense required the creation of Chinese horsemen to counter the nomads, an innovation begun by the king Wuling (325–299 BCE) of the early state of Zhou, who, in the process, revolutionized Chinese fashion by having his horsemen wear nomad's trousers instead of Chinese robes. But when Zhang Qian told Emperor Wu of the large horses of Fergana, Chinese and nomad cavalries were pretty evenly matched on what we might today call ponies. The horses of Fergana were larger than those of the sparse central Asian grasslands, which shriveled on winter pasture, because Fergana horses were raised on alfalfa that was harvested for hay in the winter. Whether or not they actually sweated blood[1] to do it, Fergana horses ate year-round. Emperor Wu wanted to know how he could get his hands on such animals.

Zhang Qian had another story that suggested an answer. When he followed the

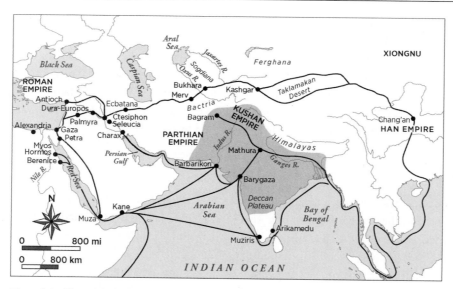

Map 4.1 The trade route normally called the "Silk Road" extended from the Chinese capital at Chang'an westward, around the great Takla Makan Desert to Kashgar and Bactria to the Roman Empire. But, as this and the map of India in the previous chapter show, there were many land and sea routes that connected east and west.

Yuezhi westward from Fergana to Bactria, he met many merchants who had traveled to India and the Mediterranean. One of their most prized commodities was a silk that Bactrian merchants thought to be Indian but Zhang recognized as Chinese.[2] Zhang realized that Chinese silks doubled their value in India and then doubled it again when they reached Bactria. On hearing Zhang's account, Emperor Wu resolved to take control of the silk trade and exchange silk for horses. He sent another envoy to the Yuezhi chief, who rebuffed the offer, then sent an army that was repelled and retreated. But Wu gave orders barring his defeated army from reentering China, forcing them to fight another day. This time they defeated the Yuezhi and brought back the first 3,000 of many Fergana horses.

The Silk Road may have begun as a trade of silk for horses, as this old story suggests; but it soon included many other commodities. In addition to silk, Chinese lacquerware, bronzes, and ceramics traveled west. In addition to horses, central Asian jade, the deep blue stone lapis lazuli from Afghanistan, and Mediterranean wools and glassware traveled to China. The northerly route from China to the Mediterranean ran north of the Himalayas and south of the deserts of Mongolia. Near Bactria, a southerly route crossed the Himalayas into India, introducing scented woods, spices, and tropical products. At every stop, traders added local products like the rock crystal and peaches of Samarkand, the date palms and tapestries of Persia, and the almonds and slaves of Mongolia. Yet the importance of silk cannot be overestimated. The luster and smoothness of silk clothing was an indulgence of the rich, sometimes forbidden to others. Rolls of silk were an economic measure of value, equal to so many slaves, paid as ransom or stipulated in treaties. Silk had been prized by women in ancient Egypt as early as 1000 BCE. A thousand years later, silk gowns were favored by Cleopatra. A Roman emperor was said to wear nothing but silk clothing. Roman senators complained that their wives' preference for silk was bankrupting both personal fortunes and the public treasury.

The heyday of the ancient Silk Road lasted as long as China was able to maintain a monopoly on silk production and keep the secret of how the cocoons of silkworms, fed on mulberry leaves, could be fashioned into precious threads. In 550 CE, two Nestorian Christian monks traveling from China to Byzantium smuggled the eggs of silkworms in bamboo shafts and the Byzantine government began to make its own silk, as did the Persians. The northern Silk Road lost its monopoly. Water "silk roads" in the southern oceans proved cheaper and safer as new generations of nomadic peoples moved across the northern steppe.

## The Spread of Salvation Religions

The routes that carried precious commodities from one side of Eurasia to the other, by land and sea, also carried new ideas. At the end of the classical age (around 200 CE), religions swept over the walls that had separated the great classical civilizations. It was as if suddenly religion replaced older systems of identity and meaning. People who had been Greeks or Indians or Romans or Chinese became Christians and Buddhists. It was not as if religion itself was entirely new. All the classical civilizations had priests, temples, and religious festivals. All worshiped the appropriate deities, paid tribute to the gods, and celebrated their feast days. Chinese sons worshipped at the altars of their fathers, Indian Brahmins supervised age-old rites, and Greek and Roman priests made offerings and interpreted oracles.

But during the classical age—in fact, during most of the previous thousands of years of urban civilization—religion was a matter for the specialists, and the role of the common person was limited. Further, most people rarely took their religions beyond their own clan or town.

The new religions leapt old boundaries and entered people's hearts. And it was not just the hearts of officials and priests that turned toward the new gods but the hearts of people who had previously given little thought to such matters—poor people, lower castes, women, and merchants. The appeal of these new religions was so powerful that the followers established new networks. Monasteries sprouted over vast areas, connecting pilgrimage routes to holy sites but paying little regard to the boundaries of territorial states.

Governments ignored these new forces at their peril. Only those that seized the initiative and supported the new religions survived. Even then, their people often thought of themselves as Christians or Buddhists rather than Romans, Greeks, Indians, or Chinese. We call these new religions "universal" and "salvation" religions. Christianity and Buddhism offered salvation to anyone who chose to participate, regardless of caste, class, birth, or background. The ministers and monastics of these new religions counseled the sick, poor, and dispossessed. They nursed the suffering, gave alms to the needy, and offered an alternative to the world of sin and illusion. The Christian heaven and the Buddhist nirvana promised a more satisfying future than an ailing world could deliver.

## Classical Collapse and Hard Times

Signs of an ailing world were abundant in the centuries after 200 CE. Nomadic tribes from the grasslands of central Asia toppled both the

Chinese and Western Roman empires between 200 and 500 CE. Depleted cities were looted and left for dead. Epidemic diseases took their toll on the survivors.

*Population Decline.* World population had grown at a healthy pace during the classical era. A world of about 50 million people in 1000 BCE doubled to 100 million by 500 BCE and then at least doubled again to 200 million or more by the year 1 CE. But by 200 CE, global population numbered only about 250 million. After the collapse of the Han dynasty in 220, Chinese population declined precipitously. By 500, when the Western Roman Empire had also been overrun by nomadic tribes, world population had fallen back to fewer than 200 million. Despite the recovery of China after 600 and the continuation of the Eastern Roman, or Byzantine, Empire at Constantinople, world population recovered very slowly. Not until 900 or perhaps even 1000 did world population surpass the level of 200 CE. This 700- to 800-year period was the longest era of population stagnation since before the urban revolution. Nothing like it has happened since.[3]

*Weather or Not?* Was the decline of 200–900 part of a global environmental change or merely the impact of the nomads of central Asia? We do not know. Global temperatures seem to have cooled during this period after warming during the classical age, but the data are not complete enough for a conclusion. It is interesting that some areas of the Americas experienced prosperity in this period. In fact, the centuries between 200 and 800 were the golden age of the Maya in Mexico and Guatemala, decline setting in after 800. In addition, in Mexico during this period, the Toltec city of Teotihuacan prospered, becoming one of the largest cities in the world before its collapse in 750. Even in Eurasia, some civilizations

prospered during these centuries. The Eurasian population gainers between 200 and 800, in addition to northerly Korea and Japan, were mainly in the south. Iran, India, South Asia, and Southeast Asia grew in size and prosperity, leading one historian to label the period as one of "Southernization."[4]

# Southernization

The nineteenth and twentieth centuries have sometimes been described as an age of "westernization." The term refers to the impact of the many peoples, ideas, and institutions that were exported from western Europe to the rest of the world in this recent "age of Western expansion." By analogy, we might define the period between 200 and 800 as an age of "southernization" since so many new ways of doing things spread from South Asia northward to the rest of Eurasia.

## Southern Sanctuaries

Why did India, South Asia, and Southeast Asia grow and prosper between 200 and 800 while northern Europe and Asia were overrun by nomadic armies of Goths and Huns? One answer may be the relatively warmer weather of South Asia, but better answers would be "the Himalayas" and "large horses."

*Himalayas and Horses.* The Himalayan Mountains shielded India and Southeast Asia from the nomadic "barbarians" who traveled east and west across the grasslands. Waves of nomadic archers swept through settled cities on the swift small horses that thrived in the grasslands. Just south of the central grasslands, in Iran, marauding tribes preyed on farmers and city dwellers until these settled people learned to raise larger horses on the richer diet of the grasses and grains of the agricultural belt. These horses were descended from the large animals that had been discovered by Zhang Qian in Fergana.

## Iran: Between Two Worlds

Iran was the successor of classical Persia. The change in name signifies a shift in power from the classical empire centered on the city of Fars (or Pers) in the southwest near the Persian Gulf to the postclassical empire centered on the great Iranian plateau in the northeast that stretched to Fergana and Afghanistan. This northern empire combined characteristics of the grasslands that stretched in every direction but south and the older Persian empire that faced south toward the Persian Gulf, the Mediterranean Sea, and the Indian Ocean. Iran was a land in between.

*Iranian Society.* In Iran, the kings of the Parthian Empire (247 BCE–224 CE) gave large tracts of land to nobles who raised large horses for armed cavalries. They planted alfalfa, which added nutrients to the soil and provided enough hay to feed the large horses in the winter. With the use of underground irrigation tunnels called *qanats*, these nobles could raise thirsty alfalfa on relatively dry land. The large horses of Iran were able to support heavy suits of armor that protected Iranian horsemen from the arrows of the nomadic cavalry.

Large horses and armored knights were to become the medieval missile shield against the periodic invasions of nomadic horsemen. Thanks to the use of stirrups, probably invented by northern Chinese nomads about the fourth century, armored horsemen could also go on the offensive, wielding battering rams or lances that might otherwise throw them off their mounts.

The Iranian deterrent to nomadic invasions came at a cost. Since Iranian nobles raised their own horses and equipped their own armies, they, rather than the king, held the reins of power. The Parthian Empire and the succeeding Sassanid Empire (247–642) were almost feudal societies where power was ultimately local and tribal, the king a subordinate to his nobles. The same drawbacks later hindered western Europe when it adopted the Iranian system of feudal armies of armed knights.

*Iranian Religions.* Iranian religions were the first to spread across the large region of Southwest Asia. In the classical age of Achaemenid Persia, that religion was Zoroastrianism. The religion of Zoroaster was an important step toward universal religion. Zoroastrians were not strictly monotheistic since they believed in both Ahura Mazda, the god of light, and Angra Mainyu, the god of darkness. But key Zoroastrian ideas of a final conflict (between light and dark), the end of the world, the last judgment, the resurrection of the dead, personal salvation, and eternal life gained a wide following among non-Zoroastrians of Southwest Asia, including Jews and Christians. The spread of religious ideas from Persia can be seen in the names of the Parsees of India and the Pharisees of ancient Israel.

In Parthian and Sassanid times, however, Zoroastrianism answered Persian and Iranian national interests. While many of its ideas circulated widely, the teachings of Zoroaster and his priests remained Iranian. This was not the case with the reformulated version of Zoroastrian dualism presented by a later Persian, the prophet Mani (216–272), who actively sought converts of all nations. Believing his Manichaeism was a synthesis of the teachings of Jesus and the Buddha, Mani created a universal salvation religion that, during his lifetime, was more successful than the Buddhism and Christianity from which it sprung. Combining the roles of both Jesus and Paul in his own person, Mani traveled from his native Babylon throughout the Sassanid Empire to establish cells of followers from India to North Africa. St. Augustine (354–430) was a Manichaean before he converted to Christianity, as were many others in the Roman Empire in the fourth century. Manichaeism, like the Zoroastrianism from which it derived, provided consolation in a dangerous world by explaining the power of evil. Especially to young searching minds, like Augustine's in his student days at Carthage, the idea of life as constant struggle between the forces of goodness and evil supplied a drama that matched the rhythms of youth as well as the threats of a hostile world. Manichaeism was to later spread to central Asia and China, and philosophies that paid tribute to darkness were never entirely extirpated by the monotheistic and universal salvation religions—Christianity, Islam, and Buddhism—that swept Eurasia in the following centuries.

Thus, Iran, with its empires of large horses, served as a protective buffer between the grasslands of invaders and the Indian subcontinent. As a middle ground between the pastoral grasslands of nomad confederacies and the lands that pointed to tropical seas, Iran also prepared the way for universal faiths and new ways of life that were carried, sometimes with monsoon force, by winds from the south.

## India and Southeast Asia

The Himalayan Mountains, the highest in the world, also protected India and Southeast Asia from the sort of massive nomadic invasions that undermined classical China and the Western Roman Empire. South Asia did not

Figure 4.2 This first-century CE statue of the Buddha from Gandhara during the Kushan Empire shows Greek artistic influence in the depiction of the Buddha, who had been marked in early Indian art by his absence—an empty throne or footprint. Here the Buddha takes on the form of a Greek god with Mediterranean curly hair and topknot, draped clothing, stance, and serious demeanor of the realistic Greek style. With the Greek halo, this Buddha, like the human gods of Greek mythology, became an object of worship in the Mahayana tradition of Buddhism that spread into central Asia. *bpk, Berlin/Art Resource, NY. Museum für Asiatische Kunst, Staatliche Museen, Berlin, Germany.*

escape incursions completely, but, in general, the more threatening peoples, like the Xiongnu (Huns), pushed the more settled ones, like the Yuezhi, before them. The Yuezhi, already settled in the area of Bactria by the time of Zhang Qian's visit, adopted elements of Greek and Indian culture in forming the Kushan state, which protected India from the Huns.

*The Kushan Prelude.* If the winds of hemispheric integration blew from the south, perhaps the first gusts came from the Kushan state. During the most intensive period of nomadic pressure from the Eurasian grasslands (200–400), the Kushan kingdom was one of the most sophisticated states in the entire world. Under Kanishka, who ruled around 100, the Kushans governed what is today Afghanistan, Pakistan, and northern India.[5] The combination of Indian and Greek traditions, the legacy of Alexander the Great, was a heady brew in Kushan culture. The Kushans evolved Ayurvedic medicine from Indian Vedic knowledge of botany and Greek science. Similarly, the collision of the two languages— Greek and Sanskrit—led Kushan thinkers to the first analysis of grammar and language structure in any language. And the different artistic traditions of Greece and India inspired Kushan artists to devise the first images of the Buddha and Boddhisatvas (Buddhist saints) as well as images of halos that were adopted by early Christians. In the end, the Kushanas gave India not only a respite from northern nomads but also a leg up when Indian political revival came after 320. And even before a new dynasty of Indian kings reunified the territories of the Mauryans, Indian merchant guilds and families were creating one of the most vibrant economies of their age. In sum, the forces of southernization between 200 and 1000 came from India even more than Iran, and they were as material as they were spiritual.

*Monsoon Winds.* One engine of Indian expansion was the seasonally variable winds. The principle is simple: oceans moderate air temperatures, cooling in the summer and warming in the winter. That is why the temperature of coastal areas is always more moderate than inland areas. Lands that are far from oceans become especially cold in winter and unbearably hot in summer. The area on the planet farthest from oceans is central Asia. Cold air is heavy and dense, warm air light and porous, so, as warm light air rises, cooler air pushes its way in and under. As the land area of central Asia cools in the winter, its dense air expands, displacing the warmer air over the southern oceans. This process is reversed in the summer when the hot air of central Asia rises and creates a vacuum that pulls in the cooler ocean air from the south. Consequently, from December to March, the prevailing winds blow south from cold central Asia across India and Southeast Asia to the Indian Ocean, the Gulf of Thailand, and the South China Sea. From May to August, the cooler winds flow north from the southern oceans toward the hot interior.

This rhythm has a profound impact on South Asian growing patterns. The summer winds from the oceans are laden with moisture, which they dump on land as far as the Himalayas (also creating the deserts on the northern "rain shadow" side of the mountains). In India and mainland Southeast Asia, this "monsoon season" is one of frequent and heavy rains. The winter winds are cool and dry as they cross the Himalayas and India, but over the oceans they pick up moisture to bring another monsoon season to coastal Southeast Asia and the islands. The heavy rain provides lush vegetation and allows a rice-based agriculture that can support a dense population. The predictability of the monsoons punctuates the growing seasons (since planting must be accomplished before or after the rains) and allows two or even three crops a year in some areas. But in the rare years when the rains fail, drought and famine are particularly disastrous.

Another consequence of the monsoons was that once sailors had mastered the winds, they were able to take advantage of an enormous natural energy source for travel and trade. These were the winds of southernization.

*Malay Sails.* The sailors of the Malay Peninsula learned to navigate the monsoon winds sometime in the first millennium BCE. Malay and Malay-Polynesian peoples were the first in the world to navigate the open seas, and they did so long before the invention of the compass. They were able to sail the vast Pacific by careful observation of the stars, ocean waves and swells, cloud patterns, bird movements, and the fish and plant life in the water. Able to sense islands 30 miles away, they settled the islands of the Pacific from the coasts of Southeast Asia to Easter Island. Others charted the Indian Ocean to the coast of East Africa.

The earliest sailing ships were fairly simple. Egyptian sailors on the Nile needed only

Figure 4.3 This relief is from the eighth-century Buddhist stupa at Borobudur, Indonesia. These ships used Polynesian double outrigger hulls (side supports) for stability and Malay tilted rectangular sails designed to swivel and tack against the wind. Such sails probably inspired the triangular lateen sails of later Arab ships. Indonesian ships like this one could have sailed the Indian Ocean to West Africa. *Werner Forman/Art Resource, NY. Borobudur, Magelang, Java, Indonesia.*

to raise a square sail to catch the north winds to travel south against the current; to return, they needed only to lower the sail and follow the current north to the Mediterranean. Mesopotamian sailors clung close to the riverbanks of the Tigris and Euphrates and the ports of the Arabian Sea. Malay sailors were the first to sail the open seas. In their epic voyages across the Pacific, they invented double-hulled outrigger canoes (the ancestor of the modern catamaran) for stability in ocean swells. To tack or zigzag against the wind, they invented the balanced lug sail, a sail that looked like a blunted arrow pointed forward, the mast near the point, with the bulk of the sail rigged to a boom that could be swung out over the water so the wind could push the craft sideways. Malay sails may have inspired the Arab sailors who developed similar triangular lateen sails.

Malay sailors also pioneered the earliest water routes between India and China. Even in the classical age of the land Silk Road, Malay sailors had discovered how to ride the monsoon winds from southern India to China by way of the Strait of Malacca. From India or Sri Lanka, they would take the winter winds south through the Strait of Malacca, where they would wait for the summer winds to take them north to China, reversing the process on the return. Malay sailors also connected the products of East Africa and the Indonesian Spice Islands to the trade of the Indian Ocean, and they introduced the spices of the Molucca Islands east of Java to an international market. There—and nowhere else—grew mace, cloves, and nutmeg.

*Tropical Crops.* Imagine a world without oranges, lemons, limes, grapefruits, mangos, melons, and the dozens of other fruits that originated in India and Southeast Asia. Imagine no sugar to sweeten your tea; imagine no tea. Imagine no cotton, no pepper, no cinnamon, or no spices. That was the world of northern Eurasia before these tropical crops came from South Asia. Most of them were brought by Malay, Indian, and Iranian and other South Asian traders in the first thousand years CE.

Malay and Indian sailors brought the tropical plants of Indonesia—bananas, coconuts, taro, and yams—to the island of Madagascar, from where they entered East Africa and became staples of the African diet. Not only did these new crops fuel a population rise in Africa, but the timing coincided with and aided the great migration of Bantu speakers from their origins in western Africa throughout the continent.

*Wet Rice.* South Asian populations also grew thanks to the new crops. The most important agricultural innovation was the expansion of wet rice cultivation: transplanting young rice shoots to paddies filled with water. Wet rice yields were double those of dry rice. Planters cut down the trees of wet tropical forest areas and built dikes, canals, and paddies. Wet rice supported huge peasant societies and required their labor. As a result, wet rice spread throughout Southeast Asia as planters in areas like Thailand and Cambodia realized the potential return. Huge tax-paying peasant societies supported the ambitions of kings and priests in Cambodia, Java, Sumatra, as well as India. A kind of wet rice also spread to southern China, enabling a large increase in population growth.

*Gupta India.* The vibrant economy of the age of the Gupta dynasty (320–535) supported a political and cultural renaissance in India. The Gupta kings consolidated their rule of northern India and kept the nomads at bay for almost 300 years. While the Gupta kingdom was not quite as large as the earlier Mauryan dynasty, it was more prosperous and sophisticated. The court of one of the greatest of the Gupta rulers, Chadragupta II (375–414; also known as Vikramaditya), can serve as an example. It patronized the greatest of Indian poets and playwrights, Kalidasa, as well as astronomers and mathematicians who were the first to show the advantages of using a zero and a 10-digit decimal system. (We call our number system "Arabic," but the Arabs called it "Hindi" since they got it from India.) The Chinese visitor Faxian wrote of the great palaces and charity hospitals of Chandragupta's city of Nalanda. More recent visitors still admire a remnant pillar from Chandragupta's palace made of such a high grade of iron that it shows no rust after 1,600 years.

*Hinduism in Southeast Asia.* During the Gupta period, Indian culture spread throughout Southeast Asia. Indian customs traveled the trade routes of the Indian Ocean, following the shifting winds of the monsoons. Gupta culture was Hindu and tolerant. Merchants transplanted their caste values as they settled in tiny trading communities throughout South Asia. In general, they kept to themselves and did not try to convert non-Indians. But expansive, seemingly successful cultures always attract converts, and Indian Hindu culture was no exception. Those who traded with the Indian merchants adopted Indian culture with its innovations in mathematics, accounting, and trading practices. At the same time, the traditional rulers of Southeast Asia were attracted to Indian ideas that kingship was the divinely instituted prerogative of Brahmins. New dynasties in Sumatra, Java, and Cambodia based themselves on these Hindu traditions of divine kingship and separate merchant communities.

The founding story of the rice-rich kingdom of Funan (ca. 100–613) on the border of modern Cambodia and Vietnam expressed a common Southeast Asian theme. According to

the tale, the first king of Funan was the child of an Indian Brahmin priest who sailed east and the beautiful woman who paddled out to meet him. She turned out to be Queen Willow Leaf, the daughter of the Cambodian serpent god. Funan peaked under King Jayavarman I (478–518), after which it was challenged by kingdoms centered on the islands of Sumatra and Java. In 802, a Cambodian prince raised at the Javanese court declared an independent Cambodia. He was crowned as Jayavarman II Devaraja (god king) by a Brahmin priest. The remains of the temple complex of the kingdom can still be seen at Angkor Wat. Dedicated to the Hindu god Vishnu, devotees also worshipped Shiva. Indian Brahmin priests were invited to the royal courts to serve as advisers. In addition to teaching Brahmin religion, they taught the engineering skills used to create the irrigation system and the art of stone carving in the Indian architectural style. Hinduism spread as far east as the island of Bali, where it is still practiced today, and as far west as the east coast of Africa, where the descendants of Indian merchant families still live and work. But Hinduism was not the only Indian religion to integrate large areas of the world in the first millennium.

## Buddhism beyond India

Buddhist monks sailed the same winds as Brahmin priests. Some of the rulers of Hindu states in Southeast Asia converted to the worship of the Buddha, in some cases, like Java, only temporarily and in some cases more permanently. In Khymer Cambodia, Jayavarman VII (r. 1181–1219) changed Angkor from a Hindu to a Buddhist state, vastly expanding its territory. In addition, he created Angkor Thom and other new temple complexes and built

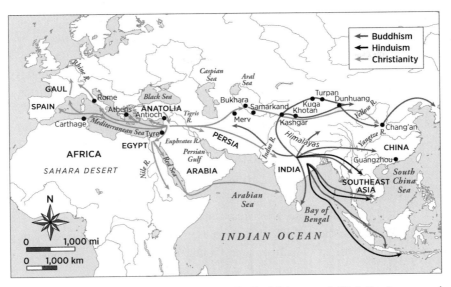

Map 4.2   Between 200 BCE and 400 CE, Buddhism and Christianity spread throughout Eurasia. Hinduism spread into Southeast Asia. By 700 CE, Christianity had reached the Chinese capital at Chang'an, and Buddhism had spread to Korea and Japan.

more than 100 hospitals and another 100 guesthouses for missionaries and travelers, a common Buddhist undertaking.

Buddhist monks founded one of the first Buddhist states on the island of Sri Lanka (Ceylon), just south of India. From there they traveled to Thailand (Siam) and Burma, where they established Buddhist societies that reflected their orthodox beliefs, principally a strict adherence to the ascetic life for all devotees. Until today in such orthodox, or "Theravada," countries, every young man was expected to don the saffron robes of the monk, carry the begging bowl for his daily rice, and live with other monks in a monastery or similar institution for at least the two or three years of early adulthood. Some men (and even some women) continue to live the monastic life into old age, and in Burma and Thailand one sees many men of varying ages in bright saffron. In a modern city like Bangkok, monasteries are

dwarfed by high-rises, and monks' robes are drowned in a sea of business suits, but the remains of a traditional Buddhist capital can still evoke a world in which spiritual matters were preeminent. Twelfth-century Pagan, on a bend of the Irrawaddy River in northern Burma, still shelters hundreds of white stone pagodas and little else. In its prime almost 1,000 years ago, one would have been overcome by the lines of men in deep orange, the sounds of their chanting, the heady smell of incense, and—the only sound one still hears today after the oxcarts have returned the tourists for the night—the music of temple bells tinkling in the wind.

## Mahayana Buddhism

Most of the monks who brought Buddhism to Southeast Asia called themselves orthodox, or Theravada, Buddhists, and most Southeast Asian societies followed the orthodox path pioneered in Sri Lanka. It was an austere and demanding tradition in which a period of monastic life was expected and each monk or nun relived the original quest of the Buddha. By contrast, a different kind of Buddhism traveled north to central Asia and later to Tibet, China, Korea, and Japan. Called by its followers "Mahayana," or "the greater vehicle," it taught of a Buddha as savior for all. Its universalism may have been shaped by contact with Zoroastrian, Greek, and possibly even Christian ideas encountered in northern India and Kushana. For Mahayana Buddhists, the Buddha offered more than a model path to enlightenment. They believed that the Buddha and numerous Buddhist saints, called Bodhisattvas, postponed their own entrances into nirvana in order to help others achieve it. Thus, anyone could achieve salvation by appealing to one of the Bodhisattvas. There is help in achieving enlightenment. One need not do it alone.

The idea of salvation was not entirely new to Mahayana Buddhism. After all, the core message of the Buddha had been the need to escape the veil of illusions that ensnared one in the world. That the root of suffering was desire, that one overcame suffering by relinquishing the world, went without saying. But Theravada Buddhists, in all likelihood Gautama Siddhartha, who became "the Buddha," and many Hindu holy men before and since sought peace in meditation, ascetic practices, and renunciation, not in the worship of a god or goddess. It was the Mahayana followers who turned the guru into the god and then prayed to him—and his Bodhisattvas—for salvation.

*Buddhism in Central Asia and China.* The Buddhist conversion of China is an unlikely story. "It is difficult to understand," a modern historian writes, "why Chinese would find any attraction in an alien faith that espoused strange ideas in an unfamiliar language."[6] The family and the state were the central institutions of Chinese society and Confucian belief. The Buddha abandoned his family, and his followers practiced celibacy in monastic communities independent of family or state. Buddhist missionaries were mendicant monks, while Chinese culture valued productive farmers. Buddhists taught that life was suffering; the Chinese taught that life was to be enjoyed.

We can almost hear this debate in the instructions of *The Disposition of Error* (450–589), a manual for Buddhist missionaries in China that resembles a modern "frequently asked questions" format:

> *The Chinese questioner will ask:* Of those who live in the world, there is none who does not like wealth and position and hate poverty and baseness, none who does not enjoy pleasure and idleness and shrink from labor and fatigue. . . . But now the [Buddhist] monks wear red cloth, they eat one meal a day, they bottle up the six emotions, and thus they live out their lives. What value is there in such an existence?[7]

The Buddhist manual's answer to this question is equally revealing: people desire rank and wealth most of all, but if they cannot obtain them in a moral way, they should not enjoy them at all. People hate poverty and meanness, but if they can avoid them only by departing from the Way, they should not avoid them at all. Laozi (Lao Tze) has said that "the five colors make men's eyes blind, the five sounds make men's ears deaf, the five flavors dull the palate."

*The Way of the Way.* Buddhist missionaries drew on a non-Confucian tradition of Chinese thought: the teachings of Laozi about "the Way," the natural path, or *Dao*. Laozi was a Chinese contemporary of the Buddha who

also disparaged worldly struggle and counseled a passive acceptance of nature's "way."
Like Buddhism, Daoism reversed the ethics of
active engagement with the world. "The way
is like an empty vessel that yet may be drawn
from, without ever having to be refilled," Laozi
wrote in the *Dao De Ching*.[8]

Buddhism was most successful at winning
Chinese converts in the centuries of instability that followed the fall of the Han dynasty.
At the beginning of the Six Dynasties Period
of Division (220–589), Buddhism was limited
to communities of foreign merchants and
monasteries mainly along long-distance trade
routes. In the second century, all the monks
in the monastery at the capital city of Luoyang were foreigners from India, central Asia,
and Parthian Persia. But by 600, China was a
Buddhist country with thousands of monasteries. Luoyang alone constructed 1,000 new
monasteries within 40 years of its rebuilding
in 494. What accounted for such a change?
Certainly the salvation message of Buddhism
fell on more willing ears in this period of
political instability, population decline, and
social disorder. Temple and cave inscriptions
from the period decry lost families, suggesting
the breakdown of the Confucian faith. Monasteries that in times of prosperity had linked
chains of merchants became, in times of need,
lifelines of support for the surrounding population, providing food and consolation. Mahayana Buddhism offered a hope of salvation
from the trying world of suffering between the
third and seventh centuries, between the collapse of the Han around 220 and the rise of the
Sui (589–618) and Tang (618–907) dynasties.

*The Uses of Magic.* In addition to translat-
ing a foreign creed into Chinese characters
by way of Daoism, Buddhist monks practiced
an age-old technique for winning converts:
magic. The very influential Buddhist monk

Figure 4.4 Buddhist deity Guanyin
(bodhisattva Avalokiteshvara). The spread of
Buddhism in China was aided by Guanyin, a
feminine version of the male Indian Bodhisatva
Avalokiteshvara. Goddesses were rare in
China. How would a figure like this increase
the appeal of Buddhism? What figure played a
similar role in the spread of Christianity?. *The
Metropolitan Museum of Art/Rogers Fund, 1913.*

from central Asia, Fotudeng, recognized the
difficulty of conveying foreign philosophical
ideas to his Chinese audience, and so, it is said,
he took a monk's begging bowl full of water,
burned incense over it, and chanted a few
words, and suddenly there appeared a water
lily in blinding blue and white.

The traditional story of the victory of Buddhism in Japan is a similar testament to the
power of association with the supernatural.
Accordingly, in the early sixth century, a Korean king sent a present of a Buddhist image
to the emperor of Japan. The emperor decided
to set up an experiment in which he gave the

image of the Buddha to a willing clan chief to see what happened. The clan chief set the image in a temple and worshipped it. Shortly afterward, however, a pestilence broke out in the land, and many people died. Deducing that the native Shinto deities were offended, the emperor took the image, threw it into the river, and burned down the temple. The Buddhist experiment had failed. In 584, however, another Korean image of the Buddha arrived in Japan. This time a monk tried to break the statue with an iron sledgehammer but broke the sledgehammer instead. Then he threw the stone in water, but it floated. In response, the monk built another temple, and Buddhism grew in Japan.

*Monks, Missionaries, and Monarchs.* These stories follow the route of Buddhist expansion from central Asia to China, Korea, and then Japan. Buddhism always entered a kingdom as a foreign religion, but it always entered from nearby. Consequently, Buddhism often first attracted those who were drawn to foreign ideas. Before Buddhism swept through China, it won over some of the nomadic peoples in central Asia and the kings and religious leaders of the northern kingdoms who were only marginally part of Chinese culture. The rulers of the Northern Wei dynasties (386–354) declared each new dynasty to be an incarnation of the Buddha. Within China, Buddhism first attracted foreign merchants, immigrant communities, and people out of power.

Buddhism brought different things to different people. The early monasteries in Silk Road oasis towns brought agricultural produce, trade goods, and urban culture to nomadic peoples. For rulers of nomadic dynasties, such as the Toda, Buddhism offered a common ground with their Chinese subjects. To the tribal leaders and minor monarchs of northern China, Buddhism conferred spiritual

legitimacy and provided literate advisers and luxury markets. For illiterate Confucian Chinese peasants, Buddhist festivals, like the popular Feast of All Souls, included ancestor cults. Chinese Daoists added the Buddha to their pantheon of protectors. In times of political instability or famine, all benefited from the refuge and reserves of the monasteries.

*Pilgrims and Writings.* While most Buddhists, like most people in any premodern religion, were illiterate, the spread of Buddhism owed much to the travels of literate missionaries and pilgrims. Stories about the Buddha, reported sermons and sayings of the Buddha, and stories and theological texts written by the Buddha's followers all played an important role in the development of Buddhism. Buddhism became increasingly bookish in China, the land that invented paper in the first century and printing in the eighth to ninth centuries. In fact, the spread of Buddhism to Korea may have generated the world's first example of printing as early as the ninth century. Earlier Theravada Buddhists in Southeast Asia spread their stories in stone monuments at places like Borobudur on the island of Java and Angkor in the Khmer kingdom of Cambodia. By contrast, the Mahayana monks in China built less graphic if often larger Buddhas,[9] and they more often studied manuscripts for literary meanings. This may reflect different levels of literacy or differences in classical Indian and Chinese culture—the Indian more tactile and plastic, the Chinese more visual and literate. It is interesting, in any case, that of the thousands of Buddhist missionaries and pilgrims who traveled between India and China, the only extant written accounts come to us from the Chinese pilgrims to India.

Indian missionaries first went to central Asia and China to bring the word orally, to establish communities, and to trade. Later,

Chinese pilgrims traveled to India to read and copy the sacred texts and visit the sacred sites where the Buddha lived and his early followers built monasteries, schools, and hospitals. The first Chinese pilgrim whose story we have was Faxian (334–420), who traveled to India in 399 and returned 15 years later with copies of numerous texts that he translated from Sanskrit to Chinese. In 645, the Chinese Buddhist Xuanzang (596–664) returned from India after nineteen years with 22 horses loaded down with texts, relics, and statues. The monk Yijing (635–713), after almost 25 years in India and Southeast Asia, translated 230 volumes of texts and wrote biographical sketches of 56 other Chinese pilgrims in India. In addition to the scriptures, the Chinese monks also brought back stories of Buddhist communities from northern India to Java. This Chinese attention to the sacred writings kept Chinese Buddhism close to the original Sanskrit meanings. Indian Buddhism was translated into Chinese through the language of Daoism, but it remained distinct from Daoism.

*Temple and State.* The ideal philosophy for ensuring the legitimacy of and popular support for the emperor was certainly Confucianism. It celebrated hierarchy, monarchy, patriarchy, rituals, and the status quo. According to Confucian doctrine, the emperor ruled with the Mandate of Heaven. Especially in times of prosperity or stability, that mandate was unquestionable. Nevertheless, Chinese Buddhists were well placed, when politics became more stabilized, to serve the interests of monarchs and dynastic officials as well as merchants, intellectuals, and the poor. The emperor Wu (502–549) of the Liang dynasty took the unusual step of ransoming himself to a Buddhist monastery, much to the chagrin of the Confucians, but in return the monks treated the emperor as a being to

be obeyed and venerated. The founder of the Sui dynasty, Sui Wendi, was a Buddhist, even though the official ideology of the government was Confucianism.

Under the more stable conditions of the Tang dynasty (618–907), Buddhism received waves of imperial support. The empress Wu Zetian (625–705), who seized power for herself late in life after the death of her son, endowed numerous Buddhist temples and cave statues in addition to practicing Daoist rituals.

Just as Buddhism had succeeded in India as an economic power that eschewed politics, so in China Buddhist monasteries became depositories of wealth that transcended political alliances. The landholdings of Buddhism constituted about a third of Chinese farmland. Buddhist wealth was created not only through the trading networks and pawn shops at monasteries but also through the donation of gold and treasures that were converted to statues of the Buddha and richly appointed temples. One Chinese critic of Buddhism estimated that Buddhists controlled seven-eighths of the wealth of the empire, even though the number of followers was low.

In 845, Chinese protests against "foreign religions" led to the expulsion of all imported faiths. Even Buddhism came under attack. The emperor Wuzong of Tang declared,

> We have heard that the Buddha was never spoken of before the Han dynasty; from then on the religion of idols gradually came to prominence. So in this later age Buddhism has transmitted its strange ways and has spread like a luxuriant vine until it has poisoned the customs of our nation, Buddhism has spread to all the nine provinces of China; each day finds its monks and followers growing more numerous and its temples loftier. Buddhism wears out the people's strength, pilfers

their wealth, causes people to abandon their lords and parents for company of teachers, and severs man and wife with its monastic decrees. In destroying law and injuring mankind indeed nothing surpasses this doctrine.

Now if even one man fails to work the fields, someone must go hungry; if one woman does not tend her silkworms, someone will go cold. At present there are an inestimable number of monks and nuns in the empire, all of them waiting for the farmers to feed them and the silkworms to clothe them while the Buddhist public temples and private chapels have reached boundless numbers, sufficient to outshine the imperial palace itself.

Having thoroughly examined all earlier reports and consulted public opinion on all sides, there no longer remains the slightest doubt in our mind that this evil should be eradicated.

But Buddhism was not eradicated. Rather, its political power was crushed. Buddhism was the only "foreign" religion not to be expelled from China. Under the Song dynasty (960–1279), Buddhism contributed to the trappings of the emperor's authority, turning some emperors into venerated Bodhisattvas. In addition, the neo-Confucianism of Zhu Xi (1130–1200) and others integrated Buddhist ideas into the Confucian tradition.

More than Hinduism, perhaps even more than Indian textiles, tropical fruits, and wet rice, Indian Buddhism—in two varieties—conquered the world of South and East Asia in the centuries between 200 and 1000. For the first time, people from the islands of Ceylon and Java shared a common faith with desert nomads in central Asia and the princes and peasants of China, Japan, and Korea. For the first time in world history, entire societies directed their affairs according to sacred books. And though their interpretations might differ, they were united in the conviction that these writings could save them from the travails of a shifting world.

## Christianity beyond Palestine

Christianity, the other great salvation religion of the age of instability, spread across the Mediterranean, Europe, and the Middle East, while Buddhism spread through central, eastern, and southeastern Asia. Some early Christians traveled to India and China and established small Christian communities in East Asia, but Christianity did not take hold in China until after a second wave of missionaries arrived 1,000 years later.

### *Hellenization*

Hellenization is a shorthand for the spread of the Greek language and Greek mythology and philosophy, especially science, reason, cosmopolitanism, and universal values. If the spread of Buddhism throughout Asia was prepared by the monsoon winds and merchant sailors of the Indian Ocean, the spread of Christianity was prepared by Hellenization.

In fact, one might argue that Hellenization was the source of universalism in both Europe and Asia 2,000 years ago. Neither Hinduism nor Judaism was a universal religion: neither claimed allegiance beyond the tribe or tradition, neither attracted or encouraged converts, and neither offered salvation beyond this world. It was not Theravada Buddhism that offered the world salvation but the Mahayana Buddhism that developed north of India in the Hellenized Kushan area. Similarly, it was not the apostles of Jesus in Jerusalem who called Jesus the savior of mankind but the Hellenized Jew, Paul of Tarsus (in modern Turkey).

Hellenism was a universal outlook before Buddhism and Christianity.

*Paul versus Peter.* The letters of Paul in the New Testament detail the conflict among the early followers of Jesus. Peter and the Jews of Jerusalem expected only observant Jews to join their community. Paul, an outsider, was conscious of preaching a different faith: to Jews and Gentiles, open to all regardless of their ancestry. His faith in Jesus as the Christ, his belief that Jesus died for the sins of mankind, and his conviction that anyone could be saved by believing in Jesus—these ideas were all more Greek than Jewish, and they mobilized Gentile communities as well as synagogues from Syria to Rome. History is full of "ifs," but one of the biggest is this: if Paul had not universalized the importance of Jesus, would there have been Christianity? There would have been a group of Jewish followers, many of whom perished by the time of the Roman conquest and destruction of the Jerusalem temple in 70 CE. But Paul's insistence that Jesus was more than a Jewish rabbi, that one did not have to be Jewish to accept Jesus, and that faith in Jesus offered salvation to all humanity was a prerequisite to success beyond the Jewish community. In addition, Paul traveled the Mediterranean visiting Gentile groups as well as synagogues to create the religious communities that became the first Christians. From his first Christian church in Antioch, Syria, he planted churches in Cyprus, Greece, and throughout what is today Turkey.

*Healing and Miracles.* Like Buddhist monks, Christians provided healing in this world as well as salvation beyond. The Gospels told of Jesus healing the sick and reviving the dead. Similarly, early Christians were often called to heal the afflicted.

Most Greeks and Romans did not belabor distinctions between mere healing and working miracles. Gods and their representatives were expected to show their power by various demonstrations of medicine, magic, or miracles. A typical account of this mix was given by the apostle John. At Ephesus, John converted unbelievers by healing the sick. He then claimed that he entered the temple of Artemis, where he called on God to cast out the Greek god. Immediately, the altar of Artemis split into pieces, and half the temple fell down, killing the priest. In response, the assembled Ephesians declared, "There is only one God: the God of John. We are converted."[10]

*Jews and Christians.* Jews had a complicated relationship with their Roman occupiers. In Judea, Jews were largely left to their own devices, a policy that Romans practiced with most of their colonies. Jews outside Judea posed more difficult problems. Like Christians, they did not worship Roman gods, but because Romans recognized that Jews had their own religion, Jewish separateness was generally accepted. At times, Jews were admired; at times, they were banned from living in certain areas, like the city of Rome. From the Roman perspective, the Christians were much more problematic because they did not seem to accept Jewish or Roman religion, they worshipped a convicted Jewish troublemaker from a minor Roman province, they refused to participate in Roman civic functions, and they constantly tried to convert others to their subversive beliefs. This made them politically dangerous in Roman eyes.

As a consequence, Christians often found themselves on the wrong side of Roman law and tradition. Sometimes Roman governors were as confused as Christians about what their proper relationship should be. Pliny, governor of the Roman province of Bithynia, wrote to the emperor Trajan (98–117) to ask if it was proper to seek out Christians for

Figure 4.5 The Coptic Christians of Ethiopia carved their churches out of the living rock of cliffs and mountains. Approached from the land above, they were literally underground. *Werner Forman/Art Resource, NY. Lalibela, Ethiopia.*

persecution or respond only when they were brought to trial. Trajan urged restraint, but other emperors did not. Nero (54–68) stocked the gladiatorial slaughters with willing martyrs. "Sometimes they were killed with the axe," the Christian historian Eusebius wrote. "Sometimes they were hung up by the feet over a slow fire."[11] The story of young Perpetua of Carthage may not have been uncommon. Having survived the attack of a wild animal and the unsteady sword of the executioner,

she grabbed the blade herself and directed it to her throat.[12] The example of Christian martyrs would be a memory with which others might build the faith, and their blood would fortify the soil in which the Christian community would be raised.

## Conversion of the Roman Empire

It would be interesting to know if Christianity spread rapidly under the relatively tolerant policies of Trajan and his successors from 90 to 160. Or did Christianity thrive more in the harsh years that began with Marcus Aurelius in 161, when the "barbarian" attacks and war with the Parthian Empire brought an end to the century of peace? The years of war, economic crisis, and plague could have increased the following for all religious cults, including Christianity, but their prominence likely increased the popular reaction against them. These were years in which Marcus Aurelius sought refuge in his *Meditations* in Stoicism (a philosophy not unlike Christianity in that it counseled acceptance, even surrender to adversity). But the years after the plague of 165 also witnessed an increase in Christian persecutions, even demonstrations where mobs chanted, "Christians to the lions," a scapegoating that might also indicate a greater prominence for the new faith.

The fact is that we know little about how quickly Christianity grew. The historian Gibbon estimated that about 5 percent of the Roman population was Christian in 250; modern historians think the percentage was much less. Constantine's biographer, the historian Eusibius, saw three surges in Christian conversions: the early period of Paul and the apostles, the era of the great theologians in the 180s, and the period just before Constantine's conversion in 312. But like us, he had no records or statistics and may have been more impressed by the proliferation of theological works in these periods.

*The Eastern Roman Empire and Beyond.* Christians were more numerous in the Eastern Roman Empire. This might be surprising because Americans and western Europeans usually envision a map of Christianity centered on Rome. But such a map would include only Roman or Latin Christianity. Before the rise of Islam, there were numerous Christian traditions. Greek, Syrian (Nestorian), and Armenian Christian churches prospered throughout eastern Europe and Asia. Egyptian (Coptic) and Ethiopian Christianity spread in Africa before Europe. A map of early Christianity might best be centered in Syria, where it began, and from where adherents established churches in Mesopotamia, Persia, central Asia, India, and even China, as well as the Mediterranean, North Africa, and Europe.

East of Rome, even east of Athens, lay all the Hellenistic cities with their ancient Jewish communities as well as legions of soldiers. From Syria to Persia, great cities attracted peoples from Rome to India. Christianity thrived in this land of cities; Christians used the word *pagans*, for "country people"—to designate non-Christians. The cities of the Middle East were cauldrons of changing faiths and newly forged sects. A modern historian describes one group of ancient Christians near modern Basra, Iraq, that demonstrates their variety:

> During the second and third centuries, groups of Baptists [Christians] could be found in the district between the mouth of the Euphrates and Tigris rivers, where they lived under the nominal control of the Parthians. They acknowledged Christian teachings among severe beliefs which had the stamp of Jewish influence. Here, they had presumably begun as a splinter group from Jewish settlers and we have come to know only recently how they combined a respect for Jesus with a strong stamp of Jewish practice and an honour for their original leader, the prophet Elchesai, who had taught in Mesopotamia c. 100–110 A.D.[13]

From a community like this came the prophet Mani, whose Manichaeism combined elements of Christianity and Persian

Zoroastrianism. From here, missionaries sailed out the Persian Gulf to India, where Christian communities traced their origins back to a first- or early second-century apostle called Judas Thomas. In the middle of the second century, Christians in India wrote to Syria asking for a bishop since their previous one had died. The early Christian world was one of great diversity.

*Soldiers and Emperors.* Like Buddhism, Christianity was ultimately successful thanks to the support of important political leaders: kings and emperors. Even before the Roman emperor Constantine supported Christianity in 312, kings in Syria had converted, contributing legitimacy and numerous followers.

We do not know precisely why Constantine supported Christianity after 312. Probably no more than 10 percent of the empire's inhabitants were Christians when Constantine embraced the faith. Many were no doubt women, his mother among them. But soldiers also converted to Christianity, especially in the eastern and African provinces. The story is told of Constantine's predecessor, the emperor Maximian, relying on a legion from Upper Egypt to conquer the tribes of the Alps. To celebrate their success, Maximian asked them to execute some Christian captives. But all the 6,600 men of the Theban legion were also Christians. Under their leader Maurice, they refused and offered their own necks to Roman swords. To commemorate the sacrifice of this Egyptian legion, the town of Aquanum (in modern Switzerland) changed its name to St. Maurice, or St. Moritz. For Maximian's successor, the loyalty of Roman troops would have been a matter of great importance.

In 312, the historian Eusibius tells us, on the night before Constantine was forced to do battle with Maximian's son to secure the crown, Constantine saw a flaming cross in the sky inscribed with the words, "In this sign thou shalt conquer." Subsequently, he embraced Christianity and won the battle. The following year (313), Constantine issued an edict making Christianity an officially tolerated religion throughout the Roman Empire. Less than a century later, Christianity was proclaimed the official religion of the Roman Empire.

*The Tribes of Europe.* An emperor may be wise to take the religion of his soldiers, and anyone who seeks the favor of the emperor would be wise to share his religion, but what of the common people of the empire? The various tribes of Europe—the Helvitii in the Alps and the Germans, Gauls, Celts, and Saxons—had their own tribal gods, festivals, and celebrations. What did they need of the emperor's religion, especially after the empire had vanished? How did the tribes of Europe become Christian? Some, no doubt, were persuaded by the idea of a single god; some embraced the Christian promise of life after death. But the language of the Christian scriptures was as Greek to the tribes of Europe as Indian Buddhism was Sanskrit to the Chinese. To make the message intelligible, Christian missionaries molded it to European tribal traditions. They adopted pagan feast days, setting, for instance, the birthday of Jesus at the time of the winter solstice and northern fire festivals that marked the returning sun. They set a place for tribal deities at the table of Christ as saints and angels, integrating their stories, attributes, and holidays. Pope Gregory the Great instructed Augustine, his missionary to England, not to destroy the pagan temples. "Only remove their idols. Then sprinkle them with holy water and build altars. Pagans will be more willing to worship the true God in familiar surroundings."[14]

Sometimes, however, tribal deities had to be confronted rather than accommodated.

After converting to Christianity, the Hessians of Germany reverted to their pagan ways. Around 719, the pope sent Boniface to bring the Hessians back to the true faith. According to the saint's disciple and biographer, Boniface gathered the people around a large oak tree, known from antiquity as the Oak of Jupiter. He then raised an ax and brought it down into the tree, slicing into the bark. Just as he did so, a great wind blew from the heavens, knocking the tree down, cutting it into four equal pieces. "At the sight of this extraordinary spectacle, the heathens who had been cursing ceased to revile and began, on the contrary, to believe and bless the Lord."[15] In gratitude, they split the logs into lumber and built a church to St. Peter, we are told. Like Buddhism, Christianity spread amid tales of miracles.

*Orthodoxy, Heresy, and Assimilation.* In order to be successful, a new religion must choose its fights carefully. Missionaries must know where to bend and where to resist. Churches must distinguish what is important from what is inconsequential. For Christians, pagan feast days, holy sites, and physical buildings were secondary. The word of God was important: the holy writ, ideas, theology, and beliefs. We have seen that Buddhists also worked to keep their sacred writings. But for Buddhists, the sacred writings constituted more of an archive than commandments. They provided continuity of tradition, not the demands of God. Chinese Buddhists continued to honor their parents and ancestors and even visit Confucian and Daoist shrines and temples.

Because Christians believed that they possessed the word of God, correct ideas were crucial. The right doctrine was everything. Especially since Christians after Paul believed that faith or belief was sufficient for salvation, what one believed was a matter of eternal life or death.

But there were many different Christian beliefs during the first Christian centuries. A basic matter like the nature of Christ was hotly debated. Some said that Jesus was a human prophet, much like John the Baptist. Others said that Christ had two natures: human and divine. Some believed that Christ was all divine. Still others said that Christ was part of a trinity that included God the Father and the Holy Ghost. In general, particular interpretations tended to hold sway in particular sees or bishops' cities. Antioch, for instance, was a hotbed for believers in a human Christ. The bishops of the great cosmopolitan cities of Jerusalem, Alexandria, Antioch, and Constantinople generally heard wider-ranging debates than did the bishops of Rome, but all sought to achieve some uniformity of belief.

The bishops called councils of church leaders together to determine which beliefs were proper and which were not. A series of these councils, many of their locations testifying to the importance of Eastern cities (Nicea, Constantinople, and Chalcedon), finally led to the designation of certain beliefs as orthodox and others as heresies.

Orthodoxy defined and fought heresy, but it also prevented assimilation. The problem is that by underlining the differences between proper and improper ideas, orthodoxy also created heresies. Some heresies had staying power, but most eventually died out, their adherents eventually assimilating or waiting for the next orthodoxy.

*Christianity in Europe and China.* We often think of Christianity as a European religion despite its obvious Middle Eastern origins. But in the early centuries, before the rise of Islam, Christianity also spread widely in Egypt and North Africa. The Egyptian and Syrian churches sent missionaries to Ethiopia, Yemen, India, and central Asia. Ethiopia to

Figure 4.6 Virgin and Child. Like Guanyin in Buddhism, the Virgin Mary, the mother of Jesus, was central to Christianity, but became more visible in the Middle Ages. Both offered salvation, for women as well as men. Both Buddhism and Christianity had nunneries for women as well as monasteries for men, but Christian religious nuns and secular female religious communities were more numerous than the Buddhist. This statue was purchased by a women's community (called a beginage) in the Netherlands in 1345. *The Metropolitan Museum of Art/Fletcher Fund, 1924*

this day hosts a large Christian population. In central Asia and China, Christians congregated in oasis towns and market cities. But Christianity, unlike Buddhism, failed to put down deep roots in China.

One historian, Jerry H. Bentley, argued that the failure of Nestorian Christianity to win China was due to the tendency of its missionaries to assimilate too thoroughly. They not only translated Christianity through Daoism but also eventually became Daoists. Bentley points to an early eighth-century document attributed to a Persian missionary who was head of the Nestorian Christian church in the Chinese capital of Chang'an:

> The treatise portrays Jesus teaching Simon Peter and other disciples, but the doctrines advanced there are specifically and almost exclusively Daoist. To attain rest and joy, according to the Jesus of this sutra, an individual must avoid striving and desire but cultivate the virtues of non-assertion and non-action. These qualities allow an individual to become pure and serene, a condition that leads to illumination and understanding. Much of the treatise explains four chief ethical values: non-desire, or the elimination of personal ambition; non-action, the refusal to strive for wealth and worldly success; non-virtue, the avoidance of self-promotion; and non-demonstration, the shunning of an artificial in favor of a natural observance of these virtues. The treatise in fact does not offer a single recognizably Christian doctrine but offers instead moral and ethical guidance of the sort that Daoist sages had taught for a millennium.[16]

Were all Nestorians as indifferent to orthodoxy or as willing to assimilate? Probably not. Earlier Nestorians taught monotheism—God as creator of all things, Jesus Christ as savior—and related many of the stories of the life of Jesus presented in the New Testament. Nestorian Christians in India maintained Christian beliefs and practices as they lived as a separate community although treated by Hindus as a separate caste. Nestorian missionaries along the Silk Road won converts among the Turkic-speaking tribes of the great grasslands. Many Mongols married into Nestorian families in fact. Only among the Mongols were Nestorian traders able to gain preferential treatment, and that provoked a Muslim reaction.[17] Elsewhere, the Nestorians lacked the close bond of merchants and political leaders that benefited the spread of Buddhism and Islam. Nowhere east of Syria did Nestorians win the exclusive political backing of a monarch or major tribal chieftain.

The Nestorian church was cut off from its political foundations in Antioch by charges of heresy and the imposition of Roman and Byzantine orthodoxy. Nestorian monasteries in central Asia and China floated in alien seas with neither local moorings nor distant, safe harbors. They breathed an atmosphere of acceptance of (or indifference to) new religious ideas. Orthodoxy seemed far away.

Christianity in Europe enjoyed the backing of the state in both Rome and Constantinople. With one exception, the emperors after Constantine were Christian. By the end of the fourth century, Christianity was the religion of the empire, east and west. Orthodoxy was enforced by the Roman emperor in the fourth century as well as by the Roman pope. After the breakdown of imperial authority in the west, the Roman pope alone held the reins of orthodoxy over the tribes of western Europe. While the Roman pope had a say with the patriarchs of other sees in doctrinal disputes east of Italy, the Roman church had a free hand in the west. Thus, even after there was no longer an emperor in Rome, the doctrines of the Roman church were taught from Ireland to Italy.

Increasingly after the eighth century, however, the patriarchs of Constantinople, Alexandria, Jerusalem, and Antioch declined to take direction from Rome. A final break came

between Rome and Constantinople in 1054, but by then centuries of separate language (Latin vs. Greek), culture, and development had created a schism that has lasted to the present day. Eastern orthodox churches tended to be more tied to national governments. The first officially Christian nation was declared by King Tiradates of Armenia in 301, 12 years before Constantine's conversion. In the Byzantine Empire, centered in Constantinople after the sixth century, the emperor often played a forceful role in the church (a political dominance that came to be known as Caesaro-Papism). But the missionaries from Constantinople brought the same doctrine to Russia that they brought to Bulgaria. Despite national differences, Orthodox churches tended to bring a similar kind of piety throughout the newly Christianized domains of the later medieval period. In piety, liturgy, and beliefs, these churches were not very different from those that spread from Rome.[18]

In summary, Christianity spread a common culture from Ireland to central Asia. Despite differences in dogma or institutional loyalties, a common identity as Christians was strong enough to encourage pilgrimages, missionaries, and (after 1095) crusades on behalf of the shared faith. In Jerusalem, Egypt, or central Asia, Christians met not only fellow Christians but also representatives of the other increasingly global cultures—the missionaries of southernization, of Buddhism, and, beginning in the seventh century, the bearers of a new universal faith called Islam.

## The Rise of Islam: The Making of a Modern World Civilization

The Islamic world was the third universal cultural system to spread across Eurasia in the first millennium CE. In many ways, it was the successor of the universal religious systems that preceded it. Islam, the religion of Muslims, was (and is) a continuation of the monotheistic salvation religion that sprang from the scriptures of Jews and Christians. For Muslims, Muhammad was the last of a line of prophets that included Abraham, Moses, and Jesus. But for Muslims, the most recent of God's revelations was received by the last and greatest of the prophets, Muhammad. The Quran (or Koran), Muslims believe, was dictated to Muhammad by the archangel Gabriel in the early seventh century CE. Muhammad recited the words, which were later compiled into the present book.

## Salvation, Endings, and Beginnings

The Quran continued to stress many of the themes of Zoroastrianism, Judaism, and Christianity. Prominent among these were the ideas of a cosmic struggle, a last judgment, and the prospect of heaven for the righteous. But the Islamic idea of salvation was much more optimistic than the Christian. Christian salvation (like Buddhist) held out a balm for a suffering world. Christians and Buddhists appealed generally to the less prosperous classes of the Roman and Chinese empires, and they entered the mainstream during the empires' decline after the second century CE.

Christianity offered salvation from a world that seemed to be ending; Islamic salvation seemed to beckon to a world just beginning. Islam sprang from a world on the move, the southern part of Eurasia that was untouched by the widespread population dislocations of the Eurasian grasslands. Between 200 and 700, a period of global population decline, the population of the Arabian Peninsula actually doubled.[19] This vitality was probably a reflection of a rising economy, resulting in part

from the redirection of trade along the "water silk road" of the Indian Ocean. Arab trade prospered from new technologies of transportation by water and land. Arab traders used Malay triangular sails to navigate the monsoon winds of the Indian Ocean. The Chinese compass allowed them to sail the open seas. Camels, the ships of the desert, had been domesticated for more than 1,000 years, but they too became more useful with the invention of a camel saddle that held a considerable array of baggage or riders with swords.

## The Prophet: Trade and Religion

Muhammad (570–632) was born into a merchant family. Orphaned at an early age, he learned the trade of a camel driver and merchant under the tutelage of a wealthy widow whom he later married. On caravan trips across Arabia, he came into contact with Jews and Christians and was drawn to the simplicity of their faith in a single God of both local and global significance. The God of Abraham was the deity of ancient nomadic pastoralists who brought their herds and people along the same routes that connected Mesopotamia and Egypt. He was also the creator of the world and of all mankind. Some Arabs recognized this and professed adherence to the faith of Moses or Jesus, but most Arabs worshipped other tribal fathers, forces of nature, and spirits called *jinns* (or genies). Muhammad was appalled by such local tribal religions and the continuous wars they engendered.

The revelation of the Quran transformed tribal conflict into a powerful force for Arab unity and expansion. Muhammad himself galvanized many of the Arabs of his native Mecca into an army of God opposed to idol worship, social inequality, political injustice, and corruption. His success threatened the ruling elite

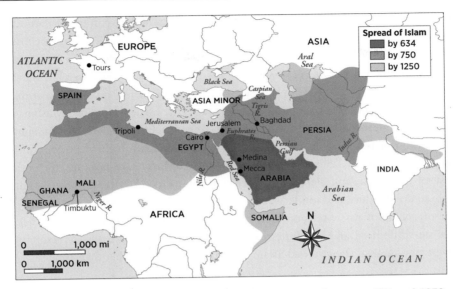

Map 4.3  Islam was the most rapidly expanding religion between 634 and 1250, changing the identity of what had previously been a largely Christian region with many Persian Zoroastrians as well as Jews, Hindus, and animists.

of Mecca, particularly the powerful leaders of the Quraish tribe who benefited from the many religious shrines of the city.

In 622, Muhammad and his followers escaped assassination by fleeing north to the city that became Medina. The flight, *hijra*, and the creation of the first Muslim community, *umma*, marked 622 as the first year of the Muslim calendar. In Medina, Islam evolved as a distinct religion, separate from Judaism and Christianity: a more robust monotheism than Christianity but attuned to Arab traditions. The "five pillars" of Islam that developed in Medina—profession of faith, prayer, fasting, charity, and pilgrimage—were unique to Islam only in the form they took. The profession of faith was not only "there is no god but God" but also "and Muhammad is his Messenger." Prayer was performed five times a day—initially facing Jerusalem but, as Muhammad in Medina separated Islam from Judaism, toward Mecca. Fasting (during the month of

Ramadan) and pilgrimage (to Mecca) also gave these practices an Arab stamp. By centering Islam (literally "submission" to God) at Mecca, Muhammad also built on traditional Arab pilgrimages to the black stone called the Kaba and took advantage of the useful influence of the Quraish tribe, which controlled the holy site and the city.

## Islam beyond Arabia

*Islamic Expansion to 750.* Religious fervor fired the initial campaigns that brought Islam to all of the Arabs of Arabia. But what happened next had as much to do with Arab armies as with religious belief. There are few historical parallels for such rapid expansion. Perhaps only the Macedonian armies of Alexander the Great (and later the Mongols) carried out a similar range of conquests in such a short period of time. Between the time of the death of Muhammad in 632 and 750, a period of little more than 100 years, the Arab armies conquered most of the territory of two of the world's great empires—the east Roman Byzantine Empire and the Persian Empire—and the peoples from Morocco and Spain in the west to the margins of India and China in the east.

It would be a mistake, however, to see the rapid expansion of Islam beyond Arabia as a religious jihad or crusade. This is because the conquest of Byzantine and Persian empires had more to do with luck and military success than the preaching of a new religion. Further, Muslims saw little need and had little reason to convert non-Arabs. They viewed Islam as Arab monotheism, akin to the monotheism of Christians and Jews. The Greek Christians of the Byzantine Empire, even the Zoroastrians of the Persian Empire, were to the Muslims fellow monotheists and "people of the Book." Like other ancient empires, Muslims also determined a system of taxation for subject peoples—at a slightly higher level for non-Muslims than Muslims. Like taxation, the enslavement of conquered peoples was also a common option of ancient empires. Muslims, however, thought it inappropriate to enslave fellow Muslims, and that too provided a reason to conquer and administer rather than convert.

Figure 4.7  Jenne and nearby Timbuktu at the southern end of the trans-Saharan salt-for-gold trade were the first and most important cities in Sudanic West Africa to become centers of Islam. *Werner Forman/Art Resource, NY. Great Mosque, Djenne, Mali.*

Arab armies dealt a significant defeat to the Byzantine Empire in 636. In 637, the Persian Sassanian Empire capitulated to Arab forces. Byzantine and Persian armies had been weakened by continual conflicts between themselves, and they faced in the Arab armies a potent and determined adversary. The fall of old empires did not have to mean a radical change in the daily lives of ordinary people, however. In Syria, Palestine, and Persia, Arab governors often used the same administrators and tax collectors who had served the Byzantine and Persian empires. Most people lived their lives as they had before. The conquering Arabs were, compared to Alexander's Macedonians, particularly insular. Arab armies stationed themselves in forts separated from the cities they had conquered. Initially, they mixed very little with the local population, using each fort as a stepping-stone to further expansion. As late as 750, only 10 percent of the non-Arab population of the Dar al-Islam (House of Islam) was Muslim, a level that testifies to the lack of religious coercion by the Arab conquerors or the disinterest of the new subjects in what they may have perceived as Arab religion.

Gradually, however, the conquered learned to appreciate the ways of the new conquerors and accept the legitimacy of the government of the caliphate. Muslims became more interested in converting their subjects to Islam, and non-Muslims found advantage in doing so. To make a contract with the new governor, perhaps to supply the troops or collect taxes, a Muslim name would be a definite advantage. Conversions began slowly but quickened in pace. The choice of a Muslim name was a clear indicator of conversion to the new faith. The historian Richard Bulliet gathered the data of name changes in Persia and discovered that Muslims grew from 10 percent to 90 percent of the Persian population between 750 and 900.[20]

Bulliet points out that this conversion rate followed a typical "S," or bell, curve where something rises slowly, gathers momentum, surges, peaks, and levels off. He remarks that the same curve would chart the popularity of a new technological innovation, such as high-definition television today. But not every innovation or new idea succeeds, and few sweep away all predecessors so stunningly. So we need to ask "why?"—or, more modestly, "how?"

*Islamic Expansion after 750.* The spread of Islam from 10 percent to 90 percent of the Persian population between 750 and 900 owed much to the power and prestige of the Abbasid caliphate that replaced the Ummayad after 750. With the Abbasids, Islam shifted its geographic center only slightly farther east, from Damascus to Baghdad. But the builders of the new city on the Tigris brought in tribes from the Iranian plateau and central Asian nomads to join with Arabs in the new faith. Under the Abbasid caliphate, Islam realized a universalism that was only potential in Arab monotheism. In opposition to the Arab favoritism of the Ummayad caliphate, the Abbasid caliphate encouraged a larger range of ethnic groups and tribes to become Muslims. In their new capital at Baghdad, the Abbasids created a cosmopolitan government and culture.

Like the other monotheistic religions, Islam included everyone from theocrats, who believed the government should institute God's will, to those who believed that spiritual matters were none of the government's business. Because of the example of Muhammad's government in Medina, perhaps more Muslims than Christians were theocrats, but Islam was a less hierarchical religion than Christianity became. In Islam, there was no equivalent of the pope or College of Cardinals. Nor were there bishops or church councils to determine orthodoxy or impose discipline. There were ulama (learned scholars) and judges, and well-respected religious leaders could issue pronouncements that their followers found binding. But a fatwa, or religious edict, rarely had the force of political law. Politically, Islam was a decentralized religion. While some of the early Abbasid caliphs thought of themselves as religious leaders, Islam spread more widely, paradoxically, under those caliphs who were more political than religious.

Ultimately, Islam's appeal was more political and cultural. It was the sophisticated urban civilization of Islam that attracted cultural converts: to the Arabic language, schools of *filosophia*, high moral standards, and the rich culture of Islam.

## The First World Civilization

Islam created the first civilization to encompass multiple states, governments, and peoples. By 750, the religion of Islam, the Quran, and the Arabic language shaped the beliefs and behavior of Berbers in North Africa and the descendants of Egyptians, Syrians, Mesopotamians, Persians, central Asians, and Indians. In the next 750 years, Islam spread to the Turks, Africans, and East Asians. A single culture united peoples across Eurasia from Spain to Indonesia. Even Jews, Christians, Hindus, and Buddhists who lived in the Dar al-Islam benefited from learning the language of the new global culture.

*Abbasid Baghdad.* The Abbasid caliphates of Harun al-Rashid (786–809) and of his son al-Mamun (813–833) were the first world cosmopolitan age. A world civilization may have been implicit in the message of Islam, but as long as that message was identified with a single ethnic group, the Arabs, its universality was muted. Al-Rashid and al-Mamun

changed the balance of Islam so that it was no longer an Arab religion ruled by sons of Arabia. Al-Rashid brought ministers (viziers) and advisers to Baghdad from throughout central Asia. The first and best known of these, from the Persian Barmakid family, were descended from Buddhist priests who converted to Islam.

The Persians and other non-Arabs of the Abbasid court turned an Arab empire into a Muslim one. Ironically, the new synthesis of Arab and Persian culture also brought the traditional trappings of Persian hierarchy and royal pomp to the palace. Some Abbasid caliphs were like divine kings. Al-Rashid turned Baghdad into a world of opulence and dramatic indulgence: extravagant gifts one moment, a brutal punishment the next. He was the prototype for the later *Thousand and One Nights*, the tale of Queen Scheherazade's nightly storytelling to curtail her evil husband's plan to execute her.

Al-Mamun, who had to defeat his brother in a civil war for the caliphate, brought a cultural renaissance to Baghdad. He created a complex called the "House of Wisdom," which included an enormous library, one of the oldest and largest universities of the world, and a center for translations from Greek, Latin, and other non-Arab and non-Persian literature. Al-Mamun's efforts saved many classical Greek works, including those of Plato and Aristotle, from oblivion.

Abbasid Baghdad also became a center of scientific and mathematical research. Arabs adopted Indian numerical notation and the Indian zero-based decimal system, which were far more flexible than Roman numerals or older Mesopotamian 12- and 60-based systems. The House of Wisdom contained an astronomical observatory, introduced the compass from China, and developed the astrolabe or sextant. Astronomers calculated the length of the solar year, the distance around the earth, and the rhythm of lunar tides. The translation center preserved the science of Greece: the astronomical writings of Ptolemy, Euclid's *Geometry*, the early medical works of Hippocrates, and the medical texts of Galen, including the first study of asthma. Scholars wrote medical encyclopedias and volumes on diseases like smallpox and measles, practiced dissection, and wrote on the optics of the eye. Indian, Persian, and Greek pharmacological knowledge led to the creation of the world's first pharmacies. Baghdad had 800 registered pharmacists. The great mathematician al-Khwarizmi introduced the study of algebra. The three Banu Musa brothers built on Greek geometry and mathematics. Geographers compiled an encyclopedia of places visited by Islamic merchants from East Africa to the Spice Islands of Indonesia.

*A Cultural Empire.* Islam was the first global civilization not because of its political empire. The Abbasid caliphate at Baghdad lasted beyond the ninth century in name only. Its top-heavy, Persian imperial court ill fitted early Muslim ideas of the equality of believers. Alternate "caliphs" challenged the authority of the Abbasids, including members of the Umayyad family who established their capital at Cordoba. Other dynasties were created by Muslims of various ethnic backgrounds and religious beliefs from Fez in Morocco to Delhi in India. The early vision of a single Muslim caliphate ceased to exist in fact. But its failure enabled the success of a cultural empire—a single civilization that embraced many people and many governments.

The cultural empire was based on a shared language and a single book. The Quran was the one authority that all Muslims shared. But the importance of the book created a culture of literacy and libraries. In addition to the

Quran, Muslims gathered the hadiths, the sayings of the Prophet reported by those who knew him. They wrote volumes on each chapter of the Quran, interpretations, analyses, and explanations. But they also continued to translate, transcribe, and build on the works of the Greeks, Byzantines, Persians, and Indians. Like the Chinese, Muslims turned calligraphy and bookmaking into art forms. By the ninth century, they had borrowed Chinese papermaking techniques, substituting linen (for mulberry bark) to make a longer-lasting cloth paper.

Writing had always been the glue that bound civilizations. Libraries not only created literate elites and cultures but also shared memories and uniform speech. Before the existence of paper, libraries the size of Baghdad's under al-Mamun were rare if they existed at all. The greatest library of the classical world was the library of Alexandria, which had probably contained between 40,000 and 70,000 scrolls (where each scroll contains a few chapters).[21] A large library in Ephesus that was burned by the Goths in 262 contained 12,000 scrolls. The library of Charlemagne, who also led a cultural renaissance in the early ninth century, numbered 256 volumes.[22] It is said that the library in Cordoba under the caliph Al-Hakem II (971–976) contained 400,000 volumes. Such numbers are hard to verify, but it is certain that the Muslim world retained and built on the literary and scientific heritage of the classical world. It is also certain that such a literary empire united Muslims and their non-Muslim residents across the largest span of land and seas and the largest number of peoples in the history of the world until that time. In the centuries that followed 1000, that Dar al-Islam expanded even farther into Africa and Southeast Asia and in the centuries after 1500 into a new world as well.

## Conclusion

The period from 200 to 1000 used to be called the Dark Ages. From the perspective of European history, especially western European history, this made a certain degree of sense. We have noted the disruptions of nomadic tribes in both western Europe and China from 200 to 600 and the accompanying population declines and loss of cities and traditional cultures. But from the perspective of southern Eurasia, this period was one of growth and expansion, both material and cultural.

The first 1,000 years of the Common Era was also a millennium of mixing. New religious and commercial relationships stretched across the borders of identity that had been forged in the previous age of classical civilizations. In many ways, the first millennium was the first global age, the first age of globalization, the first age when people became more alike rather than more different.

We have concentrated our attention on Eurasia, where these developments were most marked. Not until after 1500 did the entire world begin to become one. It remains for us to see how other parts of the world moved closer together in these and later years. Nevertheless, this world where everything is more than 1,000 years old might strike us as very familiar.

## Suggested Readings

Bentley, Jerry H. *Old World Encounters: Cross-Cultural Contacts and Exchanges in Pre-Modern Times.* New York: Oxford University Press, 1993. A leading world historian surveys Eurasian cultural interactions, especially religious conversions.

Foltz, Richard C. *Religions of the Silk Road: Overland Trade and Cultural Exchange from Antiquity to the Fifteenth Century.* New York:

St. Martin's Press, 2000. A brief overview of Silk Road religions and their relationship to trade and diplomacy.

Fox, Robin Lane. *Pagans and Christians.* New York: Harper, 1988. Rich study of pagan religions and the spread of Christianity in the second and third centuries.

Johnson, Donald, and Jean Elliot Johnson. *Universal Religions in World History: The Spread of Buddhism, Christianity and Islam to 1500.* New York: McGraw-Hill, 2007. Broad survey of these religions.

Macmullen, Ramsay. *Christianity and Paganism in the Fourth to Eighth Centuries.* New Haven, CT: Yale University Press, 1997. This is one of a number of studies of the subject by the leading scholar in the field.

Shaffer, Lynda. "Southernization." *Journal of World History* 5 (Spring 1994): 1–21. Available also in Kevin Reilly, *Worlds of History,* vol. 1 (Boston: Bedford/St. Martin's Press, 2013).

Xinru, Liu, and Lynda Shaffer. *Connections across Eurasia: Transportation, Communication, and Cultural Exchange along the Silk Roads.* New York: McGraw-Hill, 2007. A leading scholar of Chinese and Indian trade and the author of the "Southernization" essay in the previous entry discuss the cultures of the Silk Roads.

## Notes

1. Historians do not know why they were called "blood sweating," but Liu Xinru and Lynda Shaffer suggest that it may be a result of sweat oxidizing (turning orange or red) on snow. See Liu Xinru and Lynda Shaffer, *Connections across Eurasia: Transportation, Communication, and Cultural Exchange along the Silk Roads* (New York: McGraw-Hill, 2007). Other historians have speculated that a parasite may have caused lesions that bled.

2. Despite recent evidence of silk production in Harappan India before 1500 BCE, there is no evidence that it might have continued after the end of the Indus civilization about that time.

3. World population stagnated again at about 400 million between 1200 and 1300 as a result of the Mongol invasions and again at a slightly higher level from 1350 to 1450 as a result of the Black Death.

4. Lynda Shaffer, "Southernization," *Journal of World History* 5 (Spring 1994): 1–21.

5. For a map, see http://www.metmuseum .org/toah/hd/kush/hd_kush_d1map.htm.

6. Jerry H. Bentley, *Old World Encounters: Cross-Cultural Contacts and Exchanges in Pre-Modern Times* (New York: Oxford University Press, 1993), 76. Bentley actually offers a number of reasons for the spread of Buddhism in China in this useful introduction to the subject.

7. William Theodore de Bary, ed., *The Buddhist Tradition in India, China, and Japan* (New York: Random House, 1969), 132–37.

8. Laotzi or Lao Tzu ("Old Master") is the traditionally designated author of the *Tao Te Ching* or *Daodejing*, variously translated as *The Book of Changes* and *The Way and Integrity Classic*, which was written by many authors in the third century BCE.

9. The carvings of Borobudur in Java tell the story of the Buddha in hundreds of relief images. Chinese sculptors also created the fat-belly Buddhas that expressed Chinese attitudes toward food and enjoyment. Indian and Southeast Asian Buddhas were thinner and more somber.

10. The Acts of John, adapted from M. R. James, trans., *The Apocryphal New Testament* (Oxford: Clarendon Press, 1924), 42.

11. Eusebius, *The History of the Church*, trans. G. A. Williamson (Harmondsworth: Penguin, 1984), 341.

12. See Joyce E. Salisbury, *Perpetua's Passion: The Death and Memory of a Young Roman Woman* (New York: Routledge, 1997), esp. 144–47.

13. Robin Lane Fox, *Pagans and Christians* (New York: Harper, 1988), 277.

14. Adapted from Bede, *Bede's Ecclesiastical History of the English People*, ed. B. Colgrave

and R. A. B. Mynors (Oxford: Oxford University Press, 1969), 106–9.

15. Willibald, *Life of Boniface: The Anglo-Saxon Missionaries in Germany*, trans. C. H. Talbot (London: Sheed and Ward, 1954), 45. Willibald was a student of Boniface's.

16. Jerry H. Bentley, *Old World Encounters: Cross-Cultural Contacts and Exchanges in Pre-modern Times* (New York: Oxford University Press, 1993), 109. The document is called the "Sutra on Mysterious Rest and Joy." Bentley also notes that the Nestorian translations left something to be desired; for example, "Jesus" in Chinese became "Yishu," which could mean "a rat on the move."

17. Richard C. Foltz, *Religions of the Silk Road* (New York: St. Martin's Press, 2000), 138.

18. Essentially, the Orthodox Church refused to recognize Roman superiority and disagreed about minor matters of doctrine like the Immaculate Conception of the Virgin Mary and Purgatory (both of which had become canonical in the West in the Middle Ages).

19. From about 2.7 million to 5.4 million, according to Colin McEvedy and Richard Jones, *Atlas of World Population History* (Harmondsworth: Penguin, 1978), 145. According to the same source, the high of 700 was not reached again until the nineteenth century.

20. Richard W. Bulliet, *Conversion to Islam in the Medieval Period* (Cambridge, MA: Harvard University Press, 1979). See "Religious Conversion and the Spread of Innovation," the author's excerpt from the above, at "Fathom: The Source for Online Learning," http://www.fathom.com.

21. See http://www.bede.org.uk/Library2.htm# Royal. Estimates vary widely. Seneca estimated 40,000 (or 400,000 if a zero was missed by the medieval copyist).

22. See http://www.acadia.org/competition-98/ sites/integrus.com/html/library/time.html. As late as 1290, the Sorbonne library in Paris had only 1,017 volumes, and in 1475, the Vatican library contained 2,527 volumes; no European library contained more than 400,000 volumes until 1819.

# 5

# The Making of an
# Afro-Eurasian Network
## 1000 CE–1450 CE

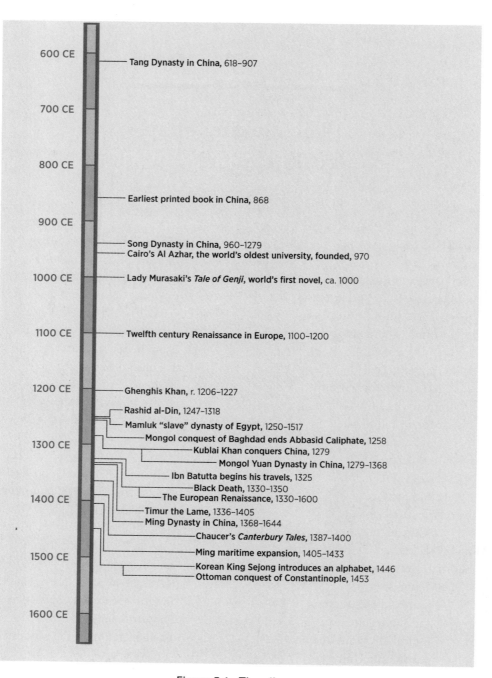

Figure 5.1 Time line.

IN 1325, Ibn Battuta, a young Muslim from Morocco, left for a pilgrimage to the holy city of Mecca. From there, he traveled through Syria, Iraq, Persia, and finally to India, where he was appointed as a judge because, although he did not speak any Indian languages, he spoke Arabic and was a jurist of the Quran. From 1333 to 1345, in his thirties and forties, he traveled extensively throughout India on official missions and to satisfy his curiosity. In 1345, Ibn Battuta sailed from India to China. At almost every port in China, he met someone he knew—the man who had first offered him money to set him up in Delhi and a Chinese envoy who had previously accompanied him on a trip from Delhi to Calicut—and on an invitation to meet the emperor, he stopped at the port of Fuzhou, where he ran into a fellow Moroccan who had lived 40 miles from his home in Morocco, a man he had recently seen in India. For Ibn Battuta, the earth was a very small world.[1]

In the age of Ibn Battuta, global travel became predictable and almost common. There were established agents, carriers, tickets, regular stops, accommodations for the traveler, places of worship for the foreign community, contacts, letters of introduction, and even souvenirs. That a Muslim who lived near the Atlantic coast could travel to the Pacific coast of China without passport or hindrance was a sign of how integrated the world had become.

Not everywhere but in numerous places—especially across Eurasia—people encountered the ways of foreigners. And in many cases, the ways of the foreigner became their own. Foreign religions, customs, clothes, crops, crafts, ideas, and even spouses won over or converted individuals, families, and communities that had for generations prided themselves on the antiquity of their ways. Change was not always voluntary or swift, and many people dug in their heels instead of opening their arms, but, ironically, as the variety of human experience became more visible for all to see, more people found common interests and identities over vastly larger regions of the planet.

This chapter is the story of how the integration of Asia, Africa, and Europe increased between 1000 and 1450. It is also the story of how that integration changed localities, states, and regions, making them both less different, one from the other, and also each more internally varied as their inhabitants increased their contacts with foreign ways and changed their own. Thus, the story of hemispheric integration is also the story of the origins of the modern world.

The previous chapters show how our world has been shaped by processes that began a long time ago. The agricultural revolution changed the way we eat and work, how many of us there are, and the lives we lead. The urban revolution multiplied our numbers and vastly increased the complexity of life. The Iron Age extended that life down the social scale and over the horizon. Our classical cultures still inform and shape us through our languages, values, and ideas. When those classical cultures were absorbed and eclipsed by a new set of ideas, techniques, and religions (the impact of southernization and universal religions), new communities emerged that were frequently both larger and more cosmopolitan than their predecessors.

In the past 1,000 years, the world has become far more integrated still. While we think of globalization as a very recent development, its roots actually go back to the first half of the previous millennium. Between roughly 1000 and 1450, the Chinese, Mongols, Muslims, Africans, and Europeans created and participated in a single network of trade, travel, and interchange. In the previous chapter, we saw the development of the early stages of this network among the Muslims and Chinese. In this chapter, we see how Africa and eventually Europe became active partners in an even more global network.

The story begins with China because it stood like a colossus over Eurasia from 1000 to 1450. Chinese technologies, manufactures, economic innovations, and organizing ideas formed the principal fuel of global interaction.

## China in the Making of an Afro-Eurasian Network

We have seen in the previous chapter how the Chinese effort to exchange silk for horses created the Silk Road, the first important link between Asia and Europe. When the Huns and other nomadic peoples of north-central Asia interrupted the flow of goods along the Silk Road between the third and sixth centuries, the trade moved south. Malays, Indians, and Arabs pioneered a route that brought southern spices as well as silks and tropical products across the South China Sea and the Indian Ocean. China was reduced to a number of smaller feuding kingdoms, not unlike the period before its unification 500 years earlier.

By the sixth century, however, the northern steppe stabilized as the nomads learned to extract payment from the caravans for protection and provisions and China reunited its empire. Under three successive dynasties, Sui (580–618), Tang (618–907), and Song (960–1279), China achieved a level of technological innovation that the world had never seen. Consequently, as trade between China and the West developed again along the northern Silk Road, China was undergoing a profound technological transformation. The new contacts between China and the West were then interrupted temporarily by the Mongol conquests, but relations resumed under the Mongol Yuan dynasty (1279–1368). Mongol rule was devastating, though in some areas—mainly maritime and military—the technology and economy of China continued to grow. The return of native Chinese rule with the Ming dynasty (1368–1644) revitalized Chinese expansion, especially during the first half of the fifteenth century.

In three key areas that have shaped the modern world—the technology of the industrial revolution, the market economy, and the modern bureaucratic state—China was centuries ahead of the rest of the world.

### *Industry and Invention*

So profound and pervasive was Chinese industrial growth from 1000 to 1450 that historians have compared it to the later industrial revolution. While historians still date the beginnings of the industrial revolution in late eighteenth-century Britain, many of the roots of that revolution lay in the industrial products and techniques of China.

*Textiles and Pottery.* Chinese silk and porcelain were the gold standards for textiles and pottery when Britain launched an industrial revolution in the late eighteenth century by producing factory-made cottons and ceramic dishes called "China." By the Song dynasty, Chinese porcelains were collected throughout the world as works of art. In the fifteenth century, East African merchants displayed Chinese blue and white dishes on the walls of their houses as a sign of prosperity. True Chinese porcelain could not be duplicated elsewhere. The luminous pottery was made from Chinese clay and feldspar, a Chinese stone. The imperial potteries established after 1000 employed over a million people by 1712, when French Jesuits smuggled the secrets to Europeans.

The secrets of silk production—feeding silkworms on the leaves of mulberry trees, then unraveling the strands of their cocoons into a fine thread—had been protected by threat of death until the sixth century. In 550, however, the secret (along with the worms and leaves) was smuggled in bamboo from China to the court of the Byzantine emperor Justinian. Constantinople established a rival silk industry that later spread throughout the Muslim world as well.

Chinese silk and porcelain attracted such a huge continental demand that these industries stimulated the development of power machinery and mass production, very much the way British industry did hundreds of years later. Already mechanized by the Song dynasty, Chinese textile producers used water-powered mills and spinning wheels by the eleventh century.

*Paper and Printing.* We have already pointed to early Chinese papermaking—from mulberry bark and bamboo fiber around 100 BCE (about 1,000 years before the Muslim world and 1,500 years before Europe). Printing with carved wood blocks may have originated in Buddhist monasteries as part of their effort to reproduce scriptures from India. The earliest of these may have been produced by Buddhist monks in Korea, but the first print shops were probably those in Chinese monasteries around 700 to 750. A million copies of the first Japanese scroll book were printed between 764 and 770, but not one was meant to be read. Rather, each was to be a miniature Buddha reciting prayers.[2] The earliest Chinese printed book to be read dates from 868. Block printing (carving a complete page at once) was particularly appropriate for Chinese with its tens of thousands of characters, and blocks could be engraved with pictures as well as words.

The use of individual pieces of movable type for printing developed later. Chinese printers experimented with wooden, ceramic, and metal type (which was probably first developed by skilled Korean metalworkers). In general, however, Chinese printers continued to use block printing. Movable type worked best where a few symbols were used frequently. Not only did the Chinese have the problem of

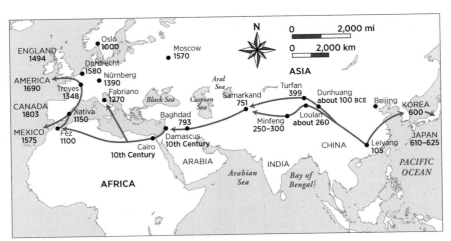

Map 5.1  Paper spread through Buddhist monasteries on the Silk Road from Dunhuang to Korea, Japan, and Tibet and west to Samarkand, from where Muslim victors brought it to western Asia and Europe.

innumerable characters, but Chinese culture also prized calligraphy, having turned the written script into an art form—one entirely lost by machinelike interchangeable typefaces. For Europeans, who had used phonetic alphabets for centuries, movable-type printing was a much greater advantage. Nevertheless, both printing and movable type came to Europe sometime after 1250, probably through Italy, possibly in the skills of slaves from Tibet or western China who were brought from the Black Sea markets to many Italian cities. The creation of a movable-type printing press by Gutenberg around 1450 combined the advantages of a mechanical press with movable type and a phonetic language that would eventually produce mass-market books and periodicals for a reading public in the millions and even billions.

*Compass and Ships.* The Chinese discovered the magnetic properties of magnetite and created magnets and compasses as early as the third century. By the eleventh century, the floating compass needle was used in Chinese ships. During the Tang dynasty, the Chinese colonized areas in the south, and by the Song dynasty, a majority of the Chinese population lived south of the Yangtze. Increasingly, relations with the peoples of the southern oceans became a matter of imperial policy. By the end of the Song dynasty, Chinese ships were sailing regularly into the Indian Ocean. Chinese vessels also sailed to the Spice Islands of modern Indonesia for the same spices that would attract Columbus 500 years later. During the period of the Mongol Yuan dynasty (1279–1368), the Mongols sent Chinese ships to invade Java and Japan. The Japanese invasion of 1281 failed, according to Japanese tradition, because of a "divine wind" (kamikaze) that sunk the Chinese ships, but recent excavations suggest that the ships, though huge by

European standards, may have been poorly constructed.

When the native Chinese Ming dynasty (1368–1644) gained control of China, shipbuilding became a major priority. Huge dry docks were constructed, new shipbuilding technologies perfected, and thousands of sailors trained. Between 1405 and 1433, the Ming emperor dispatched hundreds of "treasure ships," huge vessels, any one of which could have tucked Columbus's entire fleet of three ships into its hold. Under the command of Admiral Zheng He, a Muslim from Yunnan in southwestern China, these ships brought tens of thousands of Chinese sailors, diplomats, naturalists, artists, mapmakers, and tribute collectors on visits to foreign ports as far away as East Africa. The continual threat of invasion from northern and central Asia probably brought the ocean voyages to an abrupt close.

*Guns and Gunpowder.* In 644, an Indian monk in China showed that certain soils (containing saltpeter), if ignited, would produce a purple flame. By the eighth century, Chinese alchemists were making gunpowder. In the tenth century, soldiers packed gunpowder into bamboo tubes to launch rockets against enemy troops and fortifications. The first known cannon date from 1127. Probably the first population to share this Chinese technology was the nomadic confederacies of the steppe. Although their main weapons were crossbows fired from fast-moving horses, the Mongols also used gunpowder and Chinese catapults effectively, especially in the siege of cities. Weapons developed in warfare rarely remain secrets very long, particularly since it was common practice for each side to turn border populations and defeated troops into their own armies. Nevertheless, gunpowder did not reach European or Middle Eastern armament makers for more than 400 years. It may have come to Italy, along with printing, in the minds and skills of slaves purchased in Black Sea ports.

*Iron and Coal.* The Chinese use of iron dates from the beginning of the Iron Age in Asia, but production was relatively low before the Tang dynasty. By 1078 (toward the end of the Northern Song dynasty), China produced more iron than any country in the world before the industrial revolution. In fact, the entire iron production of western Europe did not surpass Chinese production until 1700.[3]

By the eleventh century, Chinese iron was also pure enough to be considered steel. The first ironworkers hammered soft iron into tools. Later, iron was extracted from rock and fired with wood or charcoal to remove impurities and strengthen it. But iron made this way still contained a high measure of carbon. Steel not only was much stronger but also did not rust. The making of steel, however, required much higher temperatures (about 1,600 degrees Fahrenheit). Those temperatures could be achieved only with coke, which was a concentrated block of coal (like charcoal was to wood), an intensified energy source.

The Chinese use of coal and coke for fuel may have been fortuitous. Northern China was not heavily forested, and much of the forest that did exist was cut to make charcoal during the early Song dynasty. Chinese iron production was concentrated near the northern capital of Kaifeng near abundant sources of coal. The market of metropolitan Kaifeng, a city of a million people, drove iron and steel production in the eleventh century. Iron and

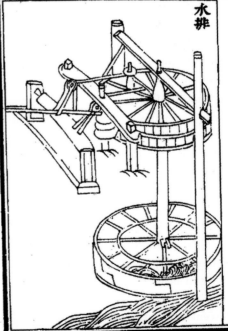

Figure 5.2  Waterwheels and Smelting Iron. As early as the first century, the Chinese were using water wheels to grind grain and (as seen here) to power the bellows of a blast furnace. This illustration comes from a book, known as the Nong Shu, written by Wang Zhen in 1313. The large book also illustrated the author's development of wooden movable type. *Waterhistory.org*

steel built a vibrant regional economy. The value of Kaifeng trade at the end of the eleventh century has been estimated at about 12.4 million British pounds; by comparison, the imports and exports of London in 1711 were worth no more than 8.4 million pounds.[4]

*Industrial Revolution?* Figures like these have led some modern historians to ask why China did not undergo an industrial revolution as Britain did 700 years later. If we restrict our inquiry to Kaifeng, the answer is fairly straightforward. Unfortunately for the people of Kaifeng, they entered a period after 1100 of a series of catastrophes that made iron production the least of their worries. In 1126, Kaifeng was conquered by the Jurchen people from the northern grasslands. In 1176 and again in 1194, the Yellow River changed its course, causing severe flooding and isolating Kaifeng from its traditional supply and trade routes. In 1233, Kaifeng fell to the Mongols after a brutal and punishing siege accompanied by plague and famine. A report of the time claimed that 900,000 coffins were carried out of the gates of the city over a five-day period. This may not be an exaggeration since the population of Kaifeng in 1330 had been reduced to only about 90,000—less than a tenth of its eleventh-century size.[5]

After the Mongol period, the Chinese economy revived, but the population shifted to the area south of the Yangtze River. While iron was no longer produced in the Kaifeng mines, it was produced in southern and central China. One problem, however, was that China's coal fields were mainly in the north. The nine provinces of the south contain only 1.8 percent of China's coal reserves.[6] Consequently, most of the iron that was produced when China revived in the fifteenth century was probably fueled with wood or charcoal. Chinese metallurgists may have even lost the craft of making coke from coal, as this was

normally passed on orally from master to apprentice. As a result, Chinese iron in the Ming and Manchu dynasties (1368–1911) was inferior to that of the eleventh-century steel.

A modern historian points to a further irony.[7] The industrial revolution that transformed Britain and the world in the nineteenth century was driven by the symbiosis of heavy industries in iron, coal, and steam. Iron became steel in blast furnaces stoked by coke. Steam engines were developed to remove water from the coal mines, then they powered the removal of the coal in wagons run on iron rails, and finally steam engines were refined to drive steel railroad cars along the iron rails laid throughout the world. The irony is that Chinese coal mines did not flood but were kept dry, so they did not have to develop steam engines. Dry mines were more dangerous and difficult to mine because the dry air full of coal dust was highly combustible. Consequently, even if China had an abundance of coal easily at hand and even if the Chinese continued to produce coke and steel, the synergy of iron, coal, and steam that jump-started the industrial revolution in Britain would have been less likely to occur in China.

Could China have begun an industrial revolution hundreds of years before it occurred in Europe? Perhaps, if there had been no Jurchen and Mongol invasions. Perhaps, if China had the global market for textiles and iron that Britain enjoyed thanks to its colonies in the eighteenth and nineteenth centuries. It is important to realize that no one foresaw the industrial revolution; no one could have planned it. Such things are much easier to copy than create. China has been industrializing quite successfully in recent decades along models borrowed from nineteenth-century Europe and late twentieth-century Asia.

But what was the relationship between medieval Chinese technological inventiveness and the industrial revolution that eventually created the modern world? If the Mongol invasion ended Chinese steel production and dramatically curtailed Chinese iron production, there was no continuity between Chinese metallurgy and the growth of the British and European iron industry. In fact, between 1500 and 1700, Chinese, Muslim, and European iron industries were relatively equal. Therefore, the precocious inventiveness of the Chinese iron and steel industry during the Song dynasty had limited global consequences.

Other Chinese inventions did begin a global history, however. While Chinese iron production was not copied by Muslims or Europeans, Chinese ceramics and silk were. Chinese ships were not copied, but the compass was. In these and many other technologies, China participated in a shared universe of technological invention and development. In an age with porous borders but no patent offices, it would be a fool's errand to trace the history of most inventions. Many transfers are as hidden from the historian as they were hidden from authorities at the time. Often technologies were stolen or captured in war. When Muslim armies defeated Chinese troops in 751, among the Chinese prisoners brought to Samarkand were Chinese papermakers. Paper appeared in Baghdad by the early ninth century and in the rest of the Muslim world by 1000. Later, paper filtered into Europe through Spain and Italy. The compass also sailed on Muslim ships before European ones, but some Chinese inventions jumped straight to Europe. Gunpowder, cannon, and block printing went directly from China to Italy in the fourteenth century, possibly brought by Mongolian or Tibetan slaves purchased by Italian merchants on the Black Sea.[8] Thus, in China, we see many roots of modern technology. And while some of these turned out to be only temporarily productive, others turned into permanent routes to the modern world.

## Commerce and Capitalism

Increasing trade is a long-term trend in world history. However, since rulers and religious institutions managed much of the trade in the ancient world, private, capitalist, market-driven trade has had a shorter history. China clearly played an important role in advancing private markets. Markets, merchants, private investors, and manufacturers were more important in Song dynasty China than ever before. But if capitalism means a society in which commercial decisions trump most others, China was not capitalist. The government directed much of the economy, and merchants were neither independent actors nor members of a self-conscious class. Rather, they operated in great family, clan, and lineage organizations that mediated individual action and restricted the role of the market.

*Money and Markets.* Song dynasty China created many of the elements of modern commercial society that we take for granted. Paper money is perhaps the most notable. Marco Polo was astounded to see paper money in China when he visited in the thirteenth century, but since appearing in 1024, paper money had already been in use for hundreds of years. Between 1265 and 1279, the government backed its paper notes with gold and silver. The Mongol Yuan dynasty (1279–1368) made paper money legal tender, the only money that one could legally use. Foreign visitors like Marco Polo and Ibn Battuta wrote of having to surrender their foreign money on arrival and convert whatever they wanted to spend into Chinese paper.

During the period of the Song dynasty, government returns from commercial activity surpassed those of agriculture.[9] This income included both taxes from private commerce and the revenues derived from government owned industries.

*Public versus Private Enterprise.* How much of this commercial activity was private, and how much government owned? Salt production was a government monopoly, as was tea, alcohol, and incense. The huge Chinese military (about a million strong) played an important role in directing the economy. In Hangzhou, the army owned 13 large and six small stores that sold alcoholic beverages. From these, it also ran taverns with state prostitutes.[10]

A class of private merchants and producers grew with the expanding Chinese economy during the Song dynasty, but it is likely that the state increased rather than decreased its control of the economy over time. There were a large number of private iron producers in Kaifeng during the eleventh century, for example. But by the thirteenth century, independent entrepreneurs had been replaced by government contractors. Then, during the reign of Kublai Khan (1260–1290) and the Mongol Yuan dynasty, these contractors were replaced by government-salaried officials. Increasingly, free laborers were replaced by slave and dependent workers.[11] Salt mines near Hangzhou employed hundreds of thousands of semi-slave workers at starvation wages. Those who were not homeless were kept in substandard public housing, six to eight in a room.

Markets also became less free during the Mongol Yuan dynasty. Merchants complained that government manufactures undersold private producers and that government purchasers paid less than full value. The government was a major buyer of armaments, clothing, and military equipment, some of which was made by government factories and some privately.

*Hangzhou.* Great cities crystallize the values of the civilization from which they spring. Hangzhou was one of the greatest. Marco Polo, who visited the former capital of the Southern Song dynasty shortly after the Mongol conquest in 1275, thought it was "the greatest city which may be found in the world, where so many pleasures may be found that one fancies himself to be in Paradise." Hangzhou offered lowly officials, foreign merchants, and native working people a variety of recreational facilities and amusements. There were many specialized restaurants: some served everything ice cold, including fish and soups; some specialized in silkworm or shrimp pies and plum wine; and even teahouses offered sumptuous decor, dancing girls, and musical lessons of all kinds. On the lake, there were hundreds of boats, many of which could be rented, according to Marco Polo, "for parties of pleasure":

> Anyone who desires to go a-pleasuring with the women or with a party of his own sex hires one of these barges, which are always to be found completely furnished with tables and chairs and all other apparatus for a feast. . . . And truly a trip on this Lake is a much more charming recreation than can be enjoyed on land. For on the one side lies the city in its entire length, so that the spectators in the barges, from the distance at which they stand, take in the whole prospect in its full beauty and grandeur, with its numberless palaces, temples, monasteries, and gardens, full of lofty trees, sloping to the shore.

While anything could be purchased in Hangzhou, many things were free. Workers, soldiers, and the poor frequented almost two dozen "pleasure grounds." Each was a large fairground with markets, plays, musical groups, instrumental and dance lessons, ballet performances, jugglers, acrobats, storytellers, performing fish, archery displays and lessons, snake charmers, boxing matches, conjurers, chess players, magicians, imitators of street cries, imitators of village talk, and specialists in painting chrysanthemums, telling obscene stories, posing riddles, and flying kites. Gambling, drinking, and prostitution were also part of the scene here as elsewhere in the city.

Market areas were equally a source of entertainment and business. Marco Polo saw so much fish in a single market that he could not imagine it would ever be eaten, but all of it was sold in a couple of hours. There were markets devoted to specialized goods and crafts that could hardly be found in the rest of China. One "guidebook" gave directions for the best rhinoceros skins, ivory combs, turbans, wicker cages, painted fans, philosophy books, and lotus-pink rice. In addition, the resident of Hangzhou could find books (hand or mechanically printed) on a fantastic variety of subjects: curious rocks, jades, coins, bamboo, plum trees, special aspects of printing and painting, foreign lands, poetry, philosophy, Confucius, mushrooms, and encyclopedias on everything.

Marco Polo's description of Hangzhou reveals a metropolis of unbridled commerce, but in praise of its architecture, Marco Polo added a note that shows the enormous power the emperor exerted over individuals, families, and private owners of property:

> And again this king did another thing; that when he rides by any road in the city . . . and it happened that he found two beautiful great houses and between them might be a small one . . . then the king asks why that house is so small. . . . And one told him that that small house belongs to a poor man who has not the power to make it larger like the others. Then the king commands that the little house may be made as beautiful and as high as were those two others which were beside it, and he paid the cost. And if it happened that the little house belonged to a rich man, then he commanded him immediately to cause it to be taken away. And by his command there was not in his capital in the realms of Hangzhou any house which was not both beautiful and great, besides the great palaces and the great mansions of which there were great plenty about the city.

Hangzhou was still the emperor's city, and China was the emperor's country. The emperor could encourage trade, support private businesses, and reward economic development, but the emperor could never be a businessperson. He could never think or behave like a capitalist. Rather, he was like a father to all the people of the Celestial Kingdom, rich and poor, powerful and weak.

Technologically, administratively, and economically, China cleared routes to modern society that others followed only recently. But China was not a modern society. Nor was China alone, large as it was, pervasive enough to change the world. The world we know evolved from the spread of these Chinese innovations and the contributions of other societies in a vast global network of trade, migration, and influences that many contemporary scholars call a "world system."

## State and Bureaucracy

The modern state was also a Chinese invention. The Chinese state is, in fact, the longest-continuing state in world history, whether we date its origins back to the Bronze Age or the formation of the Qin (Ch'in) dynasty in the second century BCE. But by the modern state, we mean something a bit different.

*The Modern State.* Our world consists almost entirely of nation-states (and the international organizations that represent these states). We take them for granted because there are no parts of the world that do not belong to a particular state. No island is too small or too far away to avoid the jurisdiction of a state. Even ships on the ocean fly the flag of a particular nation-state (though often one chosen for tax or legal purposes). But this was not always the case. A thousand years ago, there was no "France" or "Egypt" or "India." There were empires and caliphates, "no-man's-lands," stateless peoples, and frontiers beyond the control of governments. Many parts of the world were run by religious organizations, local lords, tribal leaders, or marauding armies rather than territorial sovereigns. The transformation of a stateless or tribal society into a territorial state involved a number of important steps. We have discussed some of these in our study of the ancient and classical world. Tribal, clan, or family organization

and identity had to be subordinated to state or national organization and identity, and there had to be an authority (a sovereign) able to administer the territory in some more regular and stable form than periodic plunder.

One reason why the Chinese state proved so long lasting was its development of state bureaucracy. As early as the Han dynasty, but especially during the Tang and Song dynasties, China developed a system of state administration second to none. One of the distinctive features of this centralized state administration was the Chinese civil service and examination system. We referred in a previous chapter to the origins of this system in the Han dynasty. It became especially important in the Tang and Song dynasties and had much to do with the revival of the Chinese Empire after the sixth century.

In the beginning, the old aristocracy rejected a system based on exams rather than birth, but eventually they too recognized that the system had changed. As early as the

Figure 5.3  Portrait of Jiang Shunfu, Mandarin square. The Chinese civil service exams created the first modern government of professionals. Jiang Shunfu (1453-1504) was an official (mandarin) of the first rank, as indicated by his badge of two flying cranes. His followers are probably his aides. *Anonymous.*

seventh century, one Tang emperor was said to remark, on seeing young aristocrats line up for the exams, "The heroes of the empire are all in my pocket." In fact, the battle between the palace and the old families continued throughout the Tang dynasty, and it was not until the Song dynasty that the old aristocracy was replaced by a new elite class of graduates of the highest state exams. Eventually, the sons of the old families were replaced by new names. The exam lists of 1148 and 1256 (which are unusually complete) show that less than half of the winning doctoral candidates had fathers, paternal grandfathers, or paternal great-grandfathers in the bureaucracy.

*A Bureaucracy of Experts.* The Chinese civil service exams were part of a larger process of change in Chinese society. To prepare candidates from all social classes for the exams, the northern Song emperor Shenzong (1068–1086) and his chief minister Wang An-Shih created a national university, perhaps the first in the world (although it was displaced by exam preparers in the succeeding Southern Song period [1127–1279]).

Exams may not strike modern college students as a major step forward in world history. In fact, modern society may expect exams to do too much. But in a world in which family and class stamped one for life, a test of ability or intelligence was a creative innovation. Rulers could be assured of experts, the ruled could expect fairness, and the talented could hope for success.

## Mongols in the Making of an Afro-Eurasian Network

A network is a regional system in which the various parts (countries, nations, and peoples) not only connect but also interact with each

other in a way that makes the whole more than the sum of its parts. Today, we live in a world network that embraces virtually every square foot of the planet. There are still places where one can be alone, even hide, but virtually no one on the planet anymore is unaffected by what others do and have done.

History over the very long term is a story of larger and larger spheres of interaction. The classical empires were larger than the ancient empires. The network that connected the worlds of China, the Mongols, and Muslims in the thirteenth century was larger still. This thirteenth-century network[12] was a root of the modern world network that has embraced both Eastern and Western hemispheres since 1492. Some historians call that modern network the "capitalist world system"; others might call it the beginning of globalization.

### The Mongols

The Mongols of the thirteenth century were very different from Song dynasty China. While the Mongols may have participated in the development of some Chinese technologies like gunpowder, they were in no sense industrial, bureaucratic, or capitalist. Theirs was a nomadic pastoral society: tribes of herders who periodically organized themselves to exploit "a new type of herd—human."[13] The rise of the Mongols under Temujin, who became Great Khan (Genghis Khan) in 1206, was the culmination of a series of changes that had occurred in the grasslands of Eurasia since the period of mass migrations and upheaval that had brought an end to the Han dynasty and the Western Roman Empire. Increasingly, the peoples of the steppe—Turkmen, Tatars, Uighurs, and Mongols—chose to charge transport duties and extract "protection" instead of raiding settled societies. But sometimes this more peaceful arrangement would break down. In addition, after 1000, when the tribes of the steppe broke the new balance with the settled peoples, the impact was often more lasting. This happened in the eleventh century, when the Seljuk Turks conquered most of what is today called Turkey (after them) as well as parts of Iran, Iraq, Syria, Lebanon, and Palestine. The Mongol expansion of the thirteenth century marked a similar break with the peaceful system of get and take.

The Mongols helped make the Afro-Eurasian network in two important ways: one positive and one negative.

*Death and Destruction.* The negative side of Mongol expansion was the enormous human cost and its economic consequences. When Genghis Khan died in 1227, his body was carried back across the vast empire he had created to be buried near the Mongol homeland. So that no one would reveal the burial place, however, every person along the way who aided or witnessed the procession was killed.

Genghis Khan died as he had lived. He created something very close to the world empire he envisioned when he declared himself Khan of Khans and "ruler of all who dwell in felt tents" at a Mongol meeting of the tribes in 1206. He conquered the great cities along the Asian Silk Road (Beijing, Samarkand, and Bukhara), slaughtering perhaps a million people in the process. His rules of engagement were simple. Those who surrendered immediately became slaves; those who resisted were killed. Great civilizations were lost with their cities: the Muslim Kwarezmian civilization in Samarkand and Bukhara and the Chinese-Jurchen civilization at Beijing.

After his death, his successors continued his global conquests in Russia, eastern Europe, and the Muslim heartland. In 1237, Mongol cavalries under his nephew Batu Khan swept westward to Russia, defeated the forces of Alexander Nevsky, and destroyed Russia's two largest cities, Kiev and Novgorod, in 1240. In 1241, Batu's armies conquered a combined Polish and German army and threatened western Europe. In front of the gates of Vienna, he suddenly turned back to attend the funeral of his uncle Ogedai and the selection of a new Khan in Mongolia. Europe was not threatened again, but the Muslim world was the next to feel the fury of the Mongols. In 1258, the great city of Baghdad, already living on memories, fell to the Mongols, finally bringing an end to the Abbasid caliphate. In 1279, Kublai Khan conquered China, ending the Southern Song dynasty at Hangzhou. In less than 50 years, the Mongols had conquered the known world of Eurasia.

*Trade and Tolerance.* The positive contribution of the Mongols was to bring all of Eurasia—from eastern Europe to the China Sea—under a single regime of trade and administration. The Mongols united all of Eurasia north of the Islamic lands. They permitted the free exchange of goods along the northern Silk Road, vastly reducing the costs of duties, robbery, and other risks in international trade. The northern arc of the Silk Road also completed a great Eurasian circle of trade that sped goods and ideas from China to Europe to Africa to the Indian Ocean.

The trade routes of this "Pax Mongolica" were not accidental consequences of Mongol conquests. Rather, the Mongols actively sought to increase trade and the well-being of traders. The Mongol cultural attitude toward merchants was much more positive than the Chinese Confucian attitude. Mongols benefited from the flow of goods along the Silk Road, enjoyed luxury items like silks and porcelains, profited as other central Asians had from the sale of horses and sheep, and prospered more from modest taxes than occasional plunder. In central Asia and in their conquered realms, the Mongols also aided the growth of financial instruments that have since become common. We have mentioned paper money, which the Mongol Yuan dynasty made legal tender in China. The Mongols also attempted to introduce paper money into Persia, though there they were less successful. In addition, the Mongols created a financial institution called the *ortogh*, which had elements of modern ideas of the corporation and insurance. The *ortogh* was an instrument of common ownership of a caravan; like a modern corporation, it divided costs and risks among a number of merchants or investors, allowing them to share the profits. The Mongols also encouraged the building of caravan stops and ensured that merchants would have access to food and financial needs. And for the Mongols, the lending of money for interest was not prohibited or restricted as it was in Christian and Muslim cultures.

In religion, Mongols were not monotheists; they practiced traditional rites of shamanism, ancestor worship, and respect for natural forces. Mongols were open to other religions. Many Mongols married wives from tribes that were Nestorian Christian. But they neither expected other peoples to follow Mongol religion nor disparaged foreigners who followed different traditions. Consequently, Mongols respected and eagerly learned from foreigners. Without a written language, they borrowed the script of the neighboring Uighur people and developed a written body of literature from the thirteenth century on.

Mongol hospitality to travelers was well known. The Mongol capital at Karakorum held many foreign residents, including some Christians who lived under Mongol rule because they found Mongol religious tolerance greater than in their Christian country.

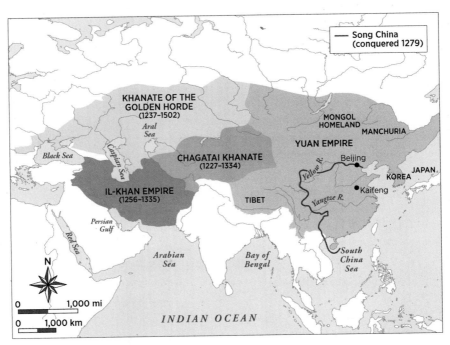

Map 5.2  The Mongol Empire around 1280: Kublai Khan's Chinese Yuan Empire and the khanates of other descendants of Genghis Khan.

*Political Divisions and Economic Unity.* By the end of the thirteenth century, almost all of Asia was ruled by a single extended family. You might think that the existence of Mongol Khans governing all the major civilizations from Baghdad to Hangzhou would have created a unified Mongol Empire. In fact, the Mongol Khanates of Persia, called the Illkanate, and China, called the Yuan dynasty, adopted many of the traits of their respective Persian and Chinese subjects. The rulers of the Illkanate eventually became Muslims. Kublai Khan did not become either Confucian or Chinese, but he and his administrators adopted many aspects of Chinese culture.

Economically, the Mongol world from 1250 to 1330 was one. Goods traveled easily across the great continent again. Chinese styles of art and architecture filtered across Eurasia and fused with traditional central Asian and Persian styles (though, interestingly, fewer Persian motifs were adopted by Chinese artists). Precious objects were made by a new class of international artists in a developing international style. One fitting symbol of the new global age was the invention of world history.

*World History for a Global Age.* Rashid al-Din (1247–1318) lived at the apex of Mongol global unity. His own life brought together the crosscurrents of global interaction. He was

Figure 5.4   Illustration of Mongol siege warfare from Rachid al-Din's world history. *bpk, Berlin/Art Resource, NY.*

born into a Jewish family in Persia. His grandfather had been an adviser to Hulegu Khan, the conqueror of Baghdad and founder of the Illkanid dynasty. At the age of 30, Rashid al-Din converted to Islam. Soon after, he began a career in his grandfather's footsteps, serving three Khans successively as court physician, steward, and vizier (chief adviser). The first two Khans were, like Hulegu, sympathetic to the Buddhists, but they also held debates among representatives of different faiths and awarded prizes to the most convincing. In 1295, the new Khan, Ghazan, chose Islam as the official faith, but in order to ensure that Mongol traditions were not lost, he commissioned Rashid al-Din to write a history of the Mongol conquests. The project grew into a multivolume encyclopedic history of all the people the Mongols encountered. Ghazan threw open the Mongol and family archives, instructed all to cooperate with the historian, brought in a Chinese historian to help with Chinese history, and instructed his emissaries to Europe and India to provide information.

The enormous compendium, the *Jami al-Tawarikh*, written in Persian and Arabic and beautifully illustrated in numerous manuscript editions, may be called the first world history book. From 1307 until his death, Rashid al-Din supervised the writing and illustrating of numerous manuscripts of his history and other works. For his efforts, he was generously rewarded by his mentor, the Khan. A later historian who knew him said that Rashid was the highest-paid civil servant in history. He was granted an entire suburb of the city of Tabriz and employed many of its residents in producing his manuscripts, he worked on the various estates that he had been given in the Caucasus and Asia Minor, he revived the efficient Mongol postal system, and he coordinated activities with his sons, eight of whom

governed major provinces of the Illkanate. At the age of 70, however, Rashid al-Din ran afoul of the jealous courtiers of a new Khan. Accused of poisoning his predecessor, he was summarily executed.

*Ecological Unity: A Dark Victory.* Ecologically, the Mongol conquest left a dark legacy. The Mongol victory had incorporated all of Eurasia into a single environment. With few exceptions (Rashid al-Din noted in his history that there were no snakes in Ireland, and so it remained), the previously local animals, plants, and pests became Eurasian, at home far from their roots. Fleas could travel across a continent by horseback; rats could live long enough in the hold of a ship to wipe out an entire crew. Within a few years of the death of Rashid al-Din, that fact was to have dire consequences.

The bubonic plague, called the Black Death because of the darkened blood-stained corpses, probably originated in China in the 1320s and spread to western Asia and Europe by 1347. Plague is an endemic disease among certain burrowing rodents like rats. When these rodent populations are disturbed by contact with humans, fleas can transfer the disease to humans or their animals. This is what happened in the wake of Mongol migrations and conquests. Plague had spread before, most notably in the sixth and seventh centuries, and it would strike again and again, but the fourteenth-century contagion had catastrophic consequences. The population of China declined from about 125 million to 90 million in the fourteenth century, partly as a result of disease. Between 1345 and 1347, the plague traveled west along the caravan routes through Russia to the Black Sea and Constantinople. From the Black Sea, it traveled by ship to Alexandria, Cairo, and Italy. Between 1348 and 1350, the plague claimed the lives of a third to a half of the population of the Mediterranean and northern Europe. Since the plague was easily spread by contact, cities lost a higher proportion of their inhabitants. Half to three-quarters of the population of Florence died the first year. The poet Giovanni Boccaccio (1313–1375) recalled in *The Decameron* "that a dead man was then of no more account than a dead goat would be to-day."[14]

After 1350, the disease had taken its toll. Those who survived had earned their immunities to future outbreaks that occurred with somewhat less virulence through the seventeenth century. But the population was slow to rise. Cities bounced back most quickly but only because the countryside emptied out. In Europe, population did not return to pre-1350 levels until 1500 or 1600.

Europe was lucky. Having escaped the Mongols, Europeans suffered only from the Black Death. The Chinese population peaked at 115 million around 1200, before the Mongols, a level it did not reach again until about 1550. Parts of Asia escaped both the Mongols and the plague. The Japanese population grew steadily throughout, tripling between 1000 and 1500. The population of the Indian subcontinent grew steadily but more gradually.

The area that suffered the most severe population losses was the Muslim heartland. The case of Iraq is most striking. Its population peaked at about 2.5 million around 800, declined to 1 million by 1300, and remained at that level until around 1850. Since that decline began before the Mongols and was not a result of the plague, it is part of a larger story.

## Islam in the Making of an Afro-Eurasian Network

The story of the Muslim world between 1000 and 1450 is one of simultaneous expansion and decline. At the core of the Dar al-Islam, the great Abbasid caliphate faded away, steppe nomads looted cities, populations stagnated, and warfare became endemic. During the same period, however, the Islamic religion spread to India, the islands of Indonesia, central Asia, the Balkans, and sub-Saharan Africa. In territory and population, the Dar al-Islam probably doubled. Further, as Islam spread, its followers created cultural and economic ties that made Islam a medieval stateless web. In place of an Arab faith and a centralized government, the Dar al-Islam became a continental civilization.

### New Muslims from the Steppe

We have seen how the history of Eurasia has been frequently shaped by the interaction of the steppe grasslands where nomadic pastoralists tended their flocks and the agriculture-based cities of China, South Asia, and Europe. Major migrations from the grasslands—in 1700 BCE, 1200 BCE, 200 CE, and, now again, 1000 CE—initiated new eras of history. In this context, the Mongol invasions of the thirteenth century were part of a larger steppe migration that began with the Seljuk Turks in the eleventh century. The Turkic-speaking pastoralists lived farther west than the Mongols and closer to the cities of the Abbasid caliphate. Consequently, they became Muslims before they displaced the armies and administration of the caliphate. In fact, many Turks had already been brought into the Abbasid army. Without much difficulty in the eleventh century, the Seljuk Turks conquered Iran, Iraq, Syria, and Anatolia (modern Turkey), leaving the Abbasid caliphate to govern in name only. Baghdad was left as a shell. Seljuk tribal leaders governed entire countries with their tribal armies.

The government of the Turks was very different from that of a bureaucratic state like the Abbasid caliphate. But it set a pattern that

would be duplicated from Egypt to India. "Thus arose," Marshall Hodgson, a leading historian of Islam, has written, "what was to be typical of much of Islamadom for several centuries, a fluid set of purely military governments most of them founded chiefly on the personal prestige of the *emir* or his father."[15] The centralized state was replaced by garrisoned troops. Emirs governed by whim and wile, their display of force the final authority. But unlike the centralized state, which presumed an evenness of command, the effective authority of the emir extended only as far as his eye could see. Beyond the view of his fort lay large areas of anarchy.[16]

*Slaves, Soldiers, and Sons.* As the Abbasid state atrophied, sultans and emirs lacked a bureaucratic system to raise taxes and soldiers. Since they were themselves tribal leaders, they could draw on a large following of retainers and troops, but they were always wary of other leaders, in their own and other tribes or clans, who were prepared to challenge their authority. This was especially problematic since, under the rules of the steppe, it was customary for brother to challenge brother in a system of election by contest that was intended to ensure that the strongest would always lead.

Who could a ruler trust? Without an institution of state loyalty, Muslim rulers developed an ingenious—but to modern sensibilities unusual—solution. It was common practice in ancient and medieval warfare for victors in battle to take the defeated as slaves. In fact, this was one of the main sources of slaves. Slavery was not necessarily permanent or inheritable, and there was a Muslim rule against enslaving fellow Muslims. Therefore, since at least Abbasid times, Muslim armies would capture non-Muslims and make them slave soldiers. Initially, Turks, Mongols, and other steppe peoples were thought prime candidates for slave soldiers. Later, captives were taken from the Christian Balkans, the "slavic" areas of eastern Europe, the Caucasus Mountains, and sub-Saharan Africa.

Now the idea of a slave soldier might seem a contradiction in terms. It would hardly seem prudent to give a slave a weapon or send him away to do battle. But the system of slave soldiers worked because the captives were enslaved rather than killed and then converted to Islam—qualifying their slave status somewhat, although they were still slaves to God and to the sultan; in addition, they were well trained and well cared for. In fact, slaves became officers and generals, even emirs and sultans. Since the government was military, slaves were trained for the most important positions in the administration of many Muslim governments.

The advantage of a class of slave soldiers and officials to the ruler was that such "foreigners" were not beholden to any clan or tribal leaders; their only loyalty was to the sultan or emir who "owned" them. Further, as slaves, they were generally prevented from having families of their own and adding to the number of competing clans. In fact, on a few occasions, former slaves revolted and created dynasties of their own. One of these was the Mamluk (literally "slave") dynasty of Egypt (1250–1517), in which Turkic and Circassian[17] slaves came to power though more through palace revolt than inheritance.

*In Place of Government.* Ironically, the medieval Muslim tradition of government as mainly a military matter created a civilization that unleashed numerous creative energies and granted Muslims a wide range of freedoms. Slave dynasties and military governments left a good bit of daily life unattended. Without a centralized bureaucracy, many matters normally regulated by government were left to other agencies.

Matters of family life were regulated by religious law and authority. In lieu of legislative bodies, Muslims followed the *shari'a*, the body of law that emerged from the Muslim community since the time of Muhammad's governance of Medina. Muslim scholars interpreted these traditions or made pronouncements based on them. Muslim courts administered and enforced the law, relying on families and clans when necessary.

Islam was a decentralized religion. There were no popes, cardinals, bishops, and church councils as there were in Christianity. The Muslim community needed little supervision because it had God's law in the Quran. Every Muslim thereby had access to the most important elements of his or her religion. The centrality of the Quran meant a high level of literacy among Muslims, at least in Arabic. Schooling in Quranic literacy was private and pervasive. Individual scholars and masters of Islam formed schools and took students. Universities, like Cairo's Al Azhar, the world's oldest (founded in 970), subsidized students from all over the Muslim world with the aid of donations.

Charity was an intrinsic part of Islam. Giving to the poor was one of the five central "pillars" of the faith. This *zakat* was collected from all Muslims and directed to the needs of the poor, infirm, and recently converted. Various private charities, called *waqf*, provided for hospitals, education, housing, welfare, burials, and other needs, public and private.

Non-Muslims were relieved of the *zakat* but instead paid a defense tax called the *jizya*, which Muslims were not required to pay. In general, non-Muslims, like Jews and Christians, were governed by their own laws, courts, and authorities.

It is important to recognize that no medieval society treated people as individuals. For instance, Jews in Muslim and European societies were treated as a corporate group. They generally lived in separate areas, pursued separate occupations, and sometimes were expected to wear clothing that established their separate identities. Freedom from arbitrary persecution was purchased with the *jizya*, but Jews and Christians in Muslim society were no more equal to Muslims than Jews and Muslims were equal to Christians in medieval Europe. Limited or military government opened more opportunities for Muslims than others, but Jews and Christians were rarely persecuted.

### Muslims, Merchants, and Markets

*A Merchant's Religion.* Like modern America, the medieval Muslim world used markets to carry out many activities normally assumed by governments. More than any of the great religions, Islam sanctioned trade and the work of merchants. The Quran may be the only one of the world's holy books that deals explicitly with matters of trade, and the merchant was a cultural model. Not only had the Prophet of Islam been a merchant, but merchants were particularly well placed to follow the demands of the faith. They could afford to give generously to the poor, they could make the pilgrimage to Mecca as part of their business travel, and they could make the necessary arrangements to pray five times a day and fast during the month of Ramadan.

Islam not only began as a merchant's religion but also facilitated the needs of merchants as it developed and expanded. Muslims shared a common set of values across what would later be many national boundaries. A comparison with Europe is enlightening. Christianity was also a universal religion, asserting common brotherhood and shared values, but Christians identified themselves as much with their particular nation, city, and church (e.g., Roman, Greek, and Nestorian) as they did with fellow Christians. Muslims had a wide-ranging network of good faith to support long-distance trade and exchange.

Certain ideas and institutions that were essential to the development of capitalist society were created or refined in this context. Banks, checks, insurance, third-party payments, accounting and bookkeeping procedures, shares of ownership, leasing contracts, the partnership, and the corporation were all refined in the Islamic world. Some of these had pre-Islamic roots but became more sophisticated under the Dar al-Islam. Virtually all of them pre-dated European ideas and instruments by a couple of centuries. Many entered Europe through Italian traders, especially from Venice and Genoa, in Cairo and Constantinople, and some, like *tarifah* (tariff) and *sakk* (check), with echoes of their Arabic names intact.

The one exception underscores the flexibility of the Islamic financial system. While Christians were forbidden to charge usurious or excessive interest, the Quran specifically forbid Muslims from charging any interest at all. Consequently, Muslims were nonstarters in the development of interest-bearing loans

Figure 5.6  In 1154, Roger II of Sicily commissioned this map by Muhammad al-Idrisi to contain the latest information on the boundaries of the known world. Here it is "upside down" to the modern eye: the south at the top. Many of the geographic details were so accurate that the map was useful for hundreds of years. *bpk, Berling/Art Resource, NY. Museum für Islamische Kunst, Staatliche Museen, Berlin, Germany.*

and the computation of variable time-sensitive interest rates. Nevertheless, with the precision of a modern American mortgage banker who charges a borrower "points" to get a loan, Muslim bankers figured in processing costs and fines for late payment (as Islamic banks still do today).

*Cairo.* The heart of the Muslim market economy in the centuries after 1000 was Cairo. Located close to the remains of ancient Egyptian Memphis and Giza, Cairo was actually a new city in the Muslim period—or, rather, a series of new cities along the Nile (separate then but today all a part of huge metropolitan Cairo).

Cairo's golden age (1294–1340) had military roots. Within a brief time, the new Turkic Mamluk slave dynasty of Egypt defeated the Mongols (1263) and reoccupied Syria and Palestine, including the Crusader states (1291). After military consolidation, the Mamluks encouraged the expansion of trade across North Africa and the Muslim heartland but especially along the southern maritime route to India, the Spice Islands, and China.

Much of our information about the merchants and advanced market economy of Cairo comes from a most unusual and fortunate source. At the end of the nineteenth century, scholars of medieval Judaism discovered a treasure trove of documents, letters, sacred and formal writings, and everyday jottings that detailed life in medieval Cairo for centuries. Because in Jewish tradition it was considered irreligious to destroy anything with the name of God written on it—and virtually any piece of writing might refer to God—a Jewish synagogue in Fustat (old Cairo) collected all discarded paper and other materials with any writing on them. The synagogue deposited every piece of writing in a storage room called a *geniza*. This pile of writings had

reached the top of the attic hundreds of years before it was rediscovered in 1896. The *geniza* yielded books and sacred writings previously unknown, intricately detailed accounts of Jewish life in medieval Cairo and a dense array of materials for reconstructing the entire kaleidoscope of Cairene life for 1,000 years, especially during the period between the ninth and thirteenth centuries.[18]

S. D. Goitein, who devoted a long life of scholarship to the Cairo *geniza* documents, concluded that they revealed a world that, especially in the eleventh and twelfth centuries, combined "free enterprise, a monetary economy, and fluid forms of cooperation" in a "comparatively salutary" society.[19] Indeed, the many records of correspondence and travel in the Cairo *geniza* show that not only Cairo but also much of the Islamic world, from Morocco and Spain to Iraq and Iran, was not unlike a modern free trade zone where one could travel without a passport, buy a home or secure employment in a foreign country, and make a contract with or send money to a stranger 1,000 miles away by means of a piece of paper. Goitein wrote,

> To sum up: during the High Middle Ages men, goods, money and books used to travel far and almost without restrictions throughout the Mediterranean area. In many respects the area represented a free trade community. The treatment of foreigners, as a rule, was remarkably liberal. . . . How is all this to be explained? To a certain extent by the fact that the machinery of the state was relatively loose in those days. . . . At the root of all this was the concept that law was personal and not territorial.[20]

The golden age of Cairo lasted until about 1340. In the 1320s, Ibn Battuta described it as the "Mother of Cities": "Mistress of broad provinces and fruitful lands, boundless in multitudes of buildings, peerless in beauty and splendor."[21] And, of course, he had been almost everywhere.

In 1347 (as Ibn Battuta was returning from China), an Egyptian ship sailed from the Black Sea bringing slaves and grain to Alexandria and Cairo. In the grain, it also carried at least one rat and fleas infected with the plague that had already swept across central Asia. The ship left with 332 on board. It arrived in Egypt with 45, all of whom died before they could leave the port.[22] The death toll was 1,000 people per day in Cairo in 1348. Normally crowded streets were empty except for funeral processions. But the difference that began to emerge between cities like Cairo and the cities of Europe was that in Cairo the plague kept returning. Between 1347 and 1513, the plague struck Cairo 50 times—once every three years on average.

The great world historian Ibn Khaldun, who lost both his parents to the plague in Tunisia, came to Cairo to understand and to help others make sense of the great catastrophe. He offered his conclusions in the last volume of his multivolume world history.

> Civilization in both the East and the West was visited by a destructive plague which devastated nations and caused populations to vanish. It swallowed up many of the good things of civilization and wiped them out. It overtook the dynasties at the time of their senility, when they had reached the limit of their duration. It lessened their power and curtailed their influence. It weakened their authority. Their situation approached the point of annihilation and dissolution. Civilization decreased with the decrease of mankind. Cities and buildings were laid waste, roads and way signs were obliterated, settlements and mansions became empty, dynasties and tribes grew weak. The entire inhabited world changed.[23]

### Islam in Africa

The Black Death did not bring an end to civilization, not even to Muslim civilization. The very size of the Dar Al-Islam by 1350 made it able to resist even pandemics.

*Islam in West Africa.* In its golden years, Cairo had many visitors besides Ibn Battuta. There were years when the Mamluk sultan held welcoming parades for what seemed a new visiting dignitary each day. But for years afterward, Cairenes remembered the spectacular entrance in 1324 of Mansa Musa from the West African kingdom of Mali. The Muslim king of Mali was on a pilgrimage to Mecca. He arrived in Cairo with a retinue estimated at over 60,000 with 80 camels carrying two tons of gold. People said that he gave away so much gold as gifts that the price of the precious metal did not recover for years afterward. This would not be surprising since Mali in the fourteenth century produced about two-thirds of the world's gold exports. By 1324, Islam had not only spread to sub-Saharan Africa but also won many followers. Ibn Battuta visited Mali 30 years later and remarked, "On Fridays, if a man does not go early to the mosque, he cannot find a corner to pray in, on account of the crowds."[24]

Camel caravans had crossed the western Sahara for 1,000 years before 1324, as long as the camel had been domesticated in the Sahara. Christian North Africans and then Arabs and Berbers crossed the wide expanse of desert by camel train for gold, slaves, and ivory. In return, the northerners provided horses and precious salt, which they (or, more often, their slaves) dug from the desert salt mines in the northern Sahara, an area that had been under water during the Pleistocene epoch 10,000 to a million and a half years ago. At first, the northerners raided and traded with black Africans, coming into increasing contact in the market cities along the Niger River like Timbuktu. With the influence of Muslim merchants and scholars in the towns and the local initiative of ambitious tribal leaders, Islam spread from the towns to the courts of kings. Mansa Musa was one of many.

Increasingly between 1000 and 1450, sub-Saharan Africa became fully integrated into the Muslim trade network. Just as trade began while black Africans were still pagan, it continued after their conversions. Raids continued especially after 1000, when Berber tribes became more numerous in the Sahara, raising and breeding camels and competing for scarce resources. But even as clashes became more frequent, the forest lands south of the Sahara became a permanent part of the Dar al-Islam.

Some elements of Islam took root in West Africa better than others. The allowance of monarchial polygamy in African society corresponded with Arab traditions, though the Muslim practice was restricted by the example of the Prophet's limit of four wives. On the other hand, Middle Eastern traditions of veiling women played poorly in African societies that prized fertility above modesty in dress. Ibn Battuta was scandalized on his visit to Mali by the sight of naked women in public.

*Swahili Culture.* In fact, the people of West Africa were relatively latecomers to the Dar al-Islam. The people of East Africa were involved from the beginning. East Africa is only about 100 miles across the Red Sea from Mecca. Long before Muhammad, Arab ships sailed back and forth between Arabia and Africa. In the ninth and tenth centuries, African villages on the offshore islands and east coast of Africa grew wealthy by trading with Arab Muslims. Initially, they traded African tortoiseshell, rhinoceros horn, and ivory elephant tusks, which were highly valued in Asia for jewelry and medicinal purposes. By the tenth century, gold mined in southeastern Africa became a profitable addition. Villagers whose livelihood had been based on fishing and farming became city merchants, steeped in Arab market culture and Islam. Their language and culture blended Arabic with their ancestral Bantu, forming something called Swahili (after the Arabic for "coastal"), and this new hybrid language became the common tongue of the East African coastlands.

In East Africa, as in Spain, the Balkans, and the Holy Land, Islam encountered Christian peoples, kings, and clerics. In Ethiopia, the Christian church was older than any in Europe, with ties through the Coptic church of Egypt dating back to the first century of Christianity. In conflict and peaceful exchange, the Afro-Eurasian network stretched down both the eastern coast and the western interior of Africa, integrating African peoples, products, and cultures with their own.

*A Single Ecozone.* The linking of sub-Saharan Africa to the Eurasian zone was also ecological. Crops and animals were exchanged with salt and gold, and eventually so were wives, and genes, and germs. Historians are not sure to what degree this had occurred by 1350. Ibn Battuta makes no mention of the plague while traveling in Mali in 1352, leading most historians to conclude that the disease did not cross the expanse of the Sahara Desert. Recent research, however, points to population decline in this period, a possible outcome of new diseases.[25]

Certainly by 1500, the people of western Africa had become part of the same biological regime as Europeans. After the European attempt to enslave American Indians failed largely because the American Indians had no immunity to European smallpox, Europeans used West African slaves almost exclusively. Clearly, West Africans had been part of the same world of microbes and diseases long enough to have developed immunities to smallpox. But the Bantu-speaking Africans of the western sub-Saharan grasslands had little contact with the Khoi Khoi San–speaking people of southern Africa, many of whom were annihilated by European diseases when Europeans settled the southern tip of Africa in the seventeenth century. The descendants of those same Europeans, however, had no immunity advantage over the Bantu-speaking Zulu and Xhosa people, whose ancestors had come down from West Africa with Afro-Eurasian microbes. As a consequence, while European settlers in the Americas largely annihilated American Indians, the Europeans who settled in South Africa faced Bantu peoples with immunities similar to their own.

## Islam in India and Indonesia

While Islam began as an Arab religion, the conversion of Persians, Europeans, Africans, central Asians, and Turks changed the ethnic balance of the faithful by 1000. During the next 500 years, Islam spread throughout South and Southeast Asia as well. As a consequence, today Muslim Arabs constitute only about 20 percent of the world's Muslims (about 10 percent of Arabs are not Muslims). The majority of Muslims today live in the Indian subcontinent and Indonesia. Those countries that today have the largest Muslim populations are Indonesia, Pakistan, Bangladesh, and India.

Muslim expansion in India and Indonesia occurred in each of the three stages we have chronicled for other areas of the world. First, Arab armies brought Islam as far as the Indus River by 750. Then, around 1000, Turkic and other central Asian tribal armies brought Islam to what is today Pakistan and northern India. And finally, from the seventh century on, especially after 1000, Muslim merchants brought Islam to southern India and Indonesia. Each of these made different demands. The early Arab armies sought to govern rather than convert. The Turks wanted both control and converts. The merchant communities sought neither, but their religious piety and economic power made them a force to be followed. In addition, Muslim merchants were often accompanied by devotees of Sufism, a form of Islam that stressed rigorous spiritual exercises while teaching love of God and respect for other faiths. The great Sufi poet Rumi (1207–1273) wrote,

> The sufi opens his hands to the universe
> and gives away each instant, free.[26]

As often happens in the winning of hearts and minds, the least demanding were the most persuasive.

Geographically, the realms of steppe-nomad Islam and maritime-merchant Islam were also quite different. The northern Muslim states were more accomplished in military might than mercantile prowess. Descended from pastoral nomads, their skills and interests led more to military maneuvers, and their economic techniques tended more to extraction than production. The armies of the northern land empires were huge, and the military officers, tribal or slave, dominated nobility, clergy, landowners, and merchants (usually in that order). In the south, especially along the sea routes, Muslim merchants played a leading role in the governance of smaller maritime states. Some of the most notable—Malacca, Hormuz, and Aden—were not much larger than the port city itself. From an economic standpoint, however, these smaller city-states turned out to hold more of the future than the vast continental empires.

Yet from a military and political perspective, the large Turkic land empires dominated the century between 1350 and 1450. Timur the Lame (1336–1405) revived Mongol ambitions of global conquest in a period of feuding khanates at the end of the fourteenth century, briefly conquering central Asia from Delhi to Greek Smyrna in the eastern Mediterranean. When European ships sailed to relieve Smyrna, Timur warned them away by filling the harbor with floating plates carrying the severed heads of the garrison defenders lit from inside the skulls by burning candles. Typical of many tribal conquests, Timur's empire did not last beyond his death. Much longer lasting, however, was the empire of the Ottoman Turks, who conquered not only Turkey but extended their control in the fifteenth century to eastern Europe and the Balkans, including Greece. Having surrounded the city of Constantinople for generations, the Ottomans finally captured the city in 1453, putting an end to the Byzantine Empire. From there, the Ottomans created a sophisticated military state and went on to threaten Europe as far west as Vienna until 1683. Seven hundred years of conflict between Christianity and the Muslims remained as unresolved as it was at the beginning of the First Crusade in 1095.

## Europe in the Making of an Afro-Eurasian Network

### *Revival and Expansion*

The European economy began to revive from the debacle of Roman decline, nomadic

incursions, and urban depopulation by the end of the eighth century. The ascendancy of Charlemagne in 800 was a sign and agent of that revival. Charlemagne brought to his court scholars from as far afield as England and Italy and was visited by representatives of the patriarch at Constantinople and Slavic and Muslim lands. Recent historians have discovered evidence of hundreds of travelers between Europe and the Byzantine and Muslim worlds in the ninth century as well as hordes of Arab and Byzantine coins that indicate a level of trade that grew from 780 to 900.[27] With little to export for such "real money" and Arab spices and pharmaceuticals, European merchants supplied their one surplus product: other Europeans, whom they sold as slaves for the bustling slave markets of Africa and the caliphate.[28]

European population and agricultural land expanded simultaneously. Between 800 and 1200, Europeans brought new lands under cultivation by reclaiming marshes, clearing forests, and colonizing new areas. The expansion of agriculture was aided by a range of new technologies. After 800, northern Europeans began using a heavy plow that could turn over the heavy soils of northern fields. A new horse collar permitted the harnessing of horses in a way that did not choke them, and teams of horses could be harnessed to the heavy plow.

An Irish legend tells of a king in the third century who supposedly brought the first water mill builder from "beyond the sea" to give a rest to the slave girl who was bearing his child.[29] Whether the legend is true or apocryphal (and the date is probably too early), it calls attention to the correlation between labor and technology. Societies that were too poor to keep slaves might be quicker to substitute machines. The use of water mills, which had been used in classical times in Rome and

Map 5.3   Compared to China, Europe was a land where numerous seas, rivers, mountains, islands, and peninsulas helped divide peoples into separate states.

Figure 5.7  This twelfth-century manuscript shows the European's use of the heavy plow as his wife prods the oxen. *The Granger Collection, New York.*

Figure 5.8 The windmill came to Europe from Persia, but the Persian windmill was a solid structure set to the prevailing winds. The European windmill rotated on a platform to catch changing winds. *Gianni Dagli Orti/ The Art Archive at Art Resource, NY. Bibliotheque Municipale Valenciennes.*

China, increased dramatically in Europe after the ninth century. Windmills are more recent, dating from about 700 in the Middle East. They were used first in the dry plains of Iran and Afghanistan, where they served the same purposes as water mills—mainly pumping water and grinding grain. Persian windmills were introduced into Europe through Muslim Spain, but by 1185, Europeans had invented a different kind of windmill. The Persian windmill was a fixed conical structure with open doors that drew the prevailing winds inside to turn the central pillar and its grinding stone. European windmills employed large exterior sails that swiveled on a horizontal axis to catch the changing direction of the wind. By the sixteenth century, the new windmill had sprung up everywhere in Europe—even in Spain, where Don Quixote imagined that the windmill sails were the threatening arms of invading giants.

*Good Weather and Good Luck.* European growth also came during a time of good weather. Between 700 and 1200, the climate of northern Europe warmed considerably. The combination of warming and abundant rainfall aided the expansion of farming into new regions, especially in the north. The Vikings settled in Greenland and Iceland. In the early 1200s, the east coast of Greenland permitted agricultural cultivation, grapes were grown and wine was produced in southern England and northern Germany, and farmers grew crops at high altitudes in Norway and Switzerland. Medieval warming was not limited to Europe, but there it coincided with a period of agricultural expansion in the northern marshes and forests. European growth slowed a bit during a colder period from the later 1200s to 1450,[30] when Viking settlement in Greenland ended and wine production and farming in high latitudes and mountain sides of Europe was curtailed.[31]

Europe also had good luck in escaping the more serious nomadic invasions of the period between 1000 and 1250. Viking attacks and Magyar (Hungarian) migrations caused serious disruption in parts of Europe in the ninth century, but after 1000, Europeans escaped the equivalent of the Jurchen, who destroyed Beijing; the Seljuk Turks, who overran much of the Byzantine Empire; and the Mongols, who overwhelmed the cities of China, central Asia, Russia, most of the Muslim heartland, and eastern Europe.

*Two Europes, Four Economies.* The expansion of settlement and farming in the north created a second Europe that had barely existed in classical times. The Greeks and Romans had colonized the Mediterranean. While Roman legions fought as far north as England and maintained a line of village forts across France and Germany, the forests of northern Europe were sparsely settled. Medieval settlement changed that balance. Around 700, the population of northwestern Europe overtook that of Mediterranean Europe for the first time, an advantage the north retained until about 1900.

The fledgling economy of Charlemagne's Franco-German Empire did not thrive much beyond his grandchildren, but in the tenth and eleventh centuries a new economy developed in France that attracted merchants, bankers, and traders from wealthy Venice. International merchants came to trade at the seasonal fairs in Champagne in central France. One of the more desired items was the cloth from

Flanders (modern Belgium), which was made from the best English wool.

The economies of Venice, Champagne, and Flanders were very different. Venice was an international banking and trading center with interests in Constantinople and the Muslim world. Venetian bankers provided much of the capital and financial know-how for the merchants at the Champagne fairs. Flanders and Champagne were local economies attached to international markets. Together, they added a European loop to the great Mongol–Muslim circle of trade.

A fourth European economy developed farther north along the Baltic Sea and the coast of northern Germany. These cities constituted themselves as the Hanseatic League and traded codfish, salt, lumber, and furs. After 1200, some of the Hanseatic port cities, like Hamburg and Lubeck, and the Belgian city of Bruges began to challenge the dominance of the European Mediterranean cities like Venice and Genoa, although Venice remained the dominant European sea power before 1450.

## Cities and States

The nomadic incursions of the fourth century destroyed not only the Western Roman Empire but also its many cities. The area of that empire became a deurbanized patchwork of agricultural estates run by local notables and worked by dependent laborers. Between the fall of Rome around 400 and the coronation of Charlemagne in 800, there was no states and few cities. Except for southern Italy, there were few cities of any size in Europe in 1000. Northern Europe was particularly rural. London and Paris were "small muddy towns" of a few thousand inhabitants in 1000, while Cordoba in Islamic Spain contained 260,000 houses, 80,000 shops, and 4,000 markets.[32]

*Urban Renewal.* Europe produced an unusual number of cities after 1000. The Hanseatic League alone included more than 60 cities at its height in the fourteenth century. The growth of cities after 1000 was due in part to the increased productivity of European agriculture and the expansion of the population.

New cities were also a product of changes in European politics and society. Feudal society allowed little freedom or social mobility. Knights, vassals, serfs, and even lords were bound by contracts, some made generations earlier. New cities grew up on the coasts and boundaries of the great agricultural estates, kingdoms, and principalities. The residents of the cities provided arts, crafts, precious goods, advice, and financial support useful to the neighboring lords and kings. In return, local rulers often gave cities control over their own affairs. City finances, courts, taxes, tariffs, and even laws were turned over to the people of the city. Kings and city leaders drew up contracts that spelled out the freedoms of the city. A common saying of the time declared that freedom was in the city air; indeed, in some cases, a serf was legally free after living in the city a stipulated amount of time. In addition to cities that negotiated their independence, there were cities that fought for it. Between 1080 and 1132, the cities of northern and central Italy, which had been ruled by German emperors since 962, declared their independence, each setting up a municipal government that they called the "commune."

*City-States and Citizenship.* Many of these late medieval cities became city-states. In northern and central Italy, the newly independent cities proceeded to control surrounding territory and create city-states that included farmland as well as urban areas. Relations between city-states were not always peaceful. Pisa and Genoa fought frequently over their mutual designs on neighboring Sardinia, to give just one example. Yet because they were independent states, they had to find a way to conduct their affairs. Often there was a leading family or group of families, sometimes even an individual, who seized control. An elite group of families governed Venice for centuries; a single family, the Medici, did the same for Florence. For a brief period in Florence, the monk Savonarola ruled—before the townspeople turned on him and burned him at the stake in the public square. Even in abeyance, the rule of the new city-states required the participation of all who lived within the walls. By contract or custom, these city-states became the first self-governing states since those of ancient Greece. These autonomous zones required a high degree of public participation. A budget for the city of Siena in 1257, which had an adult male population of about 5,000, included 860 holders of public office, including police (but not military, which would have potentially included all). City-states created the first legislative bodies since the classical era, and these too demanded a high degree of public participation. In Italy, city councils normally had a Great Council of 400 or more and an Inner Council of about 40.

Urban residents, at least men with property, were citizens, not subjects, of their city-state. They voted on issues ranging from the choice of an architect for the cathedral to matters of war and peace. They served in the city councils, staffed government offices, and fought when they called on themselves to do so. This experience—by no means universal—shaped a different idea of politics, government, and the role of the individual than commonly existed in other societies.

A Muslim like Ibn Battuta could live and work in Delhi, India, or Fez, Morocco, but he was a citizen of neither. He could even govern as a judge in India, but he played no role in making the law and served only at the pleasure of the sultan. Marco Polo was a proud citizen of Venice. Thanks to Muslim universalism and hospitality, he could travel freely anywhere in the Dar al-Islam, but he had to be much more careful in Italy; when he returned, the great Venetian was captured by rival Genoese and had to dictate his "million tales" from a "foreign" jail.

## Law and Science

Ibn Battuta did not make the law in India; in truth, no one did. In Islamic societies, there was no need for human law because there was God's law—the sunna, or summation, of the Quran and the hadiths (witness reports). Judges like Ibn Battuta might enforce or interpret the law, and they might issue a fatwa or judgment based on the law, but there was no need for humans to add to the laws, rules, and advice that God provided.

*Natural Law and Natural Reason.* When Christianity became the official religion of the Roman Empire, it adopted Roman law. Long after the empire had breathed its last, the church continued to use Latin and Roman law to run its affairs and shepherd its flock. In the early Middle Ages (400–800), Europeans followed the particular customs, rules, and laws of their clans. In addition, they were subject to the laws of the land, ruler, or government, if there was one. But when it came to religion, they talked of following the "Roman law" of the church.

Roman law, like Greek law, was a universal code based on territorial sovereignty that applied to everyone equally. Roman law was legislated, but it purported to be fair and just because it was based on principles of "natural law" accessible to "natural reason." We have

already traced this idea of a correspondence between human law and natural law back to the ancient Greeks. We have noticed the fit between the idea of an ordered universe and a society ruled by law. Greeks and Romans believed that people had a capacity to understand the laws of nature through their own powers of reason. Thus, the public sphere could be effectively managed by citizens. Some of these ideas continued to operate in the Eastern Roman Empire at Constantinople. Many Roman laws were enshrined in the code of the Byzantine emperor Justinian in the seventh century. Nevertheless, most people of medieval western Europe knew as much Roman law as most Christians today know Latin.

Along with the loss of Roman law, medieval Europeans lost much of Greek science, which also derived from the idea that laws of nature could be discovered by human reason. Early medieval Christianity was sometimes indistinguishable from the mystery religions and pagan folk customs that bubbled up in the post-Roman world. The term "dark ages" would be an appropriate characterization of the enormous loss of classical texts, knowledge, and universal law and science.

*Twelfth-Century Renaissance.* Western Europeans began to retrieve the classical texts and revive legal-scientific ways of thinking in the late eleventh and twelfth centuries. Two events in the late eleventh century revitalized awareness of natural law. One was the discovery of the Byzantine emperor Justinian's law code, showing what a vast, sophisticated, coherent, and equitable system Roman law had been. The other was a conflict between the emerging kingdom in Germany and the papacy that brought to a head the budding conflict between state and church authority. The conflict established the principle of a separation of church and state—two powers, two jurisdictions—that became an essential element of western European thought. By the beginning of the twelfth century, the Roman papacy had declared itself free of secular control, including the appointment of its clergy, which had previously been chosen by local government officials. As a result, from that time on, every western European Christian faced two governments with overlapping jurisdictions—religious and secular. Further, at least one of those governments, the church, claimed universal validity, representing God's law and natural law. Some historians have suggested that, ironically, this competition led to the beginning of the modern Western state.[33] In opposition to the claims of secular rulers who ruled because they could, the church declared itself a sovereign body, an independent public authority, with the right to make laws according to accepted principles and to administer those laws with its own hierarchy over a defined territory. The key is that it did not deny the right of other bodies like secular governments to do the same (as a Muslim caliphate or Chinese emperor would have). It therefore encouraged the development of overlapping but separate authorities, many of which could claim universal or natural validity within their own jurisdictions. The result was a world of multiple sovereignties: cities (as we have seen), states, and the church but also guilds, parishes, and corporations. Europeans grew accustomed to participating in different governing institutions in different ways. Some, like guilds and cities, were relatively democratic; others, like monasteries, were egalitarian but not democratic; and others still were neither democratic nor egalitarian, but even they had to defend their jurisdiction in terms of certain principles that would be generally recognized.

Between 1200 and 1350, Europeans created dozens of universities that were similarly independent with separate jurisdictions and hierarchies. Committees of faculty (or students in student-run Bologna) set standards, awarded degrees, and administered these institutions as corporate bodies—ministates on the model of the larger ones. The first European universities copied the earlier Muslim models, but the Muslim universities were not independent entities with faculties and degrees, and they were always administered by religious authorities.

The key ingredient of the European twelfth-century Renaissance was the retrieval of many of the works of Aristotle and some of the Greek scientists. All these had been available in the original Greek or in Arabic translations but were unknown to Europeans before the twelfth century. Aristotle gave Europe a complete set of natural laws, internally consistent, logical, and sweeping in coverage but fundamentally at odds with much of church teaching. Aristotle's principles of natural law held, for instance, that the universe had no cause since something could not be created from nothing and that the laws of nature were uniform and consistent, seemingly ruling out God and miracles in two easy assumptions.

The idea of a world of nature knowable to human reason was insidious in its simplicity and persuasiveness. Muslim and Christian clerics challenged Aristotle. Islam became increasingly critical of secular philosophy after 1000. Science was called "foreign," making it an easier target for religious surveillance. Universities, madrassas, and mosque schools all emphasized Quranic education anyway; the only institution that taught Aristotle, Al-Azhar University in Cairo, eliminated it.

Christian Europe was more divided. When reading Aristotle was banned at the University of Paris, the other universities continued to teach his works. The faculty of the University of Toulouse advertised its teaching of Aristotle in order to steal Parisian students away.

Eventually, Paris relented. In Europe, universities, cities, and states could act independently, even competitively. There was no emperor or caliph to impose a uniform curriculum or command. Christian Europe opened its doors enough to invite the Greek guest in because Europe had become accustomed to separate tables.

It would be a mistake to suggest that Aristotle or natural science monopolized the European mind in the twelfth century or even the fifteenth. Many of the greatest thinkers of the period sought to integrate reason and faith, science and theology, and the heritage of Athens and Jerusalem. Nevertheless, a significant part of European intellectual life was thereafter devoted to an idea of truth that required no prior commitment but could develop in a neutral space and lead where it would. "Truth in search of itself has no enemies," the philosopher Peter Abelard (1079–1142) declared, convinced that God-given human reason could lead nowhere else. To be a "friend of truth" became a frequent call among European philosophers and theologians in the thirteenth and fourteenth centuries.[34]

By the mid-thirteenth century, the works of Aristotle formed the core of the curriculum in most of the dozens of European universities. A master of arts degree at Paris or Oxford was heavily weighted with courses in logic, physics, astronomy, and mathematics. A modern historian writes,

> Since virtually *all* students in arts studied a common curriculum, it became clear that higher education in the Middle Ages was essentially a program in logic and science. Never before, and not since, have logic and science formed the basis of higher education for all arts students.[35]

*Popular Science.* From the thirteenth century, students and professors at the universities studied and practiced science, but many of their less privileged neighbors became increasingly science minded. Monotheistic religion had long established the belief in absolute truth. Christianity had nurtured faith in human reason—in part, perhaps, to require responsibility in a world that the church did not fully control. This had the effect of emphasizing the power of the individual to understand. The Judeo-Christian idea that nature was God's creation and that mankind was in charge of nature also contributed to a sense of scientific objectivity. In Christian cultures, humans were observers of nature rather than participants (as a Hindu, Buddhist, or Daoist might be). For late medieval European Christians, the world was a stage; for their ancestors and many pagans and polytheists, the world was more like a garment that one wore or the air that one breathed. Muslims, of course, shared the biblical belief in God's creation, but they also had the Quran. Their religion called on specific pieces of scientific knowledge. They studied astronomy for such purposes as marking the beginning and end of the month of Ramadan with precision. They studied geometry and geography to align the prayer mats and mosques with Mecca. But they did not need science to understand the truths contained in the Quran. For Christians, lacking "The Book," God's Truth was contained in His creation. Nature was His book. Even the Bible was only a partial guide to a greater and continuing revelation. Consequently, Christian culture became more science minded than other cultures.

Europeans probably integrated science and technology more than other cultures as well. The historian Alfred Crosby suggests that "the West had a greater proportion of individuals who understood wheels, levers, and gears than any other region on earth."[36] The Christian

Figure 5.9 An anatomy lesson from a fifteenth-century edition of a thirteenth-century text by Mondino de Liuzzi, who restored public dissection in anatomy instruction, a practice shunned for 1,000 years. *Universal Images Group/Getty Images.*

intellectual class valued manual labor more than the masters of Confucianism. "To work is to pray" was the motto of the Benedictine monastic order.

By the fourteenth century, European society was full of machines. The most important for the development of science-mindedness was not the latest windmill or water mill but rather the mechanical clock. We do not think of the clock as a machine because it seems to do no more than tell time. But the clock is an elaborate mechanism of moving wheels, balances, and springs, and it does something

that no other machine can do: it abstracts time. With the mechanical clock, time was abstracted from nature. Time was no longer slower in summer, lighter or darker, or cloudy or bright; it was a series of equal moments—abstract, interchangeable, neutral, and merely mathematical. Instead of the time the creek thaws or the mare foals, people began to tell time by numbers. Days were divided into hours, not prayer times or eating times, and those times came at different hours and minutes each day. Once the clocks were installed in the town square and in the church steeple, the bells would chime the hour, and the prayers and meals would follow the chimes. In the fourteenth century, European towns installed public clocks like there was no to-morrow—at least none to be wasted. The philosopher Nicola Oresme (ca. 1323–1382) coined a metaphor that would stand for the modern universe: he wrote that the "heavenly machine" was a kind of "clockwork."[37]

Beginning in the fourteenth century, Europeans abstracted space as well. After a copy of Ptolemy's *Geographia* arrived in Florence from Constantinople around 1400, Europeans imitated the ancient use of grid maps of neutral space and applied them to lands and oceans still unknown. They drew directional "plumb lines" for navigation charts and invented three-dimensional perspective in painting. They created lenses, spectacles, and, after 1600, telescopes. To think of things abstractly may be an element of scientific thinking that, once developed in one area, can be easily applied elsewhere: measurement, mathematics, alphabetization, and the notation of musical notes on gridlike staffs. All these scientific ways of thinking spread with great alacrity in Europe after 1400.

# The Formation of the Modern Network

By almost any measure, western Europe in 1000 had been a backwater. We have noted signs of growth and significant changes, but no one in 1000 would have imagined that in a mere 500 years, the small cities and states of western Europe not only would have joined the world system as an equal partner but also would have begun to seize control of it. We have probed the precocious rise of western Europe. We should keep in mind that most of

the changes we have noted—the rise of cities, citizenship, modern states, the rule of law, and scientific laws and ideas—would have been unremarkable to most medieval observers. The Chinese or Muslim visitor to the West in the fourteenth century would have felt more pity than envy. We have already mentioned some of the raw comparisons: cities, libraries, and ironworks a fraction the size of those of China and the Islamic world and Europeans struggling without some of the basic conveniences of the then modern world, such as paper, printing, the classic literature of the Greeks, and ancient science and its Arabic improvements. As late as the thirteenth century, Arab astronomers were invited by the Chinese to Peking to run the Chinese observatory. As late as the fifteenth century, Chinese ships were the vessels of choice for the discriminating world traveler. As late as the sixteenth century, Europeans were still using Arab medical texts. So it would seem that the rise of western Europe was still remote.

## Death and Rebirth

We have already indicated how the late medieval period was slashed by the Black Death of 1348–1350. Europe suffered as much as China and the Muslim world. A third to a half of the population died. But we have also remarked that the people of Cairo suffered another 50 plagues in the next century and a half and that Cairo, Damascus, Baghdad, and much of the Muslim heartland was already in population and agricultural decline long before 1300. European agriculture and population may have peaked around 1280, but most parts of western Europe gradually recovered after 1350. Later plagues were far less frequent and less severe; they returned every 10 or 15 years, not every three. Temperatures cooled, farm yields shrank, and famine dogged those on the margins. To make matters worse, the ruling dynasties in England and France fought the Hundred Years' War, which did not end until 1453.

Nevertheless, European society revived after the plague. Survivors found their labor in great demand. Dependent laborers gained leverage in negotiating with their "betters." Despite the more challenging climate conditions, the average European lived better in 1450 than in 1300.

*The Renaissance.* Europe also experienced a cultural renaissance in the 200 years after the plague. Even before the plague, Italian painters like Cimabue (d. 1302) and Giotto (d. 1337) filled churches and canvases with strikingly unmedieval three-dimensional figures. They and their successors before 1450 still chose religious subjects for their art, their paintings and sculptures gracing altars, sacristies, and church doors. But they placed their patrons, their townsmen, and even themselves around the manger of the Christ child or looking up at Jesus on the cross.

While the Italian artists filled their religious paintings with Greek gods in contemporary Renaissance clothing and crafted meticulous spaces with scientific accuracy, artists in Flanders put a mirror to their world and each other. Dutch masters showed an Adam and Eve who in their nakedness resembled local peasants rather than Greek gods, and in the background they meticulously layered details of everyday life on a landscape so realistic that you could find your way without a map.

At the same time, the poets Dante (d. 1321), Petrarch (d. 1374), and Boccaccio (d. 1375) began the creation of a national Italian language and literature. Petrarch, who along with Boccaccio survived the plague, has been called the father of the Italian Renaissance.

Refreshed by the discovery of Latin authors like Cicero, he expressed a classical faith in human capacity and civic virtue in a new vernacular language that he "got together [with] my lime and stones and wood."[38] The younger Boccaccio crafted a Florentine Italian language as modern as yesterday into what may have been Europe's first piece of literature as entertainment, the *Decameron*, 100 tales of love and deception told by ladies and gentlemen waiting out the Black Death. Chaucer's *Canterbury Tales* (1387–1400) did much the same for a Middle English language that would be less recognizable today.[39] These Renaissance classics shock us with their modern secular tone, sexual themes, and entertaining narratives.

## The Classical and the Novel

The *Decameron* and the *Canterbury Tales* were actually modeled on a literary form that may have originated in India and became known to Europeans in the form of *A Thousand and One Nights*, or *The Arabian Nights*, which, we have already noted, was compiled in Baghdad in the tenth century, probably from older Persian stories. The Arabic work, however, was always more popular in the West than in the Muslim world, where it was disparaged as inelegant, especially in its mix of classical and vernacular languages. Classical Arabic, the language of the Quran, enjoyed a status among Muslim clerics and intellectuals that was far beyond Latin in the West. The development of a vernacular or modern Arabic was not a project that anyone encouraged. Popular vernacular expressions were to be corrected rather than imitated.

We called the *Decameron* the first piece of modern European literature. Considerably older and as modern is the Japanese *Tale of Genji*, which was written by Lady

Murasaki around 1000. It is sometimes called "the world's first novel." Why should Japan rather than China invent the novel? And why should it be written by a woman? In China, learning the characters and the classics defined the educated gentleman. The Chinese Empire and bureaucracy resisted local variations more than the plague. Classical Chinese authorized cultural expression throughout East Asia. The development of national identities was a gradual process of separation from China. In 1000, the Japanese popular vernacular was just in the process of distinguishing itself from classical Chinese. Chinese was the language of officials in Japan; it was considered inelegant for gentlemen to use the emerging vernacular. But that is why Lady Murasaki could use the popular speech and, like Boccaccio and Chaucer, invent her language as well as its literature. As a lady in waiting in the Japanese court, Murasaki was free of the pretensions of male officialdom. She and Sei Shonogon, another courtesan, were not embarrassed to write in Japanese, and they had much to say. As cultural outsiders, women could be more inventive.

## Japan and Korea

Japan was to China as Europe was to Rome, Byzantium, and the Dar al-Islam: an underdeveloped outlier where a sense of cultural inferiority encouraged eager imitation of the dominant culture but also provided the space for experimentation and innovation. Both areas, on opposite ends of Eurasia, escaped the Mongols. Both grew rapidly between 1000 and 1300 (Japan continuing apace until 1700). Japan's political geography was also similar to that of Europe in some ways: both created maritime cities rather than large land empires, and Japanese cities resembled European city-states even in their relative autonomy. The

city-states and small maritime states were the innovators of Europe as they were of the Muslim world. If East Asia had nurtured other Japans, their competition and interchange might have forced innovation more quickly.

One other potential Japan was Korea. In fact, because Korea was adjacent to China, it was more dominated by the classical Chinese language and culture than was Japan. As the Korean language diverged from Chinese, the scholars and administrators of the Korean court (which recruited officials with its own Confucian examination system) struggled using Chinese characters to write Korean.

During the first half of the fifteenth century, under the guidance of King Sejong, Korea experienced a cultural revival that bore similarities to the Italian Renaissance. The king gathered many scholars to his court, some merely to follow their stars, others to help with some of the king's pet projects in language, printing, music, and science. The common theme of the king's projects was the realization of certain principles that he believed to be in keeping with the neo-Confucian movement sweeping China. In China, neo-Confucianism meant Confucianism tempered by Buddhist meditation. To King Sejong, neo-Confucianism meant more Confucian emphasis on public welfare (and less Buddhist introspection). All his reforms, the king declared, were intended to educate and uplift the people. In two critical areas, these reforms bear a striking resemblance to a combination that was soon to transform Europe. King Sejong chose to greatly increase the use of printing with movable type, and he chose to create a Korean alphabet. He accomplished both. In the preface to his New Korean Phonetic script, the king wrote, "Because our language differs from the Chinese language, my poor people cannot express their thoughts in Chinese writing. In my pity for them I create 28 letters, which all can easily learn and use in their daily lives."[40] In addition, he dedicated his rule to the spread of knowledge through printing by metal movable type:

> To govern it is necessary to spread knowledge of the laws and the books so as to satisfy reason and reform men's evil nature; in this way peace and order may be maintained. Our country is in the East beyond the sea and books from China are scarce. Wood-blocks wear out easily and besides it is difficult to engrave all the books in the world. I want letters to be made from copper to be used for printing so that more books will be available. This would produce benefits too extensive to measure.[41]

In Europe, the combination of a phonetic script and a printing press based on movable type caused a revolution in popular literacy and linguistic invention. In Korea, it had no such effect. In fact, the two reforms were rarely combined. Despite the advantage of setting a phonetic system with movable type, most Korean books continued to be block printed, and few works were written in the new script. The book that introduced the alphabet in 1446, *The Correct Sounds for the Instruction of the People*, was block printed. During King Sejong's reign, 194 books were printed in woodblock and 114 in metal print; 70 of the latter were on the subjects of Chinese history, Chinese characters, Chinese classics and literature, and Chinese law.[42] As in Japan, the educated elite preferred the use of classical Chinese characters, while Korean women used the new Hangul alphabet in writing Korean.

King Sejong's alphabet for writing Korean sounds was uniquely innovative. The letters not only stood for particular vowels, consonants, or syllables but also were shaped to suggest the position of mouth, teeth, and tongue in pronouncing the sounds. In addition, the letters were divided into Yin and Yang types and made to represent the five elements: air, earth, fire, water, and metal. The richness of the invention, however, made other things more difficult. The Hangul script carried layers of meaning that hindered its use as a tool for abstraction in the way the European alphabets could be used to alphabetize. Very much like the original idea of the length of a king's "foot," until measurements could be completely divorced from their natural associations, scientific abstraction was encumbered.

## Imitators and Innovators

We think of imitators as the opposite of innovators, but they are not. Those who see no reason to imitate have no reason to change. Large landed empires like China and the Muslim states of central Asia were guided by people who had a greater stake in preservation. Innovation in China often came inadvertently or in response to a particular crisis. Confucianism encouraged good works, social improvements, and good government, and the Chinese state and bureaucracy could put enormous resources behind a policy or project. The private sector in China was huge because China was huge, but the government was the force behind the building of canals and cities and the adoption of new military and industrial technologies. If the social conscience of Confucianism was an advantage, the elitism of the scholar administrators was not. Mind work and manual labor marked two different worlds in China as they had in most societies, and the workers and thinkers had no place or inclination to talk to each other. New tools and new ideas rarely struck a chord much less a chorus.

In the Dar al-Islam, innovation was more a product of private initiative, mercantile trade, and individual leadership. Despite their prestige, however, the Muslim merchant class was as subject to higher authority as the Chinese. Only the authority was different: clerical and military rather than political and bureaucratic. In fact, in neither China nor the Islamic world was there an independent *class* of merchants. In both societies, business combinations were made up of families and relations whose loyalties lay with the lineage or clan.

Religious conservatism increasingly undermined innovation in the Islamic world after 1000. Chinese block printing was widely condemned by Muslim clerics who believed that books should be produced by hand, the way the Quran had been copied for centuries. The technical advantage that block printing had in duplicating images made it even more suspicious from the standpoint of those who believed that the Quran forbade visual replication.

European Christians had no such religious obstacles to printing, but they were slow to see its benefits. In fact, they were slow to recognize its existence. Block-printed seals on messages from the Ilkanid rulers of Iran to the kings of England and France seem to have gone unnoticed by their European recipients; although Marco Polo was struck by the paper money of China, he seems to have failed to notice the significance of its printing. Imitation is not automatic. One's culture prepares one to see and understand.

And cultures change. Muslim science was studied in Europe until the sixteenth century, but once Europeans translated the Greek and Arabic texts, the balance shifted decisively. By the sixteenth century, European artists were drawing precise diagrams of human anatomy taken from dissected cadavers. Islam forbade dissections of human cadavers or pigs. Islamic medical students studied vague and inaccurate depictions of the human body, while students at Bologna were cutting them open.

In Europe sometime after 1200, innovation became systematized. A range of institutions paved the way. Europeans learned to work together in civic and other nonfamilial groups. Investment corporations, merchant companies, and banks often started as family ventures, as they were commonly elsewhere, but the experience of participation in other corporate groups—civic, guild, university, and church—spilled over into business, increasing their scale and flexibility.

In Europe, merchants and bankers could not be controlled or fleeced as easily as they could by an emperor or sultan. In autonomous cities, they became a self-governing class, used to operating independently and communally to secure their fortunes and opportunities. They loaned money to princes and kings and supplied their armies with armaments and uniforms. They were indispensable. Some large merchant banks, such as the Medici in Florence and the Fuggers in Germany, were more powerful than princes, who were a dime a dozen in the patchwork quilt of competing European states. In Europe, a class of capitalists created society in their own image. A recent world history puts it well:

> Since moneyed men were continually on the lookout for anything that might turn a profit, a self-sustaining process of economic, social, and technological change gathered headway wherever political conditions allowed it the freedom to operate. Time and again, local interests and old fashioned ways of doing things were displaced by politically protected economic innovators, who saw a chance at monetary profit by introducing something new. This

situation still persists today, having transformed European society, and then infected the whole wide world, thus marking modern times off from earlier, more stable forms of society.[43]

But we have seen that merchants were not the only innovators in Europe. Poets, painters, composers, scientists, and mechanics were cultural innovators as much as preservers. The city was as much the crucible of the new order as was the market. And the yeast of change was not only greed and private profit. It was also a product of universalism and civic identity, individuality and community, and reason and faith.

Finally, as we have seen over and over again, to invent something is not to own it. Often the borrowers are able to do more with an invention than its creators. While the seedlings of the modern age dug their roots in different soils and climes, their fruits are as transferable as the apples of Kazakhstan or the peaches of Samarkand.

## Conclusion:
## The Virtues of Variety

"Social and political institutions of Europe," the historian Arnold Pacey says in a particularly felicitous phrase, "favored 'the multiplication of points of creativity' in the many small states in which the continent was divided."[44] We might generalize further and argue that cities had always favored "the multiplication of points of creativity," that the intensity of city life led to more frequent interchange, imitation, and innovation than was possible on pasture or farm. This explains the enormous inventiveness of the first cities, especially the city-states of the ancient world.

Not only did the political geography of European rivers and mountains lead to numerous small states, able to compete with each other for the most talented or ambitious, but many of those states were city-states. They were states led from the city, not the county seats of aristocratic families or ancient lineages. Their leaders were people who prized innovation, who believed that advantage was everything, and who recognized that personal, social, and civic advantage came from doing something new and different and better.

Cities activated the inventions of Chinese, Islamic, and even Mongol civilizations as well. The cities of China and the Islamic world played a major role in shaping Chinese and Islamic civilizations. Together as links of a network, these civilizations became something much more. Each new addition to the network not only added a different way of thinking or doing but also changed the ways of all. The belated addition of European cities to the network of China, the Mongols, and Islam multiplied already numerous points of creativity.

Ibn Battuta never got to Christian Europe.[45] He wrote and retired in the great city of Fez in what is today Morocco. But he began his travels with the most important pilgrimage a Muslim could make: the hajj to the holy city of Mecca. For the rest of his life, he traveled from one city to another. The full title of his account, called the *Rihla*, was *A Gift to the Observers concerning the Curiosities of the Cities and the Marvels Encountered in Travels*. Like a modern American who goes not to Europe but to London, Paris, Rome, and Venice, Ibn Battuta traveled to the great cities of his world: to Mecca, Medina, Cairo, Alexandria, Jerusalem, Damascus, Baghdad, Basra, Isfahan, Kabul, Samarkand, Bukhara, Constantinople, Kilwa, Mogadishu, Aden, Cambay, Calicut, Delhi, Chittagong, Canton, Quanzhou (Zaiton), Timbuktu,

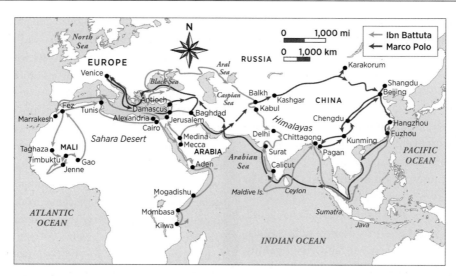

Map 5.4   The routes of two of the great travelers of the late thirteenth and early fourteenth centuries.

and many more. The Afro-Eurasian network was in fact a brilliant chain of cities, each a point of creativity that, like a string of lights on a tree, turned into something more magical and marvelous.

## Suggested Readings

Abu-Lughod Janet L. *Before European Hegemony: The World System 1250–1350.* New York: Oxford University Press, 1989. Challenging but important and influential.

Dunn, Ross E. *The Adventures of Ibn Battuta: A Muslim Traveler of the Fourteenth Century.* Berkeley: University of California Press, 1990. A fine history of the great traveler's experiences. Quite accessible.

Elvin, Mark. *The Pattern of the Chinese Past.* Stanford, CA: Stanford University Press, 1973. Accessible entry to an important debate.

Gernet, Jacques. *Daily Life in China on the Eve of the Mongol Invasion 1250–1276.* Translated by H. M. Wright. Stanford, CA: Stanford University Press, 1962. Very readable and evocative study of China in the period of Marco Polo and the Mongols.

Lopez, Robert S. *The Commercial Revolution of the Middle Ages, 960–1350.* Cambridge: Cambridge University Press, 1976. Slightly dated standard introduction to an important topic.

McClellan, James E., III and Harold Dorn, *Science and Technology in World History.* Baltimore: Johns Hopkins University Press, 1999. Thoughtful introduction to the subject.

Miyazaki, Ichisada. *China's Examination Hell: The Civil Service Examinations of Imperial China.* Translated by Conrad Schirokauer. New Haven, CT: Yale University Press, 1981. Fascinating readable study by a leading scholar of China.

## Notes

1. See Ross E. Dunn, *The Adventures of Ibn Battuta: A Muslim Traveler of the Fourteenth Century* (Berkeley: University of California Press, 1990).

2. Roger S. Keyes, *Ehon: The Artist and the Book in Japan* (Seattle: University of Washington Press and the New York Public Library, 2006).

3. Robert Hartwell, "Markets, Technology and the Structure of Enterprise in the Development of the Eleventh-Century Chinese Iron and Steel Industry," *Journal of Economic History* 26 (1966): 34.

4. Robert Hartwell, "A Cycle of Economic Change in Imperial China: Coal and Iron in Northeast China, 750–1350," *Journal of the Economic and Social History of the Orient* 10, no. 1 (1967): 144.

5. Hartwell, "A Cycle of Economic Change in Imperial China," 153. Hartwell adds that the population of Kaifeng was no more than 100,000 as late as 1933. The estimate as of 2011 was almost 5 million.

6. Kenneth Pomeranz, *The Great Divergence: China, Europe, and the Making of the Modern World Economy* (Princeton, NJ: Princeton University Press, 2000), 64.

7. See Pomeranz, *The Great Divergence*, 65–67.

8. Lynn White Jr., "Tibet, India, and Malaya as Sources of Western Medieval Technology," *American Historical Review* 65 (1960): 515–26. See also his *Medieval Technology and Social Change* (New York: Oxford University Press, 1966), 85–116.

9. James E. McClellan III and Harold Dorn, *Science and Technology in World History* (Baltimore: Johns Hopkins University Press, 1999), 123.

10. Jacques Gernet, *Daily Life in China on the Eve of the Mongol Invasion 1250–1276*, trans. H. M. Wright (Stanford, CA: Stanford University Press, 1962), 81.

11. Hartwell, "A Cycle of Economic Change in Imperial China," 150–51.

12. The idea of a thirteenth-century world system is now generally accepted by world historians. The idea was first developed, however, by Janet L. Abu-Lughod in *Before European Hegemony: The World System 1250–1350* (New York: Oxford University Press, 1989).

13. This apt phrase is that of Janet Abu-Lughod, *Before European Hegemony*, 155.

14. "First Day" [041]. See http://www.stg .brown.edu/projects/decameron/engDecShow Text.php?myID=d01intro&expand=day01.

15. Marshall G. S. Hodgson, *The Venture of Islam*, vol. 2 (Chicago: University of Chicago Press, 1974), 53.

16. On this combination of military despotism and anarchy (as on so many other topics) see Hodgson, *The Venture of Islam*, 131–32.

17. People from the Caucasus Mountains, between the Black Sea and the Caspian Sea in modern southwestern Russia.

18. See especially S. A. Goitein, *A Mediterranean Society: The Jewish Communities of the Arab World as Portrayed in the Documents of the Cairo Geniza*, 6 vols. (Berkeley: University of California Press, 1967).

19. Goitein, *A Mediterranean Society*, vol. 1, *Economic Foundations*, viii.

20. Goitein, *A Mediterranean Society*, vol. 1, *Economic Foundations*, 66.

21. Ibn Battuta, *Travels in Asia and Africa 1325–1354*, trans. and ed. H. A. R. Gibb (London: Broadway House, 1929), 50.

22. Michael Dols, *The Black Death in the Middle East* (Princeton, NJ: Princeton University Press, 1977), 69.

23. Dols, *The Black Death in the Middle East*, 67.

24. Ibn Battuta, *Travels in Asia and Africa 1325–1354*. See http://www.fordham.edu/halsall/ source/1354-ibnbattuta.html.

25. Roderick McIntosh, *The Peoples of the Middle Niger* (Oxford: Oxford University Press, 1998), chap. 10.

26. *Furuzanfar #630*, in A. J. Arberry, ed., *Persian Poems* (New York: Everyman's Library, 1972).

27. See Michael McCormick, *Origins of the European Economy: Communications and Commerce A.D. 300–900* (Cambridge: Cambridge University Press, 2001).

28. McCormick, *Origins of the European Economy*, 237.

29. Robert S. Lopez, *The Commercial Revolution of the Middle Ages, 960–1350* (Cambridge: Cambridge University Press, 1976), 43.

30. Warming returned from about 1450 to 1550, followed by a dramatic "little ice age" from 1560 to 1890. Since then, global warming has returned with the addition of human causes.

31. Colin McEvedy and Richard Jones, *Atlas of World Population History* (Harmondsworth: Penguin, 1978), 28.

32. David Levine, *At the Dawn of Modernity: Biology, Culture, and Material Life in Europe after the Year 1000* (Berkeley: University of California Press, 2001), 132. Estimates on Paris and London vary between 3,000 and 25,000. At the usual ratio of four inhabitants to a house, the population of Cordoba would have been over a million.

33. Toby E. Huff, *The Rise of Early Modern Science: Islam, China, and the West*, 2nd ed. (Cambridge: Cambridge University Press, 2003), 124. Huff cites other presentations of this idea, but this chapter follows Huff's linking of law and science.

34. Huff, *The Rise of Early Modern Science*, 186–87.

35. Edward Grant, *Physical Science in the Middle Ages* (Cambridge: Cambridge University Press, 1977), 21.

36. Alfred W. Crosby, *The Measure of Reality* (Cambridge University Press, 1997), 53.

37. Crosby, *The Measure of Reality*, 84.

38. Francesco Petrarch, Seniles V-III, "On the Latin Language and Literature" and "To Boccaccio," in *The First Modern Scholar and Man of Letters*, trans. James Harvey Robinson (New York: G. P. Putnam, 1898). Available at http://petrarch.petersadlon.com/read_letters.html?s=pet07.html.

39. Compare, for instance, the opening lines in the original "Middle English" with modern English: "Whan that Aprill, with his shoures soote. The droghte of March hath perced to the roote" and "When in April the sweet showers fall That pierce March's drought to the root." See http://www.librarius.com/canttran/gptrfs.htm.

40. See http://www.mmtaylor.net/Literacy_Book/DOCS/pt2.html.

41. Kim Won-Young, *Early Moveable Type in Korea* (Seoul: National Museum of Korea, 1954), quoted in Lucien Febvre and Henri-Jean Martin, *The Coming of the Book: The Impact of Printing, 1450–1800* (London: Verso, 1984), 76.

42. Pokee Sohn, "King Sejong's Innovations in Printing," in *King Sejong the Great: The Light of 15th Century Korea*, ed. Young-Key Kim-Renaud (Washington, DC: International Circle of Korean Linguistics, George Washington University, 1992), 55.

43. J. R. McNeill and William H. McNeill, *The Human Web: A Bird's-Eye View of World History* (New York: Norton, 2003), 14.

44. Arnold Pacey, *Technology in World Civilization* (Cambridge, MA: MIT Press, 1990), 44–45.

45. He did travel to the Muslim cities of Malaga and Granada in Spain and Cagliari in Sardinia.

# 6

## Parallel Worlds of Inner Africa, the Americas, and Oceania
### BEFORE 1450

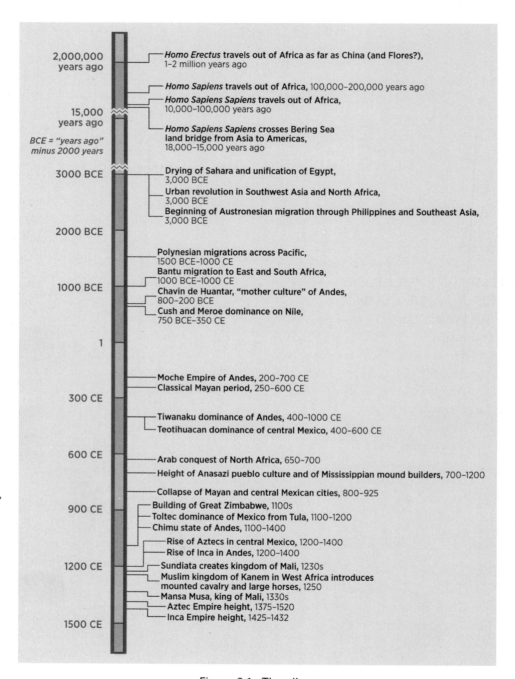

Figure 6.1  Time line.

WHILE THE Afro-Eurasian world came together as a single system between the classical age 2,000 years ago and the rise of the West 500 years ago, other parts of the world carried out their own traditions, established their own networks of interaction, and experienced their own arcs of change. We turn in this chapter to these "parallel worlds" in inner Africa, the Americas, and the Pacific Ocean because their stories are as compelling as they are separate. Indeed, their very separateness gives us a greatly expanded field of evidence and example to help us understand the human condition and historical change. To focus only on the dominant trend is very much like telling only the history of the victors. In either case, we end with a lesser sense of who we are and an even lesser sense of who we could be.

## The World of Inner Africa

"Outer" Africa—the Nile, the Red Sea and Indian Ocean ports, North Africa along the Mediterranean, and the kingdoms of West Africa—was an intrinsic part of the Afro-Eurasian world of the first millennium CE. The Nile valley was a creator of that world. The Red Sea and Mediterranean were early participants. By 1000 CE, a single zone of communication extended across the western Sahara as well, to the border of tropical rain forests just north of the equator.

Inner Africa was the interior African world that was not swept up into the Afro-Eurasian network before 1450. It constituted a large part of the African continent below the Sahara Desert. It includes all of Africa south of the equator, all of the equatorial rain forests, and the dry lands and savanna that pushed into the Sahara in central Africa.

### Geography, Race, and Language

Inner Africa had not been integrated into the Afro-Eurasian network because it was remote from the rest of Eurasia. In addition to the almost 1,000-mile width of the Sahara Desert, the rivers of Africa made contact difficult. The rivers of West Africa like the Niger and Congo flowed from uplands across cataracts and waterfalls to the Atlantic Ocean, making it difficult for outsiders to enter. In addition, the maritime path from the northern Atlantic was blocked by prevailing currents that inhibited easy access. From Asia, East Africa was easier to reach across the Red Sea and Indian Ocean. Contacts between the Arab world and the Swahili cities of the East African coast were extensive as far south as modern Mozambique.

Inner Africa was the larger part of a huge continent. The perpendicular grid of popular Mercator world maps, which magnify polar areas and reduce areas near the equator, makes it look as if Africa is about the size of Greenland. In fact, Africa is 15 times larger: 12 million square miles, compared to Greenland's total area of 840,000 square miles. By comparison, all of Eurasia amounts to 21 million square miles. Africa is larger than China, India, the continental United States, and the entire continent of Australia combined.

Africa is also far more diverse than most people imagine. Geographically, Africa contains some of the wettest and driest places on earth, snowcapped mountains, dense rain forests, and open fields as well as deserts. Biologically, Africans are more diverse than the people of any other continent. This physical diversity (measured by DNA) stems from the long period of human development in Africa before mankind populated the rest of the planet. When Europeans began classifying humans into "races," they failed to recognize this diversity. In the interest of seeing the African as dark skinned or black, they failed to recognize that they were creating a particular stereotype—based mainly on people who came from West Africa. Consequently, they missed the differences in appearance of not only the Berbers and Arabs of North Africa but also the taller people of the Nile valley, the shorter people of the Congo rain forest, and the lighter-complexioned people of the southern African desert. Europeans also failed to recognize the social and cultural diversity of Africans. They failed to recognize that even inner Africa contained empires, various kinds of states, village-based societies (without states), cities, and pastoral and agricultural societies as well as hunter-gatherers.

Today, biologists and anthropologists are not inclined to use the word *race* in classifying peoples, in part because of the tortured history of the term but also because of its lack of precision in a world shaped more by culture than biology and by intermixing more than isolation. Rather, we might see the mixtures of African peoples coming from regions of relative separation, speaking different languages, and practicing different cultures. By that measure, we might distinguish five major groups of African language and culture systems. These would be the Afro-Asian peoples of the north (including ancient Egyptians, Berbers, and, more recently, Arabs), the Nilotic-Sudanic peoples (mainly herders, often tall and thin in stature) from the Nile valley, the Niger-Congo peoples of West Africa (including speakers of the Bantu languages), the Pygmy peoples of Central Africa, and the Khoisan people in the Kalahari Desert.

## The World's Three Transformations in Africa

*Humans, Farmers, and States.* In the beginning, of course, we were all Africans. The first transformation began when some of our ancestors started moving out of Africa about a million years ago. The next transformation occurred with the development of agriculture, but since Africans were among the first to plant and domesticate crops, the only divergence between Africa and the rest of Afro-Eurasia was in the particular crops that were domesticated. The third global transformation centered on the revolution in social organization that led to cities and states. The North African Egyptian state was one of the leaders in that revolution. Here, too, African Egyptians developed their own civilization, one that they shared with neighbors to the south.

*The Nile Connection.* During the Egyptian period, contact between northern and central Africa continued as state societies were created up the Nile in Kush, Meroe, and Nubia (in what is today Sudan). About 750 BCE, a Kushite king conquered Egypt and established a dynasty that ruled the two kingdoms for 100 years. From about 590 BCE to 350 CE, the successor state of Meroe remained independent of Egypt and its various occupiers (Persian, Greek, and Roman), and cultivated a way of life that included a centralized state, pyramids, irrigation, hieroglyphic writing, and iron smelting. They were finally conquered not by the Romans but by the Christian Axumite kingdom of Ethiopia. After Meroe, Nubian kings ruled the upper Nile. They converted to the Coptic Christianity of Egypt, reestablishing close contact with Egypt between 350 and 700 CE. The patriarch in Alexandria appointed bishops and trained clergy, and Nubians studied the Coptic rite, developed an alphabetical script based on Coptic Greek and old Meroitic, and traveled back and forth frequently. Nubian inscriptions indicate knowledge of Greek as late as the twelfth century.

The flow between northern and central Africa that had continued for millennia was interrupted by two factors, one ephemeral and the other climatic. The ephemeral interruption was the Arab conquest of Egypt around 700. Sudan broke into the Arabic and Muslim north and a largely Christian south. But the Nile remained the main link between northern and central Africa because a more fundamental barrier had arisen between the Mediterranean and central Africa since the time of the first pharaohs: the Sahara Desert.

*The Saharan Separation.* The Sahara Desert is a formidable barrier today. A modern jet takes several hours to fly the more than 1,000 miles from north to south, and all you can see is sand. On the ground, the shifting hills of sand and rock outcroppings are both more treacherous and more interesting. Nothing, however, is more striking to the modern archaeologist than the appearance, hundreds of miles from the nearest water hole, of vivid and colorful rock paintings of flowers, birds, herds of antelope, cattle grazing, and humans farming and hunting. These paintings are evidence that the Sahara was at one time a garden of life, a lush environment crowded with animals and people. On the ground, geologists can see evidence that almost 10,000 years ago Lake Chad, on the southwestern border of the Sahara, was 25 times its current size.

We now realize that the Sahara has gone through alternating wet and dry stages over hundreds of thousands of years. The most recent wet period was at the end of the last glacial period and lasted from about 11,000 years ago until 5,000 years ago. The current desert dates from about 3000 BCE, the beginning of the Egyptian Old Kingdom. Egyptian culture may be descended from these Neolithic rock painters of the Sahara in some ways: there is evidence, for instance, of mummification and cattle burial in the Sahara. But the larger point about the history of Africa is that a huge

barrier appeared between the Mediterranean and the rest of Africa, just at the moment that the world was embarking on the great Bronze Age transformation. Thus, while *only* Africans participated in the first transformation into humans and many Africans, north and south, participated in the second transformation into plant and animal domestication, an enormous barrier separated the participants in the third transformation from the rest of Africa.

The history of Sudan shows that the separation was by no means complete. But the Nile River was the only route that ran from the north to the African interior. When the Arabs conquered Egypt, that connection was interrupted. Initially, the Arabs directed their attention and trade north to Syria and Iraq rather than west across the Red Sea, but eventually Arab, Indian, and even Chinese ships added the Swahili ports of East Africa to their itineraries. Still, these contacts were limited to the coast. Africans controlled the internal trade. Similarly, in West Africa, trans-Saharan trade routes integrated the cities of the Kingdom of Mali into the Dar al-Islam, but much of the hugeness of Africa was invisible to the travelers, sheiks, and salt sellers, exhausted after weeks on a camel in driving sand, having finally reached their destination near the Niger at Jenne or Timbuktu.

## The Bantu Migrations

There is a simple principle for figuring where something came from. The original site of something always has the greatest variety. Thus, Africa has the greatest variety of humans; Morocco has a greater variety of Arabs than Jenne or Timbuktu. In the same way, Niger-Congo languages and specifically the subgroup of Bantu languages are spoken over much of Africa, but they are densely

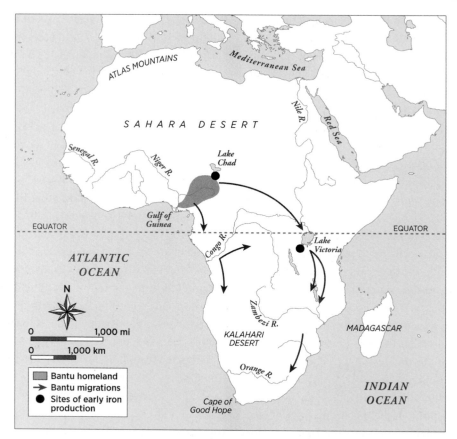

Map 6.1    From 2000 BCE to 1000 CE, Bantu-speaking peoples moved out of the grasslands of Cameroon west and south to eventually become the dominant linguistic and ethnic group in central and southern Africa. Their expansion was aided by their agriculture (in relation to forest foragers), skill with canoes, and, after 1000 BCE, their ability to make iron tools and weapons.

concentrated in the high grasslands of Cameroon. You can travel today in Cameroon a few miles from one village to the next and hear people speaking a different Bantu language. There are, in fact, more than 200 languages spoken in the Cameroon grasslands, an area smaller than the state of New Jersey. This fact shows us that the Bantu languages spoken throughout Africa south of the Sahara originated there.

*Words, Seeds, and Iron.* About 3,000 years ago, Bantu-speaking people from this area began a series of migrations that spread their descendants into East Africa and south through much of the rest of the continent by about 1000 CE. With their language, they brought their culture and tools. They brought agriculture—their knack for raising yams and palm oil trees, guinea hens, and goats. From people in central Africa, they picked up the ability to smelt iron in a furnace with bellows. From the Nilotic-Sudanic people, they borrowed the ability to raise sheep, pigs, and cattle that had been bred to survive the tsetse fly of the tropics. Their diet also expanded as they picked up the cultivation of African grains like millet and sorghum. On the east coast of Africa, they added bananas and chickens brought from Indonesia. Some of their descendants became the Swahili merchants of East African cities. Others moved into the rain forests and grasslands of southern Africa. In the mountains and tropical rain forests of central Africa, they met the Batwa (or Twa) people (sometimes called pygmies because of their small stature), who were hunter-gatherers. They exchanged their agricultural products and tools (first polished stone and then iron) for the forest products of the Batwa, especially honey, ivory, and wild animal skins. Farther south, in what is today the Kalahari Desert, they encountered the Khoisan people, who were herders and hunter-gatherers; these lighter-complexioned people spoke a "click language," so called because of its use of different dental sounds.

As Bantu speakers encountered hunting-gathering peoples in places like the Congo rain forest and the Kalahari, different things happened. In some cases, the agricultural Bantu took over the best lands, pushing the hunting-gathering people into more remote areas. The original crops of the grasslands did not grow in the rain forest, but bananas turned out to be extravagantly successful in the rain forest (as was the brewing of banana beer). In some cases, the two groups mixed together, although usually at the cost of the traditions and culture of the hunter-gatherers, who ultimately adopted the Bantu language and culture. Still, in some cases, the forest dwellers were able to use their commercial importance to achieve a certain degree of leverage in trading with the Bantu while keeping to their traditional ways.

*A Common Culture?* The spread of Bantu peoples provided a broadly common cultural background for much of inner Africa. In addition to the Bantu language family, this common culture included a set of domesticated crops and animals, iron metallurgy, and a tendency to figure inheritance from the mother but give maternally connected men important roles in councils of elders and kingship. Bantu religious beliefs generally accepted a supreme being, but most religious practices were devoted to ancestors and nature spirits. Masks were used in religious rituals, and drumming and dance were central in festive and solemn rituals.

It would be a mistake, however, to see Bantu culture as changeless. As new generations and branches of Bantu-speaking peoples migrated east and south, they adopted and added new cultural characteristics, such as a variety of round conical and rectangular housing, descent through the male as well as the female line, and a wide range of political and social institutions.

## Empires, States, and Stateless Societies

Inner Africa contained states as well as village or lineage-based societies, but clearly states were larger and more pronounced in the areas of outer Africa that were part of the Afro-Eurasian network. Why, then, were cities, states, and empires concentrated in some areas, like the Nile, and not in others areas, like central and southern Africa?

*Politics, Population, and Climate.* The long-term drying of the climate may contain part of the answer. Recent studies of ice cores from the top of Africa's largest mountain, Kilimanjaro, confirm that the cycle of drying that began about 5,300 years ago and created the Sahara extended throughout the continent (and probably into the Middle East and western Asia).[1]

Figure 6.2 This bronze plaque shows a king of Benin flanked by warriors and attendants. *Art Resource, NY. The Metropolitan Museum of Art, New York, NY, USA.*

Reductions in rainfall may have had opposite effects in northern and central Africa, increasing population centers in the north and reducing density in the south. In the north, the drying of the Sahara pushed agriculturalists and herders into the Nile valley (as well as north and south), forcing more people to contend with scarce resources. Population concentration likely resulted in state formation. Those who already enjoyed status increased their dominance in chiefdoms, kingdoms, and state societies. Kings and leading social classes formed states and systems of law to ensure their political dominance and economic expropriation.

*Lots of Land.* The impact of climatic drying in central tropical Africa was to reduce the rain forests and increase the grasslands. This was the background of the expansion of Bantu agriculturalists. Climate desiccation opened sparsely populated forests areas into new arable grasslands, attracting just the sorts of people who were looking to expand their agricultural way of life. Bantu farmers and herders "had so much more country into which they could expand," the historian Christopher Ehret points out. As West African peoples spread out

> across the immense reaches of East and southeast Africa, their settlement densities would have been very low indeed, much lower than in the western Great Lakes region from which their expansions stemmed. . . . Not until later centuries, by which time their population densities would have considerably increased, did larger chiefdoms and eventually, [after 1000] kingdoms evolve in such places.[2]

## West Africa

Virtually every political structure that emerged in inner Africa could be found in the areas of West Africa that grew in the wake of the great drying up of the Sahara after 3000 BCE. From about 300 CE to 1000 CE, West Africa enjoyed substantial rainfall, and the population grew considerably. The densest area was probably the high grasslands of Cameroon, which provided an especially healthy climate since it was above the altitude at which mosquitoes carrying malaria could flourish.

*Stateless Societies.* Nevertheless, even in these highly populated areas, West Africans (Bantu speakers and others) favored small communities without states or hierarchies. Typically, a group of 5 to 15 villages formed a *kafu*, a sort of confederation with a big man or chief. This preference for autonomy and the great availability of unoccupied lands contributed to make the Bantu and other West Africans such great migrants and colonists. A tradition whereby the eldest son inherited the family land also encouraged other sons to clear their own land from the nearby woodlands or forest. In addition, the West African custom of polygyny created families in which the men with the most land had the most wives and the most sons, all of whom had to fend for themselves.

Sometimes, a particularly ambitious chief would combine a cluster of *kafus* and create a state, declaring himself king. The great West African state of the thirteenth to fifteenth centuries, Mali, was founded this way, according to the great epic of Sundiata Keita. "From being village chiefs, the Keitas have become tribal chiefs and then kings," the poet of *Sundiata* recalled.[3] The epic also underlines the link between agricultural colonization and kingship: "Cut the trees, turn the forests into fields, for then only will you become a true king."

*Kingdoms for Horses.* We have noticed in previous chapters the close connection between state formation and horses. What role did horses play in West African state formation? We know through Saharan paintings that small horses were in North Africa before the camel was domesticated about the fourth century CE. They likely came south as well as north before the first millennium. *The Epic of Sundiata* tells us that Sundiata forged a kingdom in the 1230s with an army of free archers and cavalry forces. But the cavalries of the thirteenth century rode ponies without saddles or stirrups. By the 1330s, the time of Mansa Musa, Mali employed the heavy cavalry of Mamluk Egypt and the Islamic world. Horses were difficult to breed near the equator, and their life expectancies were shortened by tropical diseases, but these new large imported horses changed the balance between stateless peoples and states.

Equipped with saddles and stirrups, they were a formative force against standing bowmen. Introduced by the Muslim kingdom of Kanem about 1250, the combination of large horses and Islam created one kingdom after another in sub-Saharan West Africa. But the large horses had to be imported. An armed heavy cavalry was expensive, requiring heavy expropriation of settled farming populations. Since farmers could easily migrate to new lands, cavalries turned to raiding and capturing them, making them slaves and forcing them to farm for the king or his cavalry aristocracy.

The kingdoms of West Africa between 1250 and 1450 (Kanem, Bornu, Mali, and Songhai) were based on the simultaneous growth of cavalry and slaves. Slaves paid for horses, and cavalries could capture the slaves. By 1450, a large warhorse cost between 9 and 14 slaves. It is estimated that 4,000 to 7,000 slaves per year were taken up the trans-Sahara routes (including that from Darfur in East

Africa) to be exchanged for horses. Even if many died during the crossing, the value of each survivor increased five to eight times from below the Sahara to the Mediterranean coast.[4]

Stateless communities still thrived where horses could not go: in the tropical rain forests and beyond—along the coasts of West Africa. Lineage societies functioned with the aid of various strategies to maintain their autonomy: clan loyalties, councils of elders, initiation "secret societies," "age sets" of male contemporaries, systems of mediation by outsiders, ritualized war games to resolve conflicts, and communal "palaver" discussions to mediate internal disputes. Cities and ministates added more complex social institutions in places like Benin. Some were commercial centers, others the center of rituals or artistic expression. The city of Ife, on the forest border, produced glass beads, terracotta, and brass statues. Similar brass sculptures were later produced by court metalworkers in the kingdom of Benin.

## East and South Africa

Most political institutions in West Africa could also be found in East and South Africa. There were empires, kingdoms, city-states, and stateless societies. But geography and the timing of major population movements like the Bantu migration accounted for certain differences.

*Cattle and Colonization.* Perhaps the most important difference was the greater role of herders in East Africa. Bantu agriculturalists added animals to their mixed economy in central and East Africa. Cattle were introduced into East Africa by the more indigenous Nilotic-Sudanic speakers. Cattle herders like the Fulani people were common in West Africa too, but they generally remained north of the more tropical areas of agriculturalists. By

contrast, the land of East Africa is slashed by dramatic north–south rifts of mountains and deep valleys, enabling herders to introduce cattle much farther south on high plains overlooking the valleys of agriculturalists.

As a consequence, East African economies were more frequently pastoral and mixed and rarely (as was the case in West Africa) purely agricultural. In tropical regions of East Africa, the mix of herding and farming peoples in lands formerly occupied by hunter-gatherers created sharply different, often antagonistic economies side by side. Sometimes this caste-like separation had dramatic consequences, as in Rwanda and Burundi, where Tutsi herders, Hutu agriculturalists, and Twa hunter-gatherers were incorporated into single states.

In southern Africa, cattle raising took precedence over farming. Herders can form states, but their need for extensive pastureland generally means lower population densities and fewer villages or cities. In southern Africa, cattle raising tended to form chiefdoms rather than states or stateless societies. The household was the principal unit. Households gathered their round dwellings around an enclosed central cattle pen, a design less likely to lead to towns and cities than the West African shape of rectangular houses on grids of streets. These chiefdoms did sometimes coalesce into states, however, often with central cities studded with royal palaces.

*Great Zimbabwe.* The largest of these states in southern Africa between 1000 and 1450 was Great Zimbabwe, which transformed itself from a local chiefdom in the twelfth century to the leading power of southern Africa in the fourteenth. Even today, the ruins of Great Zimbabwe are impressive. The city dominates various levels of pasture from a high plateau. Building materials were stone blocks tightly placed together without mortar. The city, which contains the large royal palace, is surrounded by a huge wall that had an iron gate. In its heyday, the city probably numbered 15,000 to 18,000 people, many living inside the high walls:

> It was a city closely integrated with its surrounding countryside. Narrow pathways, dusty in the dry season and muddy in the wet, would have led in intricate ways among the crowded houses. Wandering dogs nobody much cared for, chickens scavenging in the walkways between the houses, and goats tethered at doorways would have been among the sights and background noisemakers of city life. In the later afternoon, hundreds of cooking fires would have added to the mélange of strong smells that filled the air and, if the air was still, would have created something much like smog.[5]

The fortunes of Great Zimbabwe were built on more than cattle raising and agriculture. Its chiefs learned to control and tax trade just as they had traditionally demanded cattle. First ivory and beads but eventually gold from farther up the Limpopo River valley made Great Zimbabwe the largest city of southern Africa and an empire of the Shona people. Zimbabwe traded the gold farther north, ultimately to the city of Kilwa and the Swahili cities on the coast of the Indian Ocean, where inner Africa connected to the Afro-Eurasian network.

### Inner Africa and the World

During the first millions of years of our species, inner Africa was the world. Only in the past few thousand years did inner Africa take an independent but parallel path, and in the past few hundred years our paths have merged again. Yet, even as inner Africa followed a course separate from that of Afro-Eurasia, its fortunes were connected to developments in the larger world. The Bantu migration began in an area of West Africa that had grown steeply after the desiccation of the Sahara. West Africans later connected with the people north of the Sahara who introduced domesticated camels and horses and brought salt and Mediterranean products across the desert. Later still, West Africa met bearers of the Islamic faith and founded states and empires rich in horses and gold. But by then, Bantu-speaking peoples had colonized much of the rest of Africa, bringing their crops and iron east and south. In the process, they encountered and incorporated other peoples: cattle herders of the central sub-Saharan region, farmers of Malayan and Indonesian crops like bananas and yams in East Africa, and city peoples along the East African coast who traded in the Arabian Sea and Indian Ocean.

Still, the Bantu travelers, the hunter-gatherers of tropical rain forests, and the cattle herders of South Africa created their own networks, some independent and others attached to those of the larger world. They created their own systems of social and political organization, all without writing[6] and most without the apparatus of state administration and control. The village-based societies, hunter-gatherers, and pastoral peoples of inner Africa invented a range of voluntary, lineage- and family-based, age- and gender-related institutions that offered an alternative model to the state-based societies that were increasingly shaping the world—even in outer Africa.

## The World of the Americas

The variety of the Americas before 1450 was almost as great as the variety of Africa. As in Africa, there were hunter-gatherers, part-time and full-time agriculturalists, villages, cities, states, and empires. The great empires are best known; we have already discussed some of them in the chapter on city and state formation.

## States and Empires of Middle America

The great empires of the early 1400s were the Aztec Empire of central Mexico and the Inca Empire of Peru. But these were relatively recent arrivals at locations in which previous states and empires had ruled for centuries.

*Before the Aztecs.* The Aztecs came down from northern Mexico only about a century earlier to the large lake on the high central Mexican plateau. Viewed as crude newcomers, they established themselves as successors to the Toltecs, who, in turn, claimed descent from the classical rulers of nearby Teotihuacan. From 400 to 600, Teotihuacan had dominated central Mexico politically and culturally. Its city by the same name was not only the largest in the Americas but also one of the largest cities in the world at the time, numbering possibly 200,000 inhabitants. The Teotihuacanos passed on a tradition of pyramid building that stretched back to the first Mexican states, the Zapotecs and the Olmecs.

At the time of Teotihuacan, the Mayan culture encompassed a huge area that stretched from the northern Yucatan Peninsula of eastern Mexico deep into Central America. The Mayans had no single city approaching the population of Teotihuacan, but they had many cities, some with as many as tens of thousands of inhabitants. The remains of Mayan cities like Tikal, Uxmal, Palenque, and Chichen Itza suggest a layout like the cities of central Mexico. They have central open spaces flanked by pyramids and other public buildings. But the Mayan cities do not seem to extend beyond such ceremonial centers. Most Mayan cities

were carved out of dense jungle, which has since returned to strangle the ruins, so it is difficult, without further archaeological work, to determine what may lie under the surrounding jungle. Central Mexican cities like Teotihuacan and the Zapotec's Monte Alban, by contrast, lie in open areas, and the excavated central plazas and pyramids are surrounded by mounds that are beginning to reveal the many homes of city inhabitants. The absence of extensive residential areas around Mayan cities leads to the conclusion that they were, at least in their early stages, purely ceremonial: places for rulers and priests, an idea that also fits what we know about Mayan culture.

*Classical Mayan.* Mayan writing was a colorful combination of pictures and syllable symbols that has only recently been deciphered. It reveals a culture in which priests played a major role in ensuring the proper balance of natural forces. Mayan cities contain astronomical observatories in which priests learned to predict solar and lunar eclipses and mark the changing seasons and the times for planting, burning, and harvesting. The Mayans used a 365-day calendar and figured the length of the year to within 17 seconds of modern calculations. They invented the concept of zero independently of the classical mathematicians of India, and they used a 20-base computation system (like our 10-base system). They built high step pyramids in stone, decorated with vivid sculptures of gods, jaguars, and serpents, and they painted on bark and stone walls in dazzling color. All this they accomplished with stone tools before metals came to Middle America around 900.

Recently, another side to Mayan life has come to light. Mayan rulers and priests practiced a ritualistic bloodletting in the belief that it would ensure the necessary rain for the crops. When, for instance, King Pacal died in 683, his son and successor, Chan Bahlum, presided at funeral services by cutting three slits into his penis with a sharp obsidian knife and inserting bark paper into the wounds so that the blood would flow copiously. His younger brother and other family members followed suit.

Mayan culture was otherwise not very different from that of others in Mexico. They shared many of the same gods; Tlaloc, the rain god, and Quetzacoatl, the feathered serpent, were particularly important. In addition to pyramid temples, all of them had ball courts where they played a ball game similar to that played by the Taino and ancestral to modern soccer. Competing teams could hit the small ball made of local rubber with anything but their hands. The game must have served some kind of dispute resolution function because the losers sometimes were executed, their heads displayed on spikes near the court. The idea that humans had to shed blood or give their lives to appease the gods was common in Mexican societies, though the Aztecs raised it to a new level.

*A Theoretical Interlude: Priests and Soldiers.* A modern world historian has an interesting theory that might help explain the bloodletting and human sacrifice that we frequently find in ancient civilizations. Johan Goudsblom[7] notes that many ancient agricultural civilizations give enormous power over life and death to priests. In earliest Mesopotamian urban society, for instance, priests supervised the planting and distribution of food as part of the feeding of the gods. Agriculture-based cities were highly vulnerable creations, Goudsblom argues: first vulnerable to the forces of nature and then, if successful, vulnerable to other peoples. Therefore, it should not surprise us to find cases in which priests are given inordinate powers to ensure the land is properly prepared for planting and that all the necessary rituals of farming are carried out to the letter. This would be especially important where nature was unpredictable, like the floods of the Euphrates. The people of Middle America faced the unpredictability of the rains. Rains that came too early or too late or that were too light or too heavy could disastrously limit the crops.

As city societies became larger, their dependence on reliable agriculture became greater. Priests who bled themselves and urged others to do the same might have been responding to what they perceived to be a very delicate balance between the efforts of humans and nature. In fact, the decline of Mayan society after 900 might be an indicator of how vulnerable it was. From around 800 to 1000, a number of American societies suffered from the lack of rainfall and collapsed. Mayan society was, in fact, able to reorganize along the northern Yucatan after the collapse of cities in the south, but it was never as extensive as in the earlier classical era. Similarly, Teotihuacan collapsed around 800, as did Monte Alban (and, we shall see, one of the great South American states).

Goudsblom points out that agriculture-based urban civilizations also rely heavily on soldiers but that the role of soldiers often eclipses that of priests at a later stage in their history. He suggests that this occurred after the society had some success in overcoming the threats of nature, achieved a certain level of abundance in crops and populations, and therefore confronted another level of vulnerability—the threat of outside forces, such as brigands, popular uprisings, or other societies. This would account for the rise of military regimes after priestly states in the ancient Near East. It might also explain the rise of soldiers over priests in the Toltec and Aztec states after the decline of Mayan society and Teotihuacan.

*Toltecs and Aztecs.* When the Aztecs modeled themselves on the Toltecs, they chose

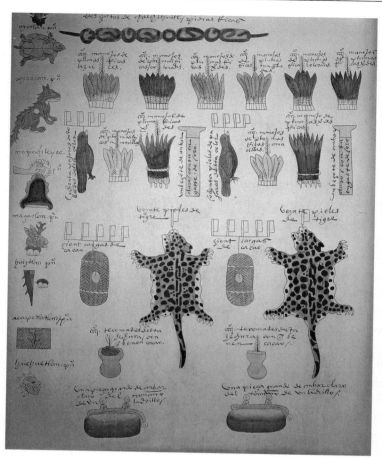

Figure 6.3  Aztec tribute lists like this itemized the goods that a subject town would have to pay the Aztecs two or four times a year. This list includes two strings of jadite stone, 4,000 handfuls of colored feathers, 160 blue-feathered birds, two gold lip piercings, 40 jaguar hides, 200 loads of cacao beans, 800 cups for drinking chocolate, and two amber bricks. *Gianni Dagli Orti/The Art Archive at Art Resource, NY. National Anthropological Museum Mexico.*

a military rather than a cultural power. The Toltec city Tula displayed symbols of a conquest state: friezes of soldiers, skulls on a rack, roaming jaguars, and eagles eating hearts. These symbols were replicated in Chichen Itza after the Toltec conquest of that Mayan city and in the Aztec capital. Toltec Tula created a large empire based on trade as well as conquest. It was the Toltec who introduced metals and metalworking to Mexico (in copper, silver, and gold), probably from their expeditions into Central America (where metals probably arrived from Peru). Although these were not durable metals, capable of being molded into tools or weapons, they encouraged trade and the making of fine art and jewelry. Toltec

state traders also founded settlements as far north as modern Arizona, bringing the Mesoamerican ball game to Phoenix (where a 900-year-old rubber ball was recently discovered) though evidently without the element of human sacrifice.

The Toltec told a story of their origins in Tula that later became an important part of Aztec lore. They told of a cultural hero or king called Topilzin Quetzalcoatl, who was a peacemaker forced out of the country (promising to return) by another powerful person, Tezcatlipoca, who became a sort of god of war and sacrifice. This conflict between Quetzalcoatl's peaceful, nurturing force and that of the god of war, conquest, bloodletting, and human

Figure 6.4   Mexican peoples believed bloodletting or human sacrifice was necessary to sustain life and agriculture. Under the direction of the war god Huitzilopochtli, the Aztecs took this belief the furthest. They brought warriors of enemies and dependent towns to their capital, where their hearts were cut out and offered to the god. *Scala/Art Resource, NY. Biblioteca Nazionale, Florence, Italy.*

sacrifice surfaced in Aztec society and was resolved in favor of the Aztec version of the god of war, Huitzilopochtli.

The followers of Huitzilopochtli believed that their god of war was also responsible for bringing the sun up every morning. To accomplish this monumental task, the god required regular sacrifices of human blood. This doctrine fueled a centuries-long Aztec expansion throughout central Mexico. The Aztec state of the fifteenth century was first and foremost dependent on the regular collection of prisoners at the ceremonial pyramids, most notably the Major Temple in Tenochtitlan (modern Mexico City), where their hearts were cut out and offered to Huitzilopochtli.

It was one of the great coincidences of history that, when the Spanish arrived in Mexico in 1519 at the end of a long religious crusade, they met an American empire driven by its own ideas of sacred warfare. The quick Spanish conquest of Mexico owed much to European "guns, germs, and steel,"[8] but the Aztecs also had many enemies in Mexico who joined the conquistadores in their march on Tenochtitlan. The Aztecs ran an empire structured in ways that made rebellion by Mexican peoples almost inevitable. It was an empire of military conquest that attempted little by way of cultural or bureaucratic integration (in contrast to the Inca, as we will see). The tentacles that stretched from Tenochtitlan to the other cities of Mexico were mainly military. It was an empire on the cheap, run as was its capital by a military aristocracy that left much of the economy to markets and merchants. Long-distance merchants (*pocheteca*) were the only other important social class at home. They also created the only alternate arteries throughout the empire along which they traded and spied for the military rulers.

The conquered peoples of Mexico and parts of what is today Central America were treated as military dependencies each required by treaty to supply stipulated amounts of raw and finished products as well as young men to be sacrificed. Without any stake in or affiliation with an Aztec society that literally bled them dry, many threw in their lot with foreign invaders who ended up taking over everything.

### States and Empires of South America

The South American Inca Empire that fell to the Spanish conquistador Pizarro in 1534 was very much like the Aztec in its origins. Like the Aztecs, the Incas were recent conquerors of other kingdoms. Like the Aztecs, they had come from obscurity in the early 1400s to rule a vast area—the four parts of the world, they called it, and it extended from Ecuador to Bolivia and from the Andes to the Pacific coast of South America. Like the Aztecs, the Inca invented ancestry from a previous power to suggest their importance. They came, they said, from Tiwanaku, the state that ruled the highlands of the Andes from around 400 to 1000. In fact, they borrowed ideas and institutions from a number of earlier states of the Andes highlands and the Pacific coast.

*Before the Incas.* Glancing at a map, it might seem strange that all the cities and states of South America before 1500 developed in the same section of the continent—along the

Pacific coast and in the Andes mountains. Today, for instance, the largest cities are along the Atlantic coast, and the largest modern states, Brazil and Argentina, were not even part of these pre-1500 states. It might seem even stranger from ground level. The Pacific coast has some of the driest, most desolate deserts on the planet, and the city sites in the Andes Mountains are in such high and forbidding places that entire cities are still being discovered in dense jungle at very high altitudes.

The earliest dense settlements in South America were along the Pacific coast in what is today northern Peru. There coastal areas were dry (though not as dry as southern Peru and northern Chile), but rivers cascading down from the high Andes provided abundant water for irrigated farming. Nevertheless, farming may have encouraged dense human settlement only after the teeming coastal fisheries had begun the process. The waters off the coast of northern Peru offered the most abundant harvests of small fish, like anchovies, and the larger fish and birds that fed on them found anywhere in the world. This was a result of the cold waters of the Humboldt Current flowing north from Antarctica along the Pacific coast, where they met the warm equatorial waters. This area may have been one of the few in the world where fisheries were abundant enough to allow dense and permanent human settlement before agriculture.[9] (The Pacific Northwest was another, as we shall see.)

If early settlements could be formed by groups of villagers who lived by fishing, hunting, and gathering, the first states and kingdoms depended on agriculture and often grazing animals as well. Even more than the pastoral societies of East Africa, the early states and kingdoms of South America were multilevel societies that took advantage of the different resources of widely varying altitudes.

Cotton and corn (after it arrived from Middle America) could be grown at low altitudes. The numerous tubers that were domesticated into potatoes and yams grew more easily at higher altitudes in the Andes. Even higher on plateaus of short grasses, llamas and alpacas were raised and grazed. In this way, compact Andean states grew vertically over desert, grasslands, lush valleys, and rugged mountains in irrigated layers of settlement.

Andean civilization seemed to climb up from the shores of the Pacific to the mountain ridges 20,000 feet above sea level. If so, it was not a straight climb, and it was not only onward and upward. First, there are two or more Andean ridges stretching north and south with large tropical rain forests in between. Second, the culture of Andean civilization shows the unmistakable stamp of peoples of eastern tropical rain forests. Places like the Amazon jungle may not have produced highly concentrated settlements, but some of their habitations may have been among the oldest on the continent, and their descendants must have helped shape Andean civilization.

*Classical Chavin.* The classical, some would even say "mother," culture of Andean civilization was centered at Chavin de Huantar (around 800–200 BCE). Some of the cultural elements of later Andean life developed earlier, but at Chavin they came together in a formative mix. The site, halfway between sea and mountaintops, at the 10,000-foot-level crossroads of ancient trade routes, was considered especially sacred. The main temple, a U shape of raised platforms with the opening facing east, uphill, and toward the mountain waters, became a model for Andean temples. At Chavin de Huantar, the temple contained secret chambers, tunnels, and a central niche with a totemlike stone pillar that contained the face of the god and imagery connected sea

and mountains and earth and sky. The role of forest peoples could be seen in the sacred depiction of jaguars, caiman crocodiles, and snakes, images replicated on stone and pottery for the following millennia that seemed to suggest that the fears and fascinations of the jungle were those of the desert and mountains as well. From the desert came a hallucinatory cactus that, according to friezes on the temple wall, would put the shaman into a sacred trance. Underneath the lower-level garden in the center of the U, one heard the rushing roar of water, the sound of the god's energy and a reminder of the miracle of irrigation that connected wet and dry and high and low.

*Moche Warrior Priests and Divine Emperors.* Beginning around 200 BCE, the Andes witnessed a series of ever-larger empires that combined the culture and religious ideas of Chavin with the techniques of military expansion and political domination. The first of these empires, the Moche (200–700), united not only upper and lower realms of the mountains but also entire valleys between mountain ridges. If Chavin was run by priests, the Moche Empire was run by warrior priests and a king who styled himself as a god, demanded human sacrifices, and commanded the work of all and the lives of some to magnify his realm and accompany him after death. Here we also see the first cases of burial distinctions in Andean society. Mummified Moche aristocrats, like the Lords of Sipan, wrapped in clothing that took another's lifetime to produce and crowned with gold-plated crescent moons, also demanded llamas, wives, and helpers in their tombs. The Moche may have initiated the *mit'a* system of forced labor for state building projects, especially the pyramid-like tombs of the rulers. They also developed metallurgy in the Americas; they did not smelt ores, but they hammered and soldered gold, silver, and

Figure 6.5 The early Peruvian Moche culture left not writing but an abundance of pottery and art. Here a priest or shaman, with feline headdress, heals or prays for someone. *Werner Forman/Art Resource, NY. Ethnologisches Museum, Staatliche Museen, Berlin, Germany.*

copper into jewelry and ritual objects that would be imitated for millennia afterward.

The end of the Moche came with a series of what we have since recognized as El Niños—sudden warming of the nearby ocean water that drastically reduced the harvests of anchovies and caused extreme conditions of drought (not incidentally causing a series of climatic changes around the world). In addition, the Andes were struck by a major earthquake sometime between 650 and 700. The Moche was not the only civilization destroyed by the desiccation and dust. The Nazca people on the coastal plains of southern Peru, known for their miles-long sand images of hummingbirds, monkeys, whales, and spiders, also disappeared.

*Incas and Their Ancestors.* When the Incas traced their ancestry back to Tiwanaku, they identified themselves with a state that had dominated the highlands of southern Peru and Bolivia from Lake Titicaca (in modern Bolivia) from around 400 to 1000. This association also meant a declaration of loyalty to Viracocha, the creator god, and to an extensive empire based on further irrigation, widespread *mit'a* service, U-shaped steppe temples that demonstrated the control of water, human sacrifice, and the imagery of jaguar and evil. In other words, Tiwanaku continued many of the elements of Andean culture from the time of the Moche and even the Chavin.

Yet each new kingdom controlled a larger area than its predecessor. One of the techniques that made this possible was an institution anthropologists call "split inheritance," which operated like a 100 percent inheritance tax each time a king died. As developed by the Chimu state (1100–1400), the immediate predecessor of the Inca, split inheritance was a system by which all *mit'a*, taxes, and tribute paid to a particular king, was channeled to his estate and the upkeep of his temple after his death. This meant that whatever son became his successor had to find entirely new sources of revenue. In other words, he had to conquer his own kingdom, adding it to his father's and those of his predecessors, thus creating his own empire. The capital of the Chimu state, Chan Chan, had 9 or 10 separate enclosed districts, each containing the temple grounds and resources of a departed king. And with each new conquest came new subsidiary cities, provincial capitals with their own local subordinates, and new aristocrats. It was an extremely effective system of imperial expansion as long as there were new lands to conquer.

The Incas used the tool of split inheritance to create an empire more than double the size of the Chimu. It encompassed all the coast and the uplands from southern Ecuador to

DEPOCITODELINGA
COLL CA

topaynga
yupanqui.

aymurusflador
suyo yoc
apo poma chaua

depocitos del ynga

como

Figure 6.6  In the absence
of other forms of writing,
Inca officials communicated
by means of colored strings.
Here a string, or quipu, reader
"translates" for an official.
*John Meek/The Art Archive at Art
Resource, NY.*

northern Chile and Bolivia. The Inca proved particularly adept at administering such a vast empire on a shoestring. Messengers ran from one station to another throughout the empire, carrying their messages on *khipus* of knotted string and sometimes (according to an older custom) engraved on lima beans.

If their technology was lean, the Inca compensated with a passion for organization. They created a system in which state sovereignty overrode kinship by dividing the empire into quarters, halves, and provinces. Then they created groups of 10,000, 5,000, 1,000, 500, and 100 taxpayers. Foremen were put in charge of groups of 50 and 10 taxpayers.

An annual census ensured proper records for taxation and military service.[10] Without wheeled vehicles, writing, or iron metallurgy, the Inca governed an empire that—because of its slopes, terraces, mountains, and valleys— covered far greater distances than the condor flies. It is estimated that the Inca built about 25,000 miles of roads.

Inca taste for organization and centralization contrasts with the loosely organized conquest states of Middle America. The Mayan civilization actually comprised a number of relatively independent cities or city-states separated by jungle and distance. The Aztec state was intentionally not integrated since Aztec sacrificial rites required a continual source of captives from nearby enemies.

## States and Peoples of North America

There were no large Native American empires in the area of what is today the United States and Canada—no large bureaucracies or militaristic imperial states on the scale of the Aztec or Inca. There were states, however, and chiefdoms, and there were abundant forms of political and social organization, including stateless societies and alliances of independent states.

The smaller size of North American political units was due in part to a lower population density. Population figures for the Americas before 1500 are largely guesswork, but estimates for North America vary from 2 million to 18 million. The entire Western Hemisphere (North, Middle, and South America) contained 40 million to 100 million people. The lower population density in North America corresponded to the widespread use of slash-and-burn agriculture, especially in the vast woodlands east of the Mississippi and to the limits of the dry and desert lands of the west. Nevertheless, there were areas where hunter-gatherers created large, settled tribal communities of significant sophistication (most notably along the rich fisheries of the Pacific coast) as well as agricultural areas where

Figure 6.7   Cahokia, on the Mississippi River opposite modern St. Louis, was the center of a North American society. This painting shows what the city might have looked like at its height around 1200. The temple of the Great Sun sits atop a palace mound surrounded by a wall that also encloses the palaces of nobility and a ball court, common in American societies. Outside the wall are numerous homes of commoners and a wooden sun calendar on the far left. *Cahokia Mounds State Historic Site, painting by William R. Iseminger.*

people created cities without irrigation or plows and draught animals.

*Peoples and Places.* One of the reasons why it is difficult to know the size of the precontact American populations is that many Native Americans were wiped out by European diseases after 1492. North American estimates pose an additional problem. English colonists in North America created a mythology that they had come to an empty or "virgin land," largely because they wanted to settle their families permanently in the "new world." Spaniards in Middle and South America were generally more interested in converting souls and exploiting labor. North American settlers had a greater interest in removing the Indian population—physically and mentally—making later accountings more difficult.

Compared to Middle and South America, North America, at least east of the Mississippi, is a land where the original people are neither seen nor heard. In Mexico, Central America, and most of South America, Indian peoples are everywhere. In much of the United States, outside of Indian reservations, most Indian faces are those of Mexican or Central and South American immigrants. But the signs of a previous habitation line every street and highway as if they were still the Indian trails they frequently trace. The names of 23 states, four Great Lakes, and thousands of rivers, lakes, mountains, and cities in the United States and thousands more in Canada (named after *kanata*, an Iroquoian word for "settlement") are Indian words. Dozens of the hundreds of Indian languages once spoken are still in use. Among those that are extinct, many of their words are still used without any idea of their origins. In much of North America, we build our lives in a haunted landscape.

*Rich Pacific Fisheries.* The *first* Americans probably settled along the Pacific coast of what is today Canada and the United States after crossing the frozen Bering Strait from Asia. There they encountered the same sort of ideal conditions that others were soon to find farther south along the Pacific coast of Peru. Ocean currents ensured moderate temperatures and abundant fish and wildlife. Salmon (rather than anchovies), seals, and whales provided an almost unlimited source of protein, and (unlike Peru) the banks of the Pacific were rich in animals and plants. Women harvested pine nuts and acorns and ground them into meal. Men harvested abundant forests to build wooden houses and canoes. These peoples enjoyed a comfortable material life, with specialists and chiefs and even slaves who were captured from foreign tribes and used for household duties. Although they grew no crops (except for tobacco), the hunter-gatherers of the Pacific coast reached population sizes and densities that were normally possible only with agriculture. Before 1500, the population of the California coast alone was about 300,000. In Santa Barbara, Chumash villages numbered more than 1,000.

Farther north on the Pacific coast, the Chinook, Kwakiutl, Nootka, and other Wakashan speakers enjoyed such affluence that they gave it away in a festival called the potlatch. To mark important events, like the erection of a totem pole or the death of an important elder, the host built a special house for the event. He designed his guest list with special care not to embarrass or slight. Guests of highest rank might be given slaves or large copper shields (each worth five slaves). Those of less rank might receive carved boxes, utensils, tools, or the valuable blankets made of mountain goat hair acquired in trade from the Athabaskan Indians of the northern interior. Hundreds of clan members would enjoy the feast: salmon, haddock, and shellfish, all dipped in the ever-present smelt sauce, and numerous varieties of berries. Following the meal, they would share tobacco, sing songs, dance, and receive the gifts. Sometimes the host ceremonially destroyed some of his wealth as a sign of his generosity (and power). Many guests stayed overnight before returning home in their canoes, which the host had loaded with more food for the journey.[11]

*Pueblos of the Southwest.* Nature was not as kind to the dry lands of what became the southwestern United States. Nevertheless, the Indians of New Mexico, Arizona, and southern Colorado developed agriculture about 3,000 years ago as the northern area of a zone of farmers that stretched deep into Mexico. They channeled light rain and generous rivers into irrigation canals where they grew beans, squash, and corn. During the relatively well watered period between 500 and 1200, the ancestors of today's Navaho, the Anasazi, created dense, well-protected pueblo settlements on highlands like Mesa Verde (Colorado) and veritable "apartment houses" for cliff dwellers at places like Chaco Canyon (New Mexico). From there, they traded with the Great Plains Indians, who hunted bison (without horses), and with Indian miners of turquoise. Sometime after 1200, however, these pueblos were abandoned. There may have been conflict with new migrants from the north (where the Anasazi had themselves originated), but the causes probably had more to do with the return of dry climate conditions. As pueblos were abandoned, the descendants of the Anasazi moved, many to the Rio Grande valley, where they became part of new communities like the Hopi. A Spanish expedition to a Hopi town in 1582 found that the Indians of the Southwest had reclaimed a satisfying standard of living:

A thousand Indians greeted us with fine earthen jars full of water, and with rabbits,

venison, tortillas, beans, cooked calabashes, corn and pine nuts, so that heaps of food were left over.[12]

*Eastern Woodland Farmers.* From the eastern edge of the Great Plains to the Allegheny Mountains, vast watered woodlands with numerous rivers and streams created a riot of plant and animal life. Much of this area from the Great Lakes to the Gulf of Mexico drained into the Mississippi River, bringing melted mountain snows and light loam silt soil to the fertile American Bottom of the Mississippi valley. The Mississippi drainage, including its tributaries like the Ohio and Missouri, covered almost a million and a quarter square miles (about the size of India).[13] The Mississippi alone extended almost 4,000 miles, about the length of the Amazon and the Nile, but since it ran almost entirely through a temperate climate zone and woodlands (instead of tropical forest or desert), the entire drainage could support a large population. The numbers elude us, but certainly the majority of Indians north of the Rio Grande lived in this area. Spaniards who accompanied Hernando De Soto's expedition from Florida to Tennessee to Arkansas and Texas in the 1540s described thousands of towns and villages.

The "Great River," as the Indian name accurately labeled it, provided for permanent human settlements, fishing, hunting, and gathering as early as 4,500 years ago, not too long after permanent settlements were established in the other great river valley civilizations on the Euphrates, Nile, Indus, and Yellow rivers. The Mississippian culture that developed in North America was, in fact, the only river valley civilization in the Americas. Whereas the other great river valleys of the world grew by domesticating plants and animals, the Americans of the Mississippi woodlands (like their settled cousins on the Pacific coast) were settled hunter-gatherers. They domesticated local grasses and gourds (mainly for the containers) and sometime after 400 began to plant Mexican corn, but not until after around 900 did corn and beans become a staple in their diet and the yeast for their population growth.

We might even speak of an urban revolution as early as 4,500 years ago, although some historians are hesitant to use the term without evidence of bronze or written languages. The earliest Indian settlement, dating from about 2500 BCE, already contained the distinctive feature of Mississippian settlements for the next 4,000 years: earthen mounds built as platforms for elite residences, temples, ceremonies, or animal-shaped mounds that communicated some sort of collective identity to strangers or the gods. At least 10,000 of these mounds could be found in the Ohio River drainage from the classical age of 500 BCE to 400 CE. All these communities displayed the elements of advanced chiefdoms. There were significant class differences between elites and commoners and a number of artisans and specialists who made pottery, hammered copper sheets, sewed clothing and wove baskets

The greatest distribution of mound-building settlements was created between 700 and 1200. The most important of these, Cahokia, near modern St. Louis, had many of the characteristics of cities despite the absence of writing or bronze. Cahokia contained 10,000 to 30,000 people and was larger than medieval London, the equivalent of Toltec Tula in Mexico. It was the largest city north of the Rio Grande before the eighteenth century. Cahokia had almost a continental trading reach, bringing it shells from Florida, copper from the Great Lakes, metals from the Appalachian and Rockies, ocean fish from the Gulf of Mexico, and bison from the Great Plains. In addition to corn and

various kinds of beans from Mexico, Cahokia adopted Mexican ball games and astronomical interests. A ring of poles organized to chart the position of the sun, chart the seasons, and predict eclipses occupied a sacred site near the most important mounds and central plaza of Cahokia: "the American Woodhenge," archaeologists call it, because of its similarity to the ancient "Stonehenge" monolith of Britain.

## Americas and the World

The history of the Americas offers a pristine parallel to the history of the Afro-Eurasian world. The peopling of the Americas was a much longer process than the repeopling of inner Africa, which occurred only in the past 2,000 years. By 2,000 years ago, some American civilizations were already able to point to distant ancestors, but none of those had experienced contact with the Old World in thousands of years.

In the Americas, the agricultural and the urban revolutions occurred independently of the Eastern Hemisphere. They produced different crops, raised fewer animals, and were limited by less adaptable technologies of writing, metalworking, and transportation. Yet the people of the Americas repeated some of the same processes that the peoples of Afro-Eurasia experienced.

Americans also developed their own networks of interaction. The use of bows and arrows came from the north to Middle America, where the Aztecs rejected them since they needed to take live captives for sacrificial rites. Middle American corn spread south and north. South American copper, silver, and gold traveled up the Pacific coast to Central America, where it was adopted by the Toltec and later Middle American states. People from the Amazon sailed into the open sea and colonized the islands of the Caribbean. The great number of American languages underscores the diversity of peoples, the remoteness of some settlements, and the huge size of the Western Hemisphere. Nevertheless, crops, cultures, deities, social systems, and ball games spread far from home.

## The World of the Pacific

The Pacific Ocean covers a third of the world. For most of history, its 10,000 islands were unoccupied, but human settlement of Australia and New Guinea began soon after humans began to migrate out of Africa. Most of the further islands were colonized in a final wave of human settlement that began about 3,500 years ago.

### *Islands and Settlers*

Recently, a team of anthropologists on the Indonesian island of Flores startled the world with the discovery of the skeletons of what appears to be an entirely different human species, which they are calling *Homo florensis*. At this writing, scientists disagree as to whether these three-foot-tall people, who lived on Flores as recently as 13,000 years ago, are descendants of *Homo erectus* who traveled from Africa to Asia over a million years ago, arriving on Flores about 840,000 years ago, or the descendants of later *Homo sapiens*. In either case, however, all the adult skeletons of *H. florensis* are much smaller than their African ancestors.

*Islands.* Scientists explain this apparent shrinking of *H. florensis*—at the same time they were getting smarter, learning to make stone tools—as a process of evolution that sometimes takes place on islands. Given a limited environment, as the human population

on the isolated island grew to the carrying capacity of the island, nature selected downsizing as a coping mechanism. The same thing happened to the large elephants that swam to the island: their descendants reduced to the size of cows.

Islands do not always induce shrinking, however. Sometimes an enclosed environment that offers abundant food and no natural predators can induce a species to become giants. This explains how the carnivorous lizards that came on natural rafts to the neighboring island of Komodo attained the size to be known as the Komodo dragons.

Islands are natural laboratories that stretch the boundaries of more interactive worlds. As such, they can sometimes tell us more than vast continents about what nature and humans can do.

*First Wave.* If *H. erectus* ventured into the Pacific or Flores a million years ago, we have no other evidence. The first wave of *H. sapiens* did not arrive before the last 100,000 to 50,000 years. This was the period of the last ice-age glaciation when the thickening ice reduced ocean levels as much as 100 yards below today's. As a result, Southeast Asia was connected to most of Indonesia; Australia, which was not too far away, was connected to New Guinea and Tasmania. The settlement of this island continent would have required migration by sea from the Afro-Eurasian landmass (or Indonesian islands). In fact, there is some evidence on islands off the coast of India that Africans used rafts or boats even before getting to Southeast Asia and Australia.

After the glaciers melted and the oceans rose, these first modern human settlers became three different peoples on New Guinea, Australia, and Tasmania. The people of Australia and Tasmania remained hunter-gatherers. The Tasmanians seem to have lost the ability to make rafts or canoes with their Stone Age tools. New Guinea also lacked animals that could be domesticated for food, but the people of the world's second-largest island, alone of the three first-wave settlers, became farmers. Their most important crop turned out to be domesticated sugar, which is today the world's largest crop by tonnage (more than the next two—wheat and corn—combined). The people of New Guinea also raised banana and coconut trees and two root crops: yams and taro. We do not know if these staples of the Pacific were first domesticated in New Guinea or in Southeast Asia. In any case, this New Guinean cultural complex, along with the domesticated chicken, pig, and dog that Austronesian travelers brought from Southeast Asia, nurtured a large and dense population in New Guinea, especially in highland areas where seafood was less available.

*Australia.* Australia was a less suitable candidate for domestication, especially after the first settlers killed off the large birds and mammals (including the many marsupials or pouched mammals related to the kangaroo). No native plants or animals were domesticated by the Australians (although sometime after 1500 BCE they adopted the Austronesian dog, or "dingo"). Australian soils were not very fertile, and much of the continent was dry desert. Australian aborigines hunted and gathered because few native plants were edible or easy to domesticate. Even today, modern scientific methods have led to the domestication of only one native plant—the macadamia nut. Nevertheless, Australian hunter-gatherers developed certain sophisticated ways of increasing the yield of their environment. Periodically, they would burn off thickets and underbrush, stampeding available animals to be captured but also, after the burn-off, reviving grasses that would attract future prey. In addition,

Australians were one of the hunting-gathering people in the world to make use of water irrigation in ways that increased the food supply but did not yield to agriculture or settled villages. In this case, they channeled water to raise and capture eels. Still, they never developed agriculture despite the fact that they traded with the agriculturalists of New Guinea and the agriculturalists of the Indonesian island of Sulawesi (Celebes), some of whom even had iron after 600 CE.

## Austronesian and Polynesian Migrations

*Austronesian Migrations.* Long after the first settlers arrived 30,000 to 50,000 years ago, their descendants were joined by a much later second wave of agriculturalists. Around 4,000 years ago, these people came from China to Taiwan and the Philippines and then to Southeast Asia, where they cultivated coconut and banana trees, yams, and taro root and domesticated chickens, pigs, and dogs. After 1600 BCE, these Austronesian peoples brought their tropical plants, domesticated animals, sailing skills, and pottery to Indonesia, New Guinea, and the nearby islands of the Pacific. Over the next 2,000 years, their descendants, whom we call the Polynesians, ventured out to colonize the unoccupied islands of the deep Pacific: the island groups of Fiji, Samoa, Tahiti, then north to the Hawaiian Islands, southwest to New Zealand (and later Madagascar), and as far east as Easter Island. This was one of the epic migrations of world history. Once they were east of the islands near New Guinea, they traveled in open waters to unknown islands where, presumably, no humans had been before.

*Polynesian Migrations.* Like the Bantu, the Polynesians used a system of primogeniture, by which only first sons inherited land and

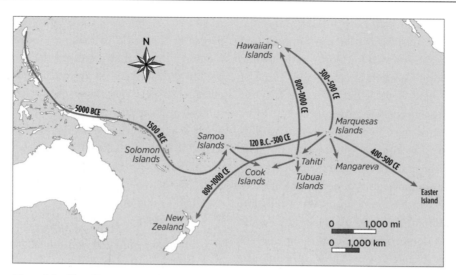

Map 6.2 The Polynesian migrations covered a greater area than any before modern times, and they were carried out without a knowledge of their destinations.

authority and encouraged younger sons to strike out on their own in search of new land to grow crops and raise their families. Traditions of seafaring, honed by generations of short voyages, enabled them to break out into the open ocean. From their Austronesian ancestors, they had learned to attach two or three canoes to a single platform, making it less likely to be capsized by heavy winds or waves. They learned how to sail against the prevailing easterly winds of the southern side of the equator by waiting for the occasional gust from the west. They read the dazzling nighttime sky like a road map. They learned to spot land birds far from shore and interpret clouds, debris, and the color of the water to find islands too distant to be seen.

Centuries later, a European sailor marveled at their ability to sail the open ocean without compass or charts:

He sees whether he has the wind aft, or on one or other beam, or on the quarter, or is close-hauled: he knows, further, whether there is a following sea, a head sea, a beam sea, or if it is on the bow or the quarter. . . . Should the night be cloudy as well, they regulate their course by the same signs; and, since the wind is apt to vary in direction more than the swell does, they have their pennants, made of feathers and palmetto bark, to watch its changes and trim sail. . . . What impressed me most in two Polynesians whom I carried from Tahiti to Raiatea was that every evening or night, they predicted the weather we should experience on the following day, as to wind, calms, rainfall, sunshine, sea, and other points, about which they never turned out to be wrong: a foreknowledge worthy to be envied, for, in spite of all that our navigators and cosmographers have observed and written about the subject, they have not mastered this accomplishment.[14]

The Polynesians had been farmers before they were sailors, so they loaded their boats with the seeds they would need in their new homes—breadfruit, coconut palms, taro,

Figure 6.8 Austronesian mariners used double-hulled ships like this, drawn by a European artist in the Pacific in 1769. *The Granger Collection, New York.*

yam, and banana—and their domesticated animals—chickens, pigs, and dogs. As each generation sailed farther, they adapted to new environments and domesticated new foods. In New Zealand, only the northern tip had a tropical climate similar to that of equatorial islands. They were able to move south to cooler areas when they learned to plant the South American sweet potato, which had crossed the Pacific either on natural rafts or on Polynesian ships.[15]

## Language and Culture

Austronesian-Polynesian colonization represented the greatest expansion of a people, culture, and language family until the expansion of the Europeans that began 500 years ago. The Polynesian stage of this migration into the far Pacific (unlike the later Europeans or the Polynesians' Bantu contemporaries in Africa) was to unoccupied lands. Consequently, they could transplant their culture intact. They confronted no alternatives and did not have to meld, compromise, or adapt their own ways

with those of others. One result is the striking similarities of Polynesian language and material culture across the vast Pacific, from Tonga to Tahiti and New Zealand to Hawaii. Some of their words and customs—like tattoo and taboo—have since entered the common culture of humanity. Their common culture was a testament to the swiftness of their colonization of truly virgin lands.

The first inhabitants of the Western Hemisphere also colonized an unoccupied land,[16] but the land itself was enormous, the tools of these ancient hunters were less sophisticated, and the process of settlement took much longer. Consequently, the Americas were more culturally diverse; there were far more languages, especially in mountain areas like western Mexico and remote areas like the southern tip of South America.

The degree to which the Polynesians created a single cultural sphere can be seen by comparing their achievement in the Pacific with their own roots. There had been many different cultures and languages in the Austronesian homelands—Taiwan, the Philippines,

Malaya, and Indonesia. Indeed, the areas that Polynesians did not settle remained highly diverse. New Guinea alone had 700 languages, a significant portion of the world's total.

Expansions like the Bantu and Austronesian created common cultures very much the way the expansion of Indo-Europeans and Eurasian steppe nomads had. Austronesian peoples shared a common table of foods, similar double-hulled canoes, a pantheon of gods, rituals of harvest, sailing, sacrifice, tattooing, and an architectural style of stilt houses and outdoor platform altars. But Austronesians lacked horses (or other draft or transportation animals), and they lacked writing. Their Polynesian descendants lacked iron as well. The daring catamarans of the Pacific carried a limited range of plants and animals to islands already limited to the flotsam seedlings of Asia. Unlike the other great migrations of the world, the Polynesian adventurers sailed to a world of diminished variety. They found islands of paradise, but as history was increasingly shaped by interaction, they sailed away from the main event. They conquered the world's greatest sea but with a ticket stamped "One Way: Pacific Only."

## Ecology and Colonization

The colonization of new ecological environments created special challenges. The ocean did not contain an inexhaustible number of uninhabited islands. The limits of settlement were reached in Hawaii in the north, Easter Island in the east, New Zealand in the south, and Madagascar in the west. To travel farther meant open ocean or settled continents. How did the colonizers adapt to limits? Inevitably, populations increased, especially on the outer islands of Polynesian seafaring. Lean boat

crews of discoverers matured into complex, stratified societies of settlers. On the Hawaiian Islands, the descendants of the first settlers created complicated hierarchies of commoners, nobles, and royals. Complex chiefdoms, imperial ambitions, and religious rites created levels of interisland contact and organization that ran counter to the initial impulse of sailing off to the sunrise for new beginnings.

Hawaii, Tahiti, and Tonga were probably the most stratified complex chiefdoms, especially after the thirteenth century. Typically in Hawaii, chiefs claimed descent from one of the "first-boat" founding settlers, exercised both political and religious authority, and enjoyed privileges that were "taboo" for lesser nobility or commoners. Lesser-stratified societies, like that of the Maori of New Zealand (Aoteoroa), were governed by the leaders of subtribes who also traced their ancestry to first-boat arrivals but did not always combine political and religious authority and made decisions in consultation with the rest of the subtribe assembled in the sacred square, the *marae*.

With the growth of populations and more complex societies, the balance between people and nature tipped precariously. In the Maori colony that became New Zealand, species of flightless birds were hunted to extinction by people (and stowaway rats) who found them easy prey. Some societies achieved a better balance. The settlers of two of the Cook Islands, Manihiki and Rakahanga, lived together on one of the islands while they let the other remain fallow in order to replenish vegetation and fisheries. Then, after a certain number of years, they moved together to the other island and reversed the process.[17]

The story of Easter Island bodes less well.[18] Rapa Nui (Easter Island was the name given by the Europeans to mark the day of *their* discovery) lies 2,300 miles off the coast of South America. It is 1,500 miles from the nearest Polynesian island. It was the end of the great migration across the Pacific. An island full of palm trees waved to the first Polynesians 1,500 years ago. Rapa Nui offered the colonists a feast of nature—abundant vegetation and wildlife and a rich soil for Polynesian crops. The population grew to about 10,000, but as islanders cut down trees for farming and housing, the rootless soil washed into the sea, and eventually farming was limited to the areas where a few remaining trees broke the wind. Settlers cut trees for rollers so that they could move the huge sculptured heads that served as sentinels from quarry to cliff. The heads can still be seen peering out into the sea, but the people of Rapa Nui sculpted themselves into a corner from which they could not escape. Fifteen hundred miles from anywhere, in one of the most isolated parts of the planet, they managed to destroy the last tree and, with it, their food and even the material to build a raft to leave. The population crashed in famine and war. Today, the last sculptured heads still lie near the quarry, ancient stone glyphs and a system of writing that developed at the time of first European contact cry out for interpretation, and the last inhabitants survive on food and tourists flown in fresh daily.

## The Advantages of Parallel Worlds

The tragedy of Rapa Nui was that the last Polynesians inhabited but one world. At the easternmost tip of the Pacific triangle of settlement, there seemed to be no place else to go. Of course, we all inhabit only one world, and (at least given foreseeable technology) there is

nowhere else for us to go (in any significant numbers).

### The Lessons of Parallel Worlds

Even when we cannot go elsewhere, we can still learn from others who have. The Polynesians who settled closest to their Asian origins had far more opportunity to learn from others than did the people of Rapa Nui. A richly studied Polynesian people on one of the Solomon Islands, which was populated mainly by other descendants of their mutual Austronesian ancestors, proudly proclaimed "we the Tikopia"[19] do things this way at every opportunity, but only when they became aware that other people did things differently.

The opportunity to learn that there are other worlds where people do things differently is one of the great advantages of studying history. What the Tikopia could do face-to-face we can do from a distance.

What are the lessons we can draw from the three worlds that ran independent of but parallel to the world of Afro-Eurasia in the thousands of years before the world became one?

*Lessons of Similarities.* That there were parallel worlds at all is a lesson in how humans share the same variety of possibilities and move along similar paths. The parallel worlds of inner Africa, the Americas, and the Pacific display the same range of activities, institutions, and ideas that we found in Afro-Eurasia during the same period. The processes of change were also similar. In all "four worlds," hunter-gatherers increasingly became farmers and farmers learned to be more productive, usually choosing to live in more complex and densely populated societies. Everyone did not develop cities, writing, and bronze or iron metallurgy, but generally when people became aware of these developments, they sought them out and adopted them for themselves.

We have reflected on the similarities in the growth of social classes, elites, chiefdoms, monarchies, and empires. Kings became more powerful as their realms expanded. They took more wives, humiliated more subjects, demanded more grave mates, and rationalized more sacrificial offerings to more demanding gods (often themselves). Whether or not soldiers replaced priests as the dominant class entrusted with preserving the material advantage of the privileged, both classes prospered in complex societies. So did fathers. City- and state-based societies tended to be more patriarchal than agricultural societies. West African and American agriculturalists were often matrilineal. In the process of the Bantu expansion, inner African societies become more patrilineal. Native American city societies were more patrilineal. In the Pacific, the early inhabitants of Southeast Asia, including Malaya, and the Austronesian ancestors of the Polynesians tended to be matrilineal. Polynesian society was patrilineal.

*Similarities or Connections.* Travelers and amateur archaeologists have frequently speculated on the similarity of Egyptian and Mayan pyramids, a resemblance that has led some to imagine ancient travels across the Atlantic or Pacific. But similarity does not mean connection. We know that Egyptian and Mesopotamian societies were closely linked, but the Mesopotamian step pyramid, or ziggurat, was different from the Egyptian pyramid, and it performed a different function: temple rather than tomb. Mayan pyramids were also temples, as were those of the Aztecs and Incas. Ancient peoples built templelike structures for other purposes as well. Nor were they limited to city societies. North American farmers from the Mississippi to Georgia built pyramid-shaped earthen mounds, although most built rounded mounds. Polynesians built pyramid structures, although most built simple platform altars. Rather than assume connections where no evidence of contacts exists, we might see the building of temples, tombs, mounds, platforms, and pyramids as efforts to communicate with sky gods, exalt certain elites, or reflect the power, shape, or ideals of the builders and benefactors of urban and complex societies.

*Lessons of Differences.* The differences that occurred *within* these broad similarities can tell us even more. The fishing villages of the Pacific coast show that even hunter-gatherers can establish settled sophisticated societies. The people of the American Southwest and Mississippi show the upper limits of social organization possible without writing and metals. The Pacific Islanders show how much can be done with only a few seeds and a shipload of grit.

The forceful role that pastoralists played in Eurasia is echoed by the Nilotic peoples of Africa but absent from the Americas and Polynesia. The almost complete absence of animals for transportation in the Americas and Polynesia prevented the dynamic synthesis we see from the clash of the two lifestyles elsewhere. But it does not seem to have prevented the development of patriarchy or military powers in the Americas or Pacific islands.

If one conclusion seems inescapable, it is that these parallel worlds were not ignited by clashes with others—pastoralists or settled people—the way the people of central Eurasia were. The fact that they went their own way, colonizing empty or underpopulated lands, allowed them to develop the unique propensities of their own cultures but kept them away from center stage. But there is a profound irony here. The separate development that was their historical weakness when Eurasia came calling is also what makes them so valuable to the rest of the world today. Just as plants that exist nowhere else can provide the world with a cure to a global scourge, the variety of human cultures testify to the breadth of our possibilities. Recently, for instance, linguistic scholars recognized that, probably uniquely in the world, the Aymara speakers of the Andes think of the past as in front of them and the future (since it is unknown) as behind them.[20] Thus, a presumed human universal can be put to rest because a parallel world is around to tell us it need not be so. Who knows what possibilities such new ideas could help us back into?

## *The Strength of Parallel Worlds*

We have seen how the story of human history might be summarized as 100,000 years of global dispersal followed by 1,000 or 2,000 years of reconnection. That reconnection and even reintegration has been especially profound in the past few hundred years, increasing in intensity even in recent decades. The benefits in communication, coordination, and innovation are enormous. But one result is increasing sameness. Like the early agriculturalists who chose a few wild plants from hundreds of thousands of candidates in the wild, we throw off old cultures, languages, ancient beliefs, and customs like old clothes. And once they are discarded, they cannot be retrieved. We lose the capacity to try on alternatives. Parallel worlds provide alternatives at virtually every step. The irony, of course, is that their value is in their accessibility, and that is also the cause of their demise.

## Suggested Readings

Adams, Richard, E. W. *Ancient Civilizations of the New World*. Boulder, CO: Westview Press, 1997. A good introduction to the Americas.

Diamond, Jared. *Collapse: How Societies Choose to Fail or Succeed*. New York: Viking, 2005. Good popular discussion of the environmental theme, including an Easter Island case study.

Ehret, Christopher. *The Civilizations of Africa: A History to 1800*. Charlottesville: University Press of Virginia, 2002. Good introduction to history of inner Africa.

Finney, Ben R. *Voyage of Rediscovery: A Cultural Odyssey through Polynesia*. Berkeley: University of California Press, 1994. Great read that shows how Polynesians sailed from Hawaii to New Zealand—by doing it.

Niane, D. T. *Sundiata: An Epic of Old Mali*. Translated by G. D. Pickett. London: Longman, 1965. The great West African classic.

Shaffer, Lynda Norene. *Native Americans before 1492: The Moundbuilding Centers of the Eastern Woodlands*. Armonk, NY: M. E. Sharpe, 1992. Excellent introduction to Native Americans of the eastern United States before Columbus.

## Notes

1. Lonnie G. Thompson et al., "Kilimanjaro Ice Core Records: Evidence of Holocene Climate Change in Tropical Africa," *Science* 298 (October 18, 2002): 591, http://www-bprc.mps.ohio-state.edu/Icecore/589.pdf.

2. Christopher Ehret, *An African Classical Age: Eastern and Southern Africa in World History 1000 B.C to A.D. 400* (Charlottesville: University Press of Virginia, 1998), 296–97.

3. D. T. Niane, *Sundiata: An Epic of Old Mali*, trans. G. D. Pickett (London: Longman, 1965), 62.

4. John Iliffe, *Africans: The History of a Continent* (Cambridge: Cambridge University Press, 1995), 75.

5. Christopher Ehret, *The Civilizations of Africa: A History to 1800* (Charlottesville: University Press of Virginia, 2002), 255.

6. Swahili was a written language using an Arabic orthography with the earliest extant writings dating to the eighteenth century.

7. Johan Goudsblom, Eric Jones, and Stephen Mennell, *The Course of Human History: Economic Growth, Social Process, and Civilization* (Armonk, NY: M. E. Sharpe), 1996, esp. 31–62.

8. The phrase is the title of Jared Diamond's popular work about Western dominance generally. See Jared Diamond, *Collapse: How Societies Choose to Fail or Succeed* (New York: Viking, 2005). Of course Spanish iron was not steel.

9. This "maritime foundations" hypothesis was presented in Michael Mosely, *The Maritime Foundations of Andean Civilization* (Menlo Park, CA: Cummings, 1975). See also the author's *The Incas and Their Ancestors* (New York: Thames and Hudson, 2000).

10. The system is described in Richard E. W. Adams, *Ancient Civilizations of the New World* (Boulder, CO: Westview Press, 1997), 120.

11. Mary Giraudo Beck, *Potlatch: Native Ceremony and Myth on the Northwest Coast* (Anchorage: Alaska Northwest Books, 1993).

12. Adapted from Stephen Plog, *Ancient Peoples of the American Southwest* (London: Thames and Hudson, 1997), 170–71.

13. Lynda Norene Shaffer, *Native Americans before 1492: The Moundbuilding Centers of the Eastern Woodlands* (Armonk, NY: M. E. Sharpe, 1992).

14. B. G. Corney, ed., *The Quest and Occupation of Tahiti by Emissaries of Spain during the Years 1772–6*, 3 vols. (London: Hakluyt Society, 1913–1919), 2:284–87. The account is from the journal of Andia Y. Varela, who visited in Tahiti in 1774, and is slightly modernized.

15. *D. E. Yen, in The Sweet Potato and Oceania*, Bernice P. Bishop Museum Bulletin, 236 (Honolulu: Bishop Museum Press, 1974), argues that Polynesians sailed to South America about 1000 CE and brought the sweet potato back.

16. Silvia Gonzalez, a Mexican anthropologist at John Moores University in Liverpool, England, most recently argued that early Australians sailed across the Pacific and were the first settlers in the Americas, citing stories of a "long-faced" people on the Pacific coast of Mexico who were wiped out by the Spanish conquest (Reuters, September 6, 2004).

17. Ben Finney, "The Other One-Third of the Globe," *Journal of World History* 5, no. 2 (1994): 284.

18. See Diamond, *Collapse*, 79–119.

19. "We the Tikopia" is the title of Raymond Firth's classic study of this people. Published in 1936, it was one of nine books he wrote on the Tikopia.

20. James Gorman, "Does This Mean People Turned Off, Tuned Out and Dropped In?," *New York Times*, June 27, 2006, F3, commenting on Rafael E. Nunez and Eve Sweetser, "With the Future behind Them: Convergent Evidence from Aymara Language and Gesture in the Crosslinguistic Comparison of Spatial Construals of Time," *Cognitive Science* 30 (2006): 401–50.

# Index

Hong Kong, 393
Hong Xiuquan, 323
horticulture, 43
"House of Wisdom," 138–39
Huitzilopochtli, 201, *201*
Human Development Report, of United
    Nations, 395
humans: animal extinctions tracking
    movement of, 9; Bering Sea land bridge
    crossed by, 9; cave paintings and, *10*, 11;
    cultural adaptation of, 11–12; cultural
    differences of, 12–14; environmental
    impact of, 398–403, *399*, *400*; European
    industrial revolution and relationship of
    nature with, 292; first clothing of, 10; first
    modern, 9–12; foraging societies and, 15–
    19; global migration of, 7–9, *8*, 332–33,
    *333*; hominid ancestry of, 6–7; languages
    of early, 14; origins of, 5–7; as products of
    culture, 7; race differences of, 12–14; skin
    pigmentation of, 12; tool making of early,
    13
human sacrifices, 48–49, 51, 199–201
Hundred Years' War, 179
Huns. *See* Xiongnu
hunter-gatherers, 15–19
Hyksos kingdom, 57–58

Ibn Battuta, 145, 151, 165–67, 174, 183–84,
    *184*
Ibo culture, 31–32
Ibsen, Henrik, 308
identity, colonialism and, 336–38
the Illkanate, 158–59
IMF. *See* International Monetary Fund
imperialism. *See* Western imperialism
Inca Empire, 53, 60, 202, 204–6, 248, *248*
India, 44, 57, 68, 75, 371, 415; Buddhism in,
    79–81, *80*; castes in, 77, 79; Christianity
    in, 132–33; cities and states in, 79–80;
    in Classical Age, 76–81; colonialism in,
    320, 330–31; famine in, 1876-1879,
    328–30, *329*; farmers in, 79; Gandhi's
    vision for, 344; Great Britain colonial
    rule and economy of, 330–31; Gupta
    dynasty in, 119–20; Himalayan Mountains
    protecting, 116–17; Hinduism in, 81;
    Islam in, 168–69; karma and reincarnation

in, 78–79; Kushan state in, 117; Malay
    sailors in, 118–19, *119*; Mauryan Dynasty
    in, 80–81; monsoon season in, 117–18;
    Mughal Empire and, 229–30, 319–20;
    patriotic sacrifice in, 87–88; politics in,
    81; population growth patterns in, 386;
    religion in, 107; Sepoy Rebellion and,
    320–21; Sikhism in, 224; social classes
    in, 77–79; tropical crops and agriculture
    in, 119; Vedic civilization in, 77–79, *78*;
    Western imperialism and globalization
    in, 328–31, *329*; Western imperialism
    confronted by, 319–21, *321*; wet rice in,
    119
Indian National Congress, 336
Indian Ocean, 271–72
Indo-Aryan nomads, 57
Indo-European languages, 76
Indonesia, 25, 272, 370, 371, 373; Islam in,
    168–69
Indus River/civilizations, 45, 76
industrial revolution: in Asia, post-World
    War II, 393; birth and death rates during
    European, *291*, 291–92; capitalism and
    European, 290–91; child labor and
    European, 294–95, *295*; communism
    and, 361–62; divergence to convergence
    with, 393–94; environmentalism and,
    401–3; in Europe, 288–95, *289*, *290*,
    315, 391–92; in France, 301; gender and
    European, 294, *295*; in Germany, 301;
    globalization and, 391–94; humanity and
    nature relationship during European,
    292; in Japan, 392–93; new wealth from
    European, 289–90; politics and European,
    295; in Russia, 302, 392; social classes
    and European, 292–94; in Soviet Union,
    392; technology and European, 288–89;
    urbanization and European, 290; in US,
    301–2; Western imperialism in age of,
    316–18, *317*
inequality: Chinese communism and, 362–63;
    in cities, 46–47, 52; gender and, 415–16;
    globalization and, 328, 395–98; in Third
    World, 396–97; in US, 396
Inner Africa: Afro-Eurasian network
    compared to, 246–47; agriculture in,
    192–93; Bantu language in, 191–93, *192*;

# About the Author

KEVIN REILLY is professor of humanities at Raritan Valley Community College and has taught at Rutgers, Columbia, and Princeton Universities. Cofounder and first president of the World History Association, Reilly wrote *The West and the World* and has edited a number of works in world history, including *Worlds of History, Readings in World Civilization,* and the *World History* syllabus collection. As a specialist in immigration history, Reilly created the "Modern Global Migrations" globe at Ellis Island's Museum of the History of Immigration. His work on the history of racism led to the editing of *Racism: A Global Reader.* He was a Fulbright scholar in Brazil (1989) and Jordan (1994) and was awarded NEH fellowships in Greece (1990), Oxford (2006), and India (2008). In 1992, the Community College Humanities Association named him "Distinguished Educator of the Year." He has served on various committees and the governing Council of the American Historical Association. In 2010, he was honored by the World History Association with a World History Pioneer award.